ALPHABET CONNECTIONS

Whole Language Activities from A to Z

by Shirley Ross, Mary Ann Hawke & Cindy McCord

Illustrated by Marilynn G. Barr

Publisher: Roberta Suid
Design: Jeffrey Goldman
Copy Editor: Carol Whiteley
Production: Susan Pinkerton
Typesetting: Santa Monica Press

Other books by Cindy McCord and Shirley Ross:
Animal Rhythms Alphabet, Animal Rhythms Vowels, Animal Rhythms Consonants.

Entire contents © 1993 by Monday Morning Books, Inc.,
Box 1680, Palo Alto, California 94302

For a complete catalog, please write to the address above.

ISBN 1-878279-52-1

Printed in the United States of America

987654321

CONTENTS

Introduction	4	Oo	193
Aa	7	Pp	207
Bb	21	Qq	219
Cc	35	Rr	233
Dd	49	Ss	247
Ee	63	Tt	259
Ff	77	Uu	273
Gg	89	Vv	287
Hh	101	Ww	299
Ii	113	Xx	312
Jj	127	Yy	313
Kk	141	Zz	327
Ll	155	Resources	341
Mm	167	Letter to Parents	342
Nn	181	Masks and Hats	343

Introduction

Alphabet Connections is a collection of activity-oriented learning experiences for young children that spans the entire early-years curriculum. The activities use the alphabet as their theme, with each letter a unit of that theme. A precursor to the book, *Animal Rhythms*, was developed in the early '70s by two of *Alphabet Connections'* authors, kindergarten teachers Cindy McCord and Shirley Ross, to teach the letters and their phonic sounds to early learners. Each letter of the alphabet was associated with an animal puppet the children made, whose name began with the letter sound it represented.

While the orginal program is still used in classrooms throughout the world, over the years it has expanded into other areas of the curriculum. The animal alphabet friends are still a major part of the program. But language arts activities that begin with each of the alphabet letters have been added, as well as science experiments, movement activities, arts and crafts projects, math activities, literature-based activities, and cooking experiences. The two original authors joined forces with another kindergarten teacher, Mary Ann Hawke, to gather all the material they had developed and added to their original program and compile it into this book, *Alphabet Connections.**

HOW TO USE THE BOOK

Alphabet Connections can be thought of as the core of your entire preschool/kindergarten program. Many teachers like to emphasize and offer the activities for one letter per week, and introduce the letters as they're presented, in alphabetical order. You may, of course, prefer to select letters and their activities at random, perhaps beginning with those whose sound is easier to hear at the beginning of words, such as m, p, or t. Or you may wish to choose letters that fit with a month, holiday, or season, such as j in January, w in any winter month, or s on a snowy day. The authors have used the program in all three ways, and have found that the children learn and enjoy the material no matter the order in which the activities are presented.

THE ACTIVITIES

Each of the main types of activities in the book—language arts, math, science, arts and crafts, movement, and cooking—provide a variety of experiences for the children that connect with the various letter sounds. A connection is also made between school and the children's homes with a homework contract that provides parents the opportunity to work together with their child. Finally, patterns and directions are included for the children to make a mask or hat depicting each alphabet animal.

LANGUAGE ARTS
Rapping the Letters

Each of the letters is accompanied by an alliterative chant that the children recite in a rap rhythm. Teach the students the rap, and say it together every day you study the particular letter. The children will internalize the sound of the letter and will soon be able to recognize it whenever they hear it.

The rhythm is the same for each of the letter raps. Say the name of the letter when it's capitalized, and say the phonetic sound when the letter is in its lower-case form and enclosed by slashes.

---

* Cindy McCord is now a kindergarten Mentor Teacher near San Diego, California; Shirley Ross and Mary Ann Hawke are Mentors and kindergarten teachers in Santa Clara, California.

Signing the Letters

An illustration of the sign language hand gesture for each letter is provided next to the letter's alliterative rap. Show the children how to sign the letter each time they say its name in the rap.

Introducing the Letters

Information on how to introduce each letter and its accompanying animal friend is included in this part, with each letter and animal introduced in a different way. For example, the children discover bear tracks on the floor of the classroom on the first day of B week. The tracks lead to a basketful of objects that begin with the B letter sound, and the children are asked to figure out what animal might have brought the objects. Bobby Bear is then introduced to the children.

Celebrating the Letters

A variety of ways are suggested for celebrating the alphabet letters. For example, the letter Q is celebrated at a quilting bee. A Wednesday is chosen as "Wacky Wednesday" when W is being studied, and the children are invited to come to school dressed in wacky clothing. Special games and activities are provided for each of the letter celebrations.

Making a Class Book

Included in each of these sections is an alliterative "sentence frame" that the children complete with a word that begins with the appropriate sound. The completed sentences are illustrated and collected in a class book.

Reading a Book

Each letter unit highlights a children's literature book that is about something that begins with that letter. Included here are a description of the book, a presentation, and several related activities you can use to follow up the reading. There are also directions for making a book with the children, and a list of additional books to read that begin with the same letter.

Making a Letter

A multi-sensory letter project is included for each alphabet letter. Begin by reproducing the letter animal page and have the students trace the letter with many different-colored crayons. This is called "rainbow writing." Then have the children make "feely letters." Duplicate the page onto lightweight cardboard stock and have the children color it lightly with crayons. Then let them glue the designated material onto the lines of the letter.

Listening and Drawing

The listening and drawing pages are designed to help young children develop listening and direction-following skills. Have them begin by using individual chalkboards or scrap paper for this activity. Draw each step with the children as you give the directions orally. Later, make a copy of the page and leave it in a center where the children can follow the directions themselves. Encourage them to add an appropriate background for each letter animal as they study the real animal and its habitat.

Letter Games

Have the children make letter games to play in class and then take home to play with their family. Duplicate the directions titled "At Home" and include them in an envelope with the sound picture cards used to play the game.

MATH

Math Activities

These are whole-class activities that include such skill development areas as estimating, counting, numerical recognition, sequencing, and classifying.

Graphing Experiences

Each letter section includes an activity that requires making a graph—either a paper one or with the children acting as a "live graph." Make a graphing grid that you can use over and over again for the paper graphing activities by ruling four columns, each about three inches wide, onto a piece of butcher paper that is between 60 and 66 inches long. Laminate the finished grid. For each activity, make a copy of the graphing question, color and laminate it, and mount it on the wall above the grid. Make 15 to 20 copies of the category picture symbols found in each letter section. Use one set as labels for the columns, and give each child a copy of the symbol that represents his or her choice to color and mount in the appropriate column. Use Post-it glue sticks to mount the symbols; they can then be easily removed for the next graphing activity.

SCIENCE

Animal Facts

The science section includes a study of the real animal associated with each letter, providing interesting facts; a "Do and Discover" experience; and a "Write a Book" activity. A children's book is listed that will provide further information about the particular animal.

Other Science Activities

The experiences in this part are drawn from the physical as well as the life sciences. The activities include such studies as learning about the wind during W week by making and observing windsocks.

ARTS AND CRAFTS

There is at least one art activity for each letter, and often two. The materials needed for each project are listed, as well as step-by-step instructions.

MOVEMENT

A variety of physical activities are included in this section, including games, dance, and movement. Some of the activities can be done indoors and some out.

COOKING EXPERIENCES

Each of the letter sections includes a recipe for something that begins with that letter sound. Most are designed so that each child can make his or her own portion, though you will need to assist in step-by-step procedures as well as measuring and use of the hot plate or oven. Whenever any cutting or chopping needs to be done by the children, be sure to provide plastic knives and lots of supervision. Some of the recipes require some preparation by an adult (in addition to gathering equipment), such as the premixing of flour and other dry ingredients for Camel Cal's Carrot Cupcakes. Duplicate copies of the recipes for the children to take home after their cooking experiences at school.

HOMEWORK

The choices of activities on the duplicatable homework contract for each letter will enable parents and their child to work at home together on a letter-related activity. The children later return the finished product to school or tell the class about what they did. A duplicatable letter on page 342 tells parents about the children's letter studies and invites them to participate in the homework projects.

MASKS AND HATS

Here you will find patterns and directions for making a hat or mask to represent each of the alphabet animals. Let the children take home their completed creations to share with their family.

RAP WITH ALLIGATOR ANN

Sign Language **A**

A is for alligator, Alligator Ann.
A /a/ /a/ /a/ /a/ /a/ /a/
Apples, ants, and Africa.
A /a/ /a/ /a/ /a/ /a/ /a/
Acrobats and animals.
A /a/ /a/ /a/ /a/ /a/ /a/
(Repeat the first two lines.)

Alligator Ann

ALPHABET STRIPS

To introduce Alligator Ann and her letter A, give every child an alphabet strip. Help them decide what all the letters together are called. Have them listen to the sound at the beginning of the word "alphabet" and discover what animal begins with the same letter sound. Discuss the order of the letters in the alphabet. Explain that the children will be meeting one alphabet animal friend for each letter.

ALLIGATOR ANN'S APPLE ADVENTURE

Celebrate Alligator Ann and her letter A by having an "Apple Adventure." Have the children bring a number of apples to school; the greater the variety, the better. Sort them in as many ways as tho children can think of (size, color, shape). Make a floor graph to find out which color group has the most apples In it. Then hold an apple tasting and ask the children to vote for their favorite kind. Have the children make apple prints as an art project. Finally, make applesauce to enjoy together.

ALLIGATOR ANN'S Aa BOOK

Brainstorm with the class words that begin with the same sound as Alligator Ann. Distribute paper and let the children each choose a word to illustrate. Have them copy the following sentence frame onto the page and write their word in the blank space. Put the pages together to make a class book.

Alligator Ann asked for an _____.

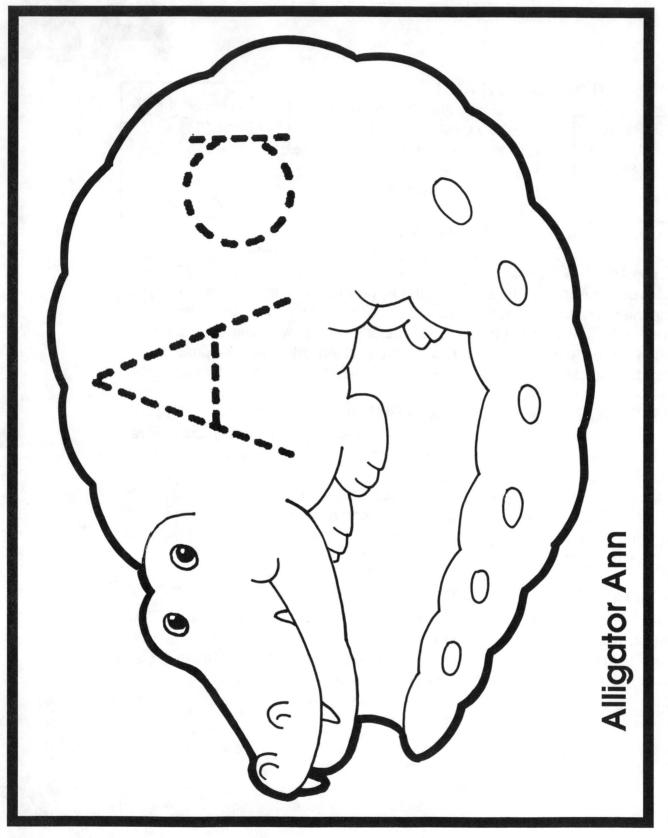

Alligator Ann

Glue alphabet noodles on the Aa's.

8

Aa
Literature Connection

READ A BOOK

Chicka Chicka Boom! Boom! by Bill Martin, Jr., and John Archambault (Simon & Schuster, 1989). *Chicka Chicka Boom! Boom!* is a whimsical ABC book that tells the story of alphabet letters climbing up a coconut tree. Its rhyme and rhythm capture children's interest immediately.

Presentation

Tell the children what the book is called, and have them practice saying "Chicka Chicka Boom! Boom!" with you several times. Let them chime in wherever this phrase appears in the book as you read it. They might also like to join in on "Skit, skat, skoodle, doot, flip, flop, flee." At the end of the book, ask the children what it was about. Discuss the idea that all the letters together are called the alphabet.

Additional Books

Eating the Alphabet by Lois Elhert (Harcourt, 1987); *Andy and the Lion* by James Daugherty (Viking, 1938); *Angus and the Ducks* by Marjorie Flack (Doubleday, 1930); *Baby Animals* by Margaret Wise Brown (Random House, 1989); *Animals Born Alive and Well* by Ruth Heller (Grosset, 1982); *Alligators All Around* by Maurice Sendak (Harper, 1962).

RELATED ACTIVITIES

Learning the Alphabet

Sing an alphabet song with the children. Print the alphabet in order on a long strip of paper and post it on the wall. Tell the children that this is the alphabet. Ask them what the first letter is, and the last. Count the letters together. Point to the letters one at a time and have the children say the names. Provide letter flash cards for the children to put into alphabetical order, and to use to spell their names.

Alphabet Big Book

Make a class alphabet book after reading *Chicka Chicka Boom! Boom!* Cut large block letters out of construction paper in a variety of colors to use in the book. Write the following sentence frame on large pieces of white paper, and give each child a copy plus one of the block letters.

Chicka Chicka Boom! Boom! Will there be enough room for _____?

Listen and Draw an Alligator

Give the children oral directions as you draw each step with them.

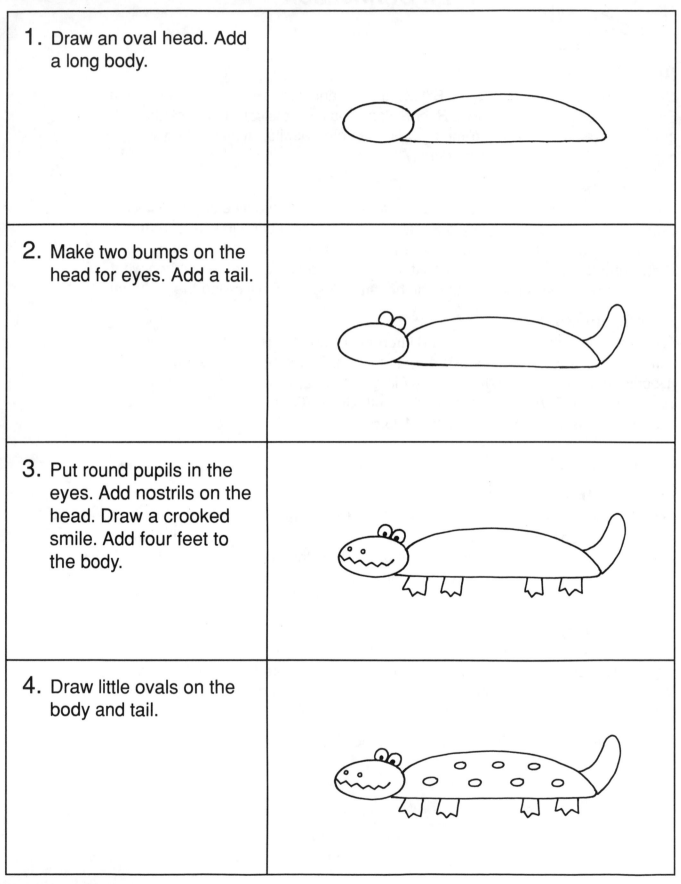

1. Draw an oval head. Add a long body.

2. Make two bumps on the head for eyes. Add a tail.

3. Put round pupils in the eyes. Add nostrils on the head. Draw a crooked smile. Add four feet to the body.

4. Draw little ovals on the body and tail.

Aa
Phonics Connection

AT SCHOOL

Copy the game board and the set of sound picture cards for The "A" Game onto oaktag for the children to color. Have them cut the cards out. Glue an envelope onto the back of the game board to store the cards and the directions for play.

Show the children how to play the game. Include the "At Home" directions when the game goes home.

- -

AT HOME

Materials:
The "A" Game game board and set of sound picture cards; a small marker for each player

Directions:
1. Place the cards face down in a pile between the players.
2. Take turns drawing from the pile. If the picture on the card begins with the long or short sound of "a," move the marker forward one space. If the picture begins with another letter sound, no move is made. If a player is lucky enough to draw Alligator Ann's card, the marker may be moved forward two spaces.
3. Reshuffle the cards each time they have all been drawn, and continue playing until someone reaches the finish line. The player who finishes first is the winner.

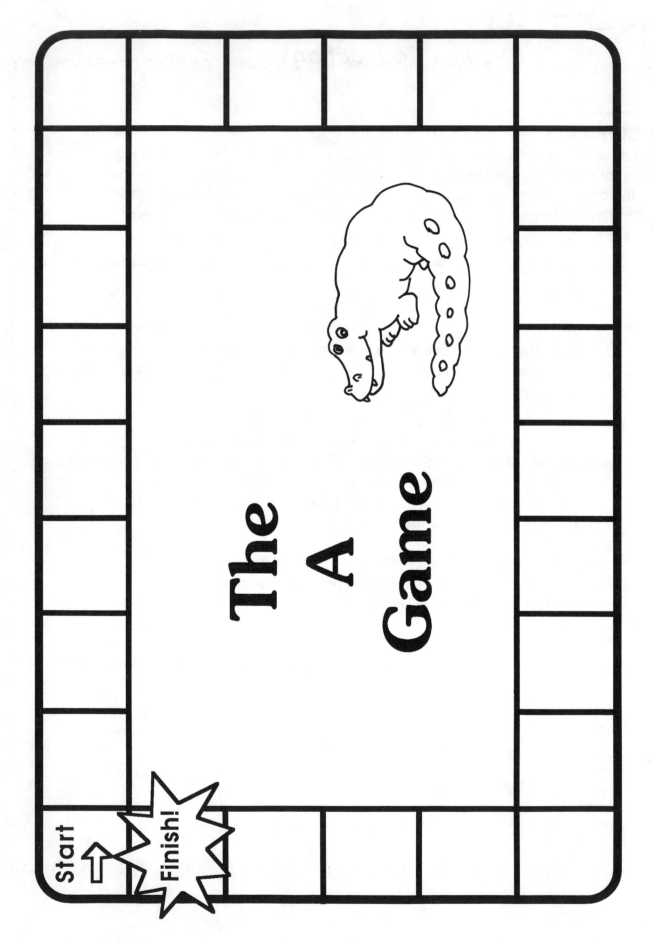

The A Game

Start

Finish!

Alligator Ann

Amy Ape

Aa
Math Connection

APPLE ESTIMATION ACTIVITIES

Bring a basket filled with apples to class and have the children estimate how many there are. Label the columns on a graph by fives (0-5; 6-10; 11-15; 16-20). Give the children sticky notes to write their guesses on, and press the estimates in the appropriate columns. Count the apples. Discuss the graph, asking questions such as, "Did more people guess too few or too many apples?" "Were there any estimates that were right on?" Finish the activity by cooking up a batch of applesauce.

Another challenging estimation activity is to have the children consider the weight of the apples rather than the number. Label the graph columns in two-pound increments (1-2 lbs, 3-4 lbs, etc.).

HOW DO YOU LIKE YOUR APPLES?

(a graphing activity)

Brainstorm with the children all the different ways that people fix apples to eat. Make a list of all the ideas presented. Reproduce the apple graph patterns on the next page and have the children select the one that represents their favorite way to eat apples.

Make a four-column graph (see the directions in the Introduction.) Label the columns: Applesauce; Raw; Apple Juice; Apple Pie. Ask the children, "How do you like your apples?" and have them tape their picture symbols into the appropriate columns.

When everyone has recorded a choice, discuss the finished graph. Begin the discussion by asking, "What does the graph show?" After the discussion, write an experience story together about the graph. Include as many of the children's observations as possible. Put a copy of the story into an experience story book and place it in the classroom library.

How Do You Like Your Apples?

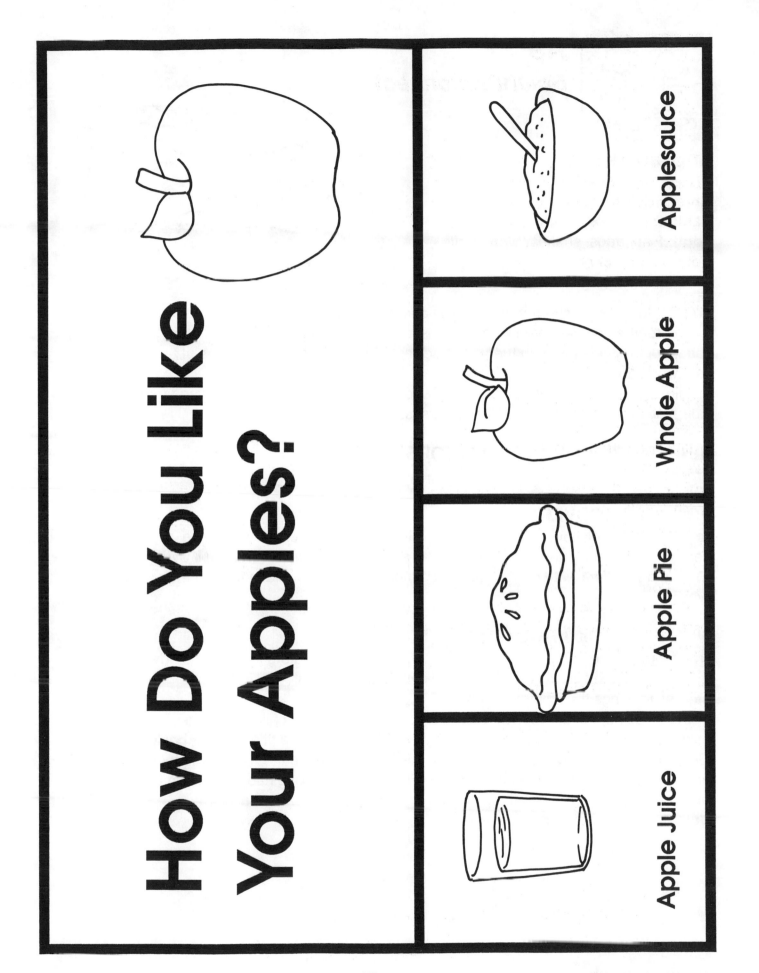

Applesauce

Whole Apple

Apple Pie

Apple Juice

Aa
Science Connection

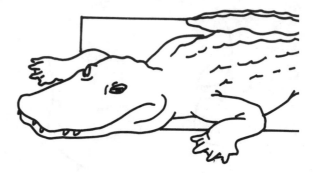

ALLIGATORS

Class: Reptile
Group: Solitary
Habitat: Swamps, rivers
Food: Fish, frogs, snakes, birds, turtles
Color: Brown or green
         (depending on the water in which they live)

An alligator is like a submarine. Its eyes and nostrils stick up above the water so it can breathe and see even when the rest of its body is underwater. Alligators lay eggs, but they do not hatch them themselves. The sun and rotting leaves of the nest warm the eggs.

Like all reptiles, alligators have tough, scaly skin. People kill alligators and use their hides (skin) to make shoes and purses.

READ MORE ABOUT ALLIGATORS

Crocodile and Alligator by Vincent Serventy (Scholastic, 1984).

DO AND DISCOVER

Let the children discover how the clear eyelids of the alligator allow it to see clearly underwater. Have the children view an object underwater with their eyes open and then try it with goggles, a diving mask, or a glass held in front of their eyes.

WRITE A BOOK ABOUT ALLIGATORS

Brainstorm all the things the children remember about alligators from their study. Make a list of the food alligators eat. Talk about their habitat. Discuss all the interesting things the children learned about alligators.

Put three pages together with a cover for a book for each child. Have the children draw a picture of an alligator on the cover and write a title for their book. (See "Listen and Draw An Alligator.") On the first page, have them draw the food that alligators eat. On the second, let them draw the alligator's habitat, and on the third draw a picture of something interesting that they know about alligators. Write or copy a sentence about each picture on each page.

Aa
Science Connection

ANTS

Take the children on a walk to find an anthill. Provide magnifying glasses. When ants are found, encourage the children to squat down near them but not to move. As the children watch the ants at work, ask questions like, "What do you think the ants are doing?" "Do you see any of them carrying something?" "Is the load the ant is carrying bigger or smaller than itself?" "Do you think the load is heavier or lighter than the ant?" Point out that ants are very strong and that most can lift objects that weigh ten times as much as they do.

Now encourage the children to choose one ant and look very closely at it with their magnifying glass. Tell them to try not to disturb the ant as it works. Ask the children, "Can you count the legs on your ant? How many does it have?"

Then say, "Look at your ant's head and tell me if you can see two little hair-like things sticking out of the top. Those are called, 'antennae.' Watch the antennae and tell me if you can see them move. Ants' antennae help them to smell, taste, feel, and hear. They are able to send messages to each other with their antennae."

Finally ask, "When two ants meet, what do you see them do?"

Allow time for spontaneous comments or questions from the children as they observe the ants.

ANTHILL MURAL

After observing ants, go back inside and have the children discuss what they saw and learned about ants. Give each child paper and crayons and have all the children draw one ant (as large as the paper allows) doing something that they observed. Help the children cut out their ants, and encourage them to make a mural of an anthill by drawing a hill on butcher paper, gluing sand on it, and adding their "ants."

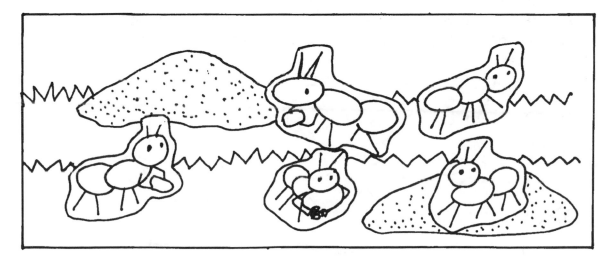

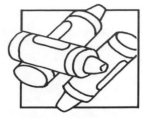

Aa
Arts and Crafts Connection

APPLE PRINTS

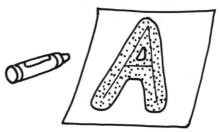

Materials:
3 apples, containers of several colors of liquid tempera, paintbrushes, paper, knife

Procedure:
1. Cut one of the apples in half crosswise, one lengthwise, and one in quarters.
2. Have the children brush paint over the cut surfaces of the apples and press them firmly onto paper to make prints.
3. Encourage the children to print different apple shapes and to use different colors until they are satisfied with their design.

Variations:
1. Give the children 4" by 12" strips of paper on which to create apple print patterns. Use the completed strips as borders around autumn bulletin boards.
2. Have the children make apple prints on bright green paper using white paint. When the prints are dry, let the children paint thin lines of red or yellow around the prints.

ALPHABET ART

Materials:
Crayons or felt pens, pencils, drawing paper

Procedure:
1. Have the children pick a letter, such as the first letter of their name, and sketch it lightly with a pencil in the middle of their drawing paper.
2. Show them how to draw a line around both the outside and the inside of the letter outline, changing the single line letter into its block form.
3. Have the children transform their letters into colorful, artistic creations with felt pens or crayons. Encourage them to decorate the background of their masterpieces as well.

Aa
Movement Connection

ANIMAL WALKS

Alligator Crawl

Have the children lie on their stomach and extend their right arm forward and their right leg straight back. Have them place their left hand on the floor close to their waist (elbow bent) and bend their left knee. Use one child as a model. When they are all in position, tell them to try to move forward like alligators, keeping their chest and tummy in contact with the floor. (Alligators move their legs cross-laterally, that is, the left front leg moves with the right back leg, and vice versa.)

Bunny Hop

Have the children squat down, placing their hands on the floor as far in front of their knees as they can reach. Show them how bunnies hop forward on their hind feet to meet their front paws, then reach out again with their front paws and hop their hind feet to meet them again. Tell them to try to keep their feet and knees close together as they pretend they are bunnies hopping through the meadow.

Crab Walk

Have the children lie on their back on the floor. Use one child as a model to show the others how to get into a "crab" position. Have the child place the palms of his or her hands flat on the floor close to the armpits and bend at the knees so that his or her feet are flat on the floor. Then help the model to push his or her back off the floor. Tell the children to keep their stomach flat and move either forward, backward, or sideways (as all true crabs do), eyes looking upward.

Duck Walk (or Waddle)

Have the children put their hands on their waist and slowly go down into a squatting position. Tell them to keep their legs bent and pretend they are ducks walking to the pond for a swim. Encourage some "duck talk" on the way.

Elephant Walk

Have the children bend at the waist and with hands clasped, dangle both arms in front of them. Show them how to move slowly forward, swinging their arms (trunks) from one side to the other with each step.

19

Aa

HOMEWORK

Name _____

Date Due _____

Put a √ by the activity you have chosen to do.

☐ Learn your **a**ddress. Draw your house. Put the house number on it, and bring the picture to school.

☐ Ask the people in your family about their favorite **a**nimals. Draw pictures of the **a**nimals. Bring the drawings to school. Tell whose favorite each **a**nimal is.

☐ Make a picture list of all the ways you can think of to fix **a**pples to eat. Bring the list to school.

_____
Signature of grown up helper

ALLIGATOR ANN'S APPETIZING APPLE

Ingredients (serves 1)
small apple half
raisins
pecan or walnut
frozen apple juice
    concentrate
cinnamon

1. Remove the core from the apple half. (Use a melon ball maker.)

2. Put 5 raisins in the hole.

3. Break the nut into pieces. Put the pieces in the hole.

4. Put 1 tsp. frozen juice concentrate in the hole.

5. Sprinkle the apple half with a dash of cinnamon.

6. Wrap the apple in a foil square.

7. Bake at 350° for 45 minutes. (You need a helping hand.)

Bb

RAP WITH BOBBY BEAR

Sign Language **B**

B is for bear, Bobby Bear.
B /b/ /b/ /b/ /b/ /b/ /b/
Busy bees and butterflies.
B /b/ /b/ /b/ /b/ /b/ /b/
Bumpy bubbles, bouncing balls.
B /b/ /b/ /b/ /b/ /b/ /b/
(Repeat the first two lines.)

BEAR TRACKS

Introduce Bobby Bear and his letter B with life-size bear tracks cut from construction paper and taped to the floor. Set up the bear tracks before school, making the trail lead from the door to a basket full of small objects that begin with /b/. Name the objects with the children and ask who might have left them. After discussing the possibilities, introduce Bobby Bear and his letter.

BOBBY BEAR'S BIG BIRTHDAY BASH

Pretend it's Bobby Bear's birthday, and give him a party. Let the children make birthday hats decorated with the letter B. Help them prepare a birthday cake with blue frosting and candles, and have the children whose names begin with /b/ blow the candles out. Then encourage everyone to sing "Happy Birthday." Give the children paper birthday cakes to color and cut out. Mount the decorated cakes in columns according to each child's birth month. Ask which month has the most birthdays, which has the least, and which, if any, have the same number.

BOBBY BEAR'S Bb BOOK

Brainstorm with the class words that begin with the same sound as Bobby Bear. Distribute paper and let the children each choose a word to illustrate. Have them copy the following sentence frame onto the page and write their word in the blank space. Put the pages together to make a class book.

Where, oh, where can Bobby Bear be?

He's buying a _____ to bring to me.

Bobby Bear

Glue beans on the Bb's.

Bb
Literature Connection

READ A BOOK
The Three Bears by Paul Galdone (Seabury, 1972). This classic story of a family of three bears and a little girl named Goldilocks has been a favorite of children for many generations.

Presentation
After reading Paul Galdone's version of the tale, ask the children to bring in any copies of the story that they have at home. Read each one as it is brought in, comparing the stories and illustrations. Ask the children why they think there are so many different books about the three bears and Goldilocks.

Additional Books
Brown Bear, Brown Bear by Bill Martin, Jr. (Henry Holt, 1983); *Bear's Bargain* by Frank Asch (Simon & Schuster, 1985); *My Brown Bear Barney* by Elizabeth Fuller (Greenwillow, 1988).

RELATED ACTIVITIES

Porridge Cookbook
Make porridge with the class. Explain to the children that porridge is like hot cereal. Take pictures of the process (or have the children draw pictures) and illustrate a class book with the photos. Develop a text from the children's descriptions of the various stages as you show them the pictures.

Dramatization
Let the children act out the story of the three bears. An elaborate set and costumes aren't necessary, though a few props are fun: a small, a medium-size, and a large bowl; a small, a medium-sized, and a large chair; and blankets in the three sizes to serve as beds. Provide the narration, and have the designated children say their respective lines. Leave the props in the dramatic play corner so that every child has an opportunity to act out the story.

Rewritten Folk Story
Ask the children what they think would happen if the three bears went to visit Goldilocks' house. Use the events in the original story as a frame for the new one, asking questions such as, "Where did Goldilocks live?" "Was she home when the three bears came?" "What did the three bears see first?" "What did they do?" Record the children's answers in narrative form (for example, "Goldilocks lived on a farm with her mom and dad. One day she saw three bears come to her door. . .". Read the new story to the class when it's finished, and tell the children you will make it into a book for the classroom library. Ask for volunteers to illustrate the new story.

Listen and Draw a Bear

Give the children oral directions as you draw each step with them.

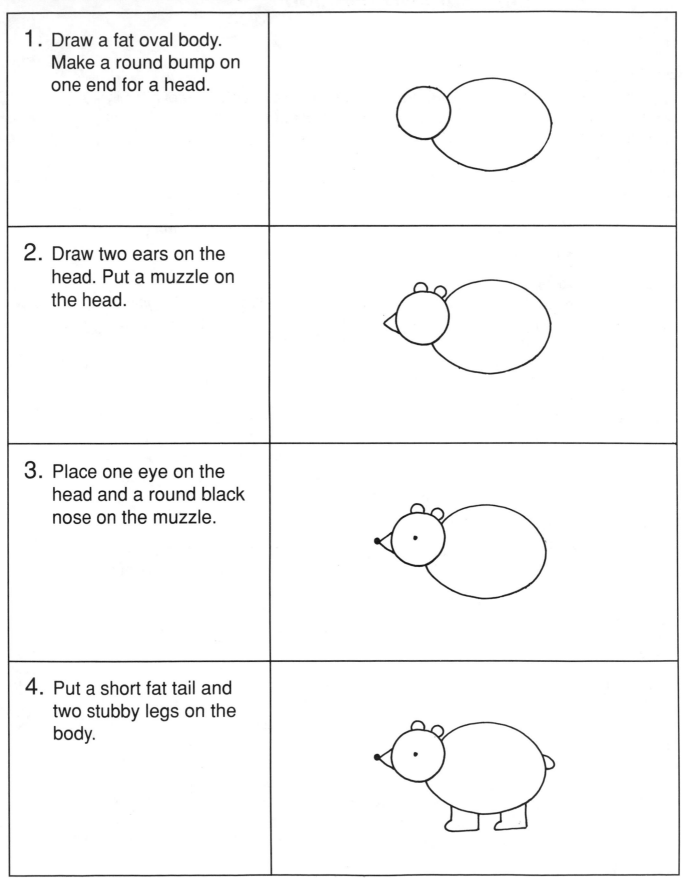

1. Draw a fat oval body. Make a round bump on one end for a head.

2. Draw two ears on the head. Put a muzzle on the head.

3. Place one eye on the head and a round black nose on the muzzle.

4. Put a short fat tail and two stubby legs on the body.

Bb
Phonics Connection

AT SCHOOL

Copy the game board and the set of sound picture cards for Bobby Bear's "B" Game onto oaktag for the children to color. Have them cut out the cards. Glue an envelope onto the back of the game board to store the picture cards and the directions for play.

Show the children how to play the game. Include the "At Home" directions when the game goes home.

- -

AT HOME

Materials:
Bobby Bear's "B" Game game board and set of sound picture cards; a small marker for each player

Directions:
1. Place the cards face down in a pile between the players.
2. Take turns drawing from the pile. If the picture on the card begins with the sound of "b," move the marker to the next space on the game board. If the picture begins with another letter sound, no move is made. If a player is lucky enough to draw Bobby Bear's card, the marker may be moved forward two spaces.
3. Reshuffle the cards each time they have all been drawn, and continue playing until someone reaches the finish line. The player who finishes first is the winner.

Bobby Bear's B Game

Start Here!

Finish!

Bb
Math Connection

BUTTON BOX ESTIMATING

Display a box of buttons. Have each child estimate the number in the box, and record all the guesses with sticky notes on a graph. Label the columns by fives or tens, depending on how many buttons are in the box. Count the buttons and discuss the graph, asking such questions as, "Were any estimates right on?" "Did more people estimate too few or too many?"

ALL SORTS OF BUTTONS

Give the children the collection of buttons and encourage them to sort them in as many different ways as they can. Help them to think of attributes less obvious than color and size, such as number of holes, materials they are made of, with or without designs.

WHICH BEANS DO YOU LIKE BEST?

(a graphing activity)

Brainstorm with the class all the different kinds of beans the children can think of. Then ask the question, "Which kind of beans do you like best?" Reproduce the graphing symbols on the next page and have each child select the one that represents his or her favorite kind of beans.

Make a four-column graph (see the directions in the Introduction). Label the columns: Lima Beans; Green Beans; Baked Beans; Refried Beans. Have the children tape the picture symbols they chose onto the appropriate columns.

When everyone has recorded a choice, discuss the finished graph together. Begin by asking the class, "What do you notice about our graph?" Then write an experience story together about the graph. Put a copy of the story into an experience story book and place it in the classroom library.

Which Beans Do You Like Best?

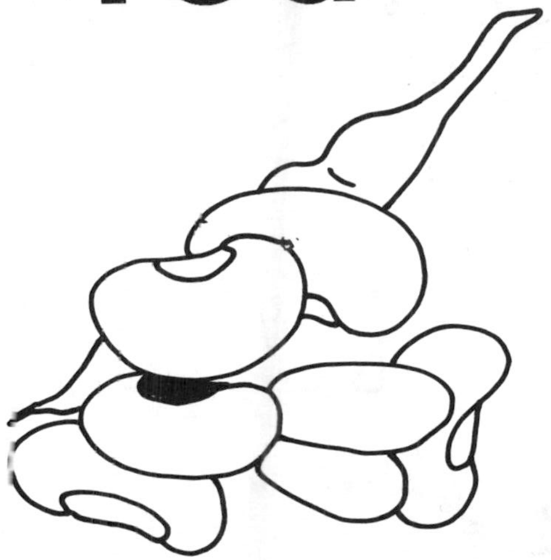

Refried Beans

Baked Beans

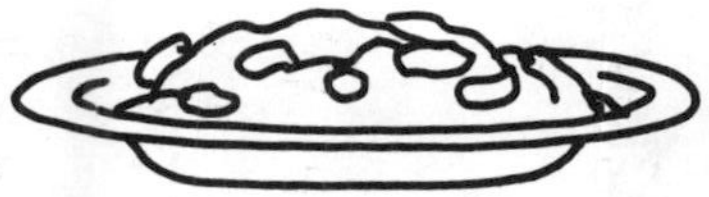

Lima Beans

Green Beans

Bb
Science Connection

BEARS

Class: Mammal
Group: Sloth (but most prefer to live alone)
Habitat: Forests
Food: Berries, fish, leaves, insects, rodents,
    snakes, honey
Baby: Cub
Color: Brown, black, white, yellowish,
    reddish, beige

Most bears are good at fishing. All large bears are good swimmers, but polar bears are best. Female bears are also good mothers. They take care of their cubs until the babies are all grown up (age two!).

READ MORE ABOUT BEARS

Bears and Other Carnivores by Ogden Tanner (Vineyard, 1977).

DO AND DISCOVER

Most large animals such as wolves, lions, and tigers walk on their toes. Bears do not. Thus they are able to rear up and walk a short way on their hind legs. Have the children get down on all fours so that they resemble animals that walk on their toes, but have them use their feet instead of their knees for "hind feet." Show them how to move without letting the heels of their hands or feet touch the ground. Ask them to stand, remaining on the balls of their feet. Discuss how it feels. Ask if they have ever seen trained dogs stand on their hind legs. Next have the children get back down on all fours (hands and feet) and try to move flat-footed like bears. Compare how it feels to moving on their hands and toes. Is it easier to rear up now, or more difficult?

WRITE A BOOK ABOUT BEARS

Brainstorm all the things the children remember about bears from their study. Make a list of the food bears eat. Talk about their habitat. Discuss all the interesting things the children learned about bears.

    Put three pages together with a cover for a book for each child. Have the children draw a picture of a bear on the cover and write a title for the book. (See "Listen and Draw A Bear.") On the first page, have them draw the food that bears eat. On the second, let the children draw the bear's habitat, and on the third ask them to draw a picture of something interesting they know about bears. Have them write or copy a sentence on each page about the picture there.

Bb
Science Connection

BONES

Display a cardboard skeleton, the kind used as decoration during Halloween. Tell the children that there are many real live skeletons hiding in the room. This should generate some interesting discussion. Ask if anyone can guess where these real skeletons are. After several children have responded, point out the display skeleton's long arm and leg bones, and encourage the children to feel their own arms and legs for these bones. At this point they should discover that the real skeletons in the room are inside themselves. Have them feel their fingers, ribs, and jaw, and ask them what it is they're feeling. Tell them about their skull, and have them feel the bone structure of their face.

Collect some chicken, fish, and meat bones. Have the children investigate them, and talk about their similarities and differences. Point out that bones give bodies shape. People would bend like rubber if they didn't have bones.

BUBBLES

Give every child a straw and a clear plastic cup filled with water. Allow the children to blow through the straws into the water. Ask what happened. Explain that the bubbles the children are blowing are filled with air.

After the class has made water bubbles, have them empty their cups; then give each child a small portion of the following soap bubble mixture: 1 cup of liquid detergent (Joy or Dawn), 3 cups of water, a small amount of glycerine. Explain that while the bubbles the children blew in water were made of air surrounded by water, the bubbles they'll be blowing with the mixture will be made of air surrounded by detergent.

Pass out pipe cleaners and have each child bend the end of one around to form a circle. Show the children how to dip the circle into the bubble mixture and blow gently into the detergent surface that forms. Have the children try additional types of bubble blowers: plastic holders from soda can six-packs, plastic berry baskets, Styrofoam cups with holes poked in the ends, and cut-up drinking straws bundled together with a rubber band.

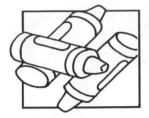

Bb
Arts and Crafts Connection

BUBBLE PRINTS

Materials:
Liquid dishwashing detergent, liquid tempera
or food coloring, water, small jars, drinking straws,
paper, measuring spoons and cups

Procedure:
1. Set out two or three small jars, each containing two tablespoons of liquid detergent, ¼ cup of water, and a teaspoon of tempera paint or five drops of food coloring. Mix thoroughly.
2. Show the children how to blow gently through a straw into the liquid to create a mound of bubbles.
3. Show them how to lower a piece of paper slowly onto the top of the jar to break the bubbles and create an imprint.
4. Be sure the children keep their original straws as they experiment with other colors.

BALLOON PRINTS

Materials:
Small, partially inflated balloons; tempera paint;
shallow pans; paper

Procedure:
1. Put a different color of paint into each shallow pan.
2. Place one balloon, knotted end up, into each pan of paint.
3. Show the children how to use the knot as a handle and dab the paint-covered side of the balloon onto paper in a bouncing motion. After several dabs, return the balloon to its original paint pan.
4. Encourage the children to repeat the process with other balloons and colors until they make a design that pleases them.

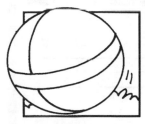

Bb
Movement Connection

BEANBAG FUN

Before giving out the beanbags, establish standards of behavior. Remind the children to hold their beanbags still while listening to directions; to wait for the starting command "Beanbags, begin"; and to "freeze" when they hear the whistle.

　Have the children find places on the playground that are not too close to each other but close enough to hear you give the directions. Then challenge them to try the following activities, stating the challenge and then saying, "Beanbags, begin!" Give them time to have fun with the activity before blowing the whistle and going on to the next.

1. Walk forward (then backward) with the beanbag balanced on your head. (shoulder, elbow, under your chin).
2. Walk with the beanbag between your knees.
3. Walk like a duck with the beanbag balanced on top of your head.
4. Bend over and walk backward with the beanbag on your back.
5. Skip while holding the beanbag behind your back with both hands.
6. Throw the beanbag in the air and catch it with two hands. Then try catching it with only one hand.
7. Toss the beanbag over your head from hand to hand.
8. Throw the beanbag in the air, clap, then catch the beanbag before it hits the ground.
9. Throw the beanbag in the air, turn around once, and catch it before it hits the ground.

Bb

HOMEWORK

Put a √ by the activity you have chosen to do.

☐ Practice **b**ouncing a **b**all. Count how many times you can do it. Show the class.

☐ Collect some **b**eautiful **b**uttons. **B**ring them to school in a **b**ag. Tell about how you can sort your **b**uttons. Tell how many you **b**rought.

☐ Make a **b**ook of things that begin with **b**. Label the pictures. Bring the **b**ook to school.

_____
Signature of grown up helper

BOBBY BEAR'S BANANA BOAT

Ingredients (serves 1)
   half a banana
   raisins or cut-up dates
   walnut or pecan
   carob chips

1. Peel back the top of the banana half.

2. Scoop out a hole.

3. Put 10 raisins or date pieces in the hole.

4. Break the nut into pieces and put them in the hole.

5. Put 5 carob chips in the hole. Fasten the peel back with a toothpick.

6. Bake at 350° for 15 minutes. (You need a helping hand.)

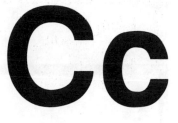

RAP WITH CAMEL CAL

Sign Language **C**

C is for camel, Camel Cal.
C /c/ /c/ /c/ /c/ /c/ /c/
Cookies, cupcakes, candy canes.
C /c/ /c/ /c/ /c/ /c/ /c/
Catching cactus carefully.
C /c/ /c/ /c/ /c/ /c/ /c/
(Repeat the first two lines.)

Camel Cal

CAMEL CAL'S SURPRISE

To introduce Camel Cal and his letter C, put a candy cane or a cookie at every child's place before school. Ask the children to try to guess which alphabet animal friend left the treats.

CLOWN CARNIVAL

Celebrate the letter C by having a "Clown Carnival" for Camel Cal. Designate the day and invite the children to come to school dressed as clowns. Set up some carnival-type activities for the children to enjoy (ring toss, beanbag throw, penny pitch, balloon pop). Ask for volunteers to staff the booths. Provide a face painting area where the children can decorate their own faces.

CAMEL CAL'S Cc BOOK

Brainstorm with the class words that begin with the same sound as Camel Cal. Distribute paper and let the children each choose a word to illustrate. Have them copy the following sentence frame onto the page and write their word in the blank space. Put the pages together to make a class book.

Camel Cal counts 1, 2, 3.

Camel Cal counts _____ with me.

Camel Cal

Glue cotton balls on the Cc's.

36

Cc
Literature Connection

READ A BOOK

Corduroy by Don Freeman (Viking, 1968). This favorite is about the adventures of a toy bear in a department store, searching for the button that came off his overalls. The book is also about love and friendship; it's an endearing story to read again and again.

Presentation

Read the story to the children. Then discuss all the places Corduroy went in the department store as he looked for his lost button. Ask the children how they think Corduroy got his name. Bring a piece of corduroy fabric to school for the class to examine.

Additional Books

Millions of Cats by Wanda Gag (Putnam, 1928); *Caps for Sale* by Esphyr Slobodkina (Harper, 1940); *The Carrot Seed* by Ruth Krauss (Harper, 1945); *The Very Hungry Caterpillar* by Eric Carle (Philomel, 1981).

RELATED ACTIVITIES

Cloth Collages

Discuss many different kinds of fabric with the children. Encourage them to examine and name the material their own clothing is made of: denim, flannel, velvet, cotton, lace, satin, wool, seersucker, etc. Ask the children to bring swatches of as many kinds of cloth as possible to share with the class.

Have the children make collages with the cloth pieces they bring in (you may need to supplement them). Give the children pieces of cardboard, and show them how to arrange and glue down their choice of swatches into designs. Be sure that there is at least one piece of corduroy for each child to include. Let the children embellish their collages with buttons, snaps, bits of trim, ribbon, and other notions.

Button Book

Discuss with the children where Corduroy might have lost his button. Then give each child a page with the following sentence frame on it to make into a class book:

Corduroy lost his button _____.

Have the children draw a picture showing where they think Corduroy lost his button. Then let them glue a real button on their pictures, and complete the sentence frame. Bind the pages together and complete the book with a picture of Corduroy on the cover.

Listen and Draw a Camel

Give the children oral directions as you draw each step with them.

1. Draw a hill with a straight line across the bottom.	
2. Add a small oval and a curved neck between the oval and the hill. Draw two ears on top of the oval.	
3. Make an eye in the middle of the oval. Add a line for a nose and two more lines for a mouth. Add a tail to the side of the hill.	
4. Make two long legs under the hill.	

Cc
Phonics Connection

AT SCHOOL

Copy the game board and the set of sound picture cards for Camel Cal's "C" Game onto oaktag for the children to color. Have them cut out the cards. Glue an envelope onto the back of the game board to store the picture cards and the directions for play.

Show the children how to play the game. Include the "At Home" directions when the game goes home.

AT HOME

Materials:
Camel Cal's "C" Game game board and set of sound picture cards; a small marker for each player

Directions:
1. Place the cards face down in a pile between the players.
2. Take turns drawing from the pile. If the picture on the card begins with the sound of "c," move the marker forward one space. If the picture begins with another letter sound, no move is made. If a player is lucky enough to draw Camel Cal's card, the marker may be moved forward two spaces.
3. Reshuffle the cards each time they have all been drawn, and continue playing until someone reaches the finish line. The player who finishes first is the winner.

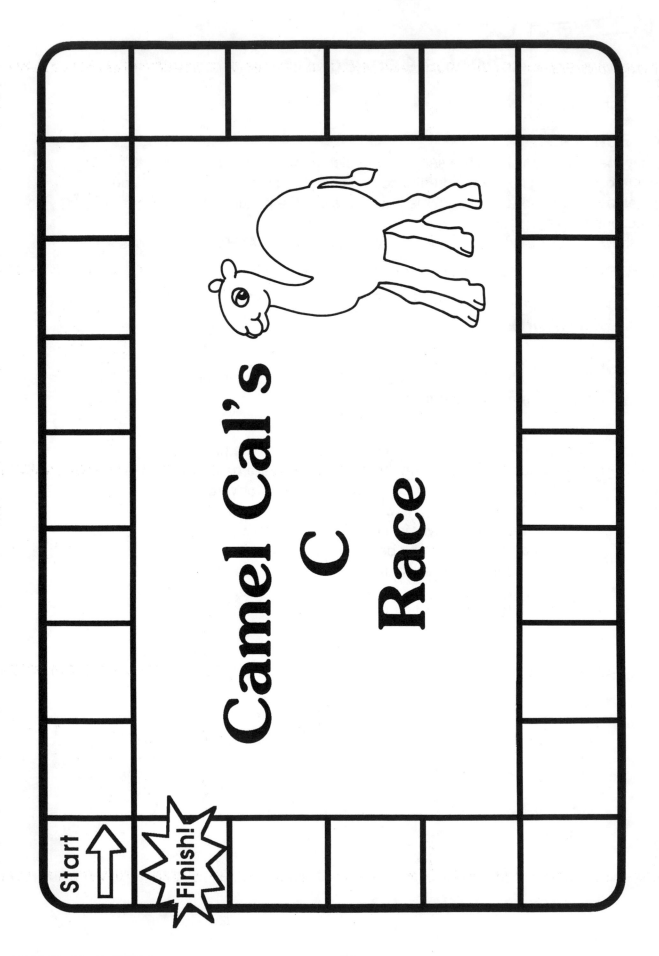

Camel Cal's
C
Race

Start

Finish!

Cc
Math Connection

CANDY CORN ESTIMATING

Show the children a measuring cup filled with candy corn and ask them to esti-mate how many candies there are. Have the children count the candies into groups of ten, and then count by tens to find out the total number. Ask the class to figure out a way to divide the candy equally among all the children.

CLAP AND COUNT

Have the children practice the counting sequence by clapping as they count. Have them throw their hands up on the last number in the agreed-upon series, and turn around as they begin again—all without missing a beat.

WHAT IS YOUR FAVORITE COLOR?

(a graphing activity)

Ask the children if any of them has a favorite color. Give everyone the chance to respond. Provide 2" by 2" construction paper squares of all the selected colors, and have the children record their choices in the appropriate columns of a pre-pared graphing grid.

When the graph is completed, begin a discussion by asking, "What do you see on this graph?" After the discussion, write a class experience story together about the graph. Put a copy of the story into an experience story book and place it in the classroom library.

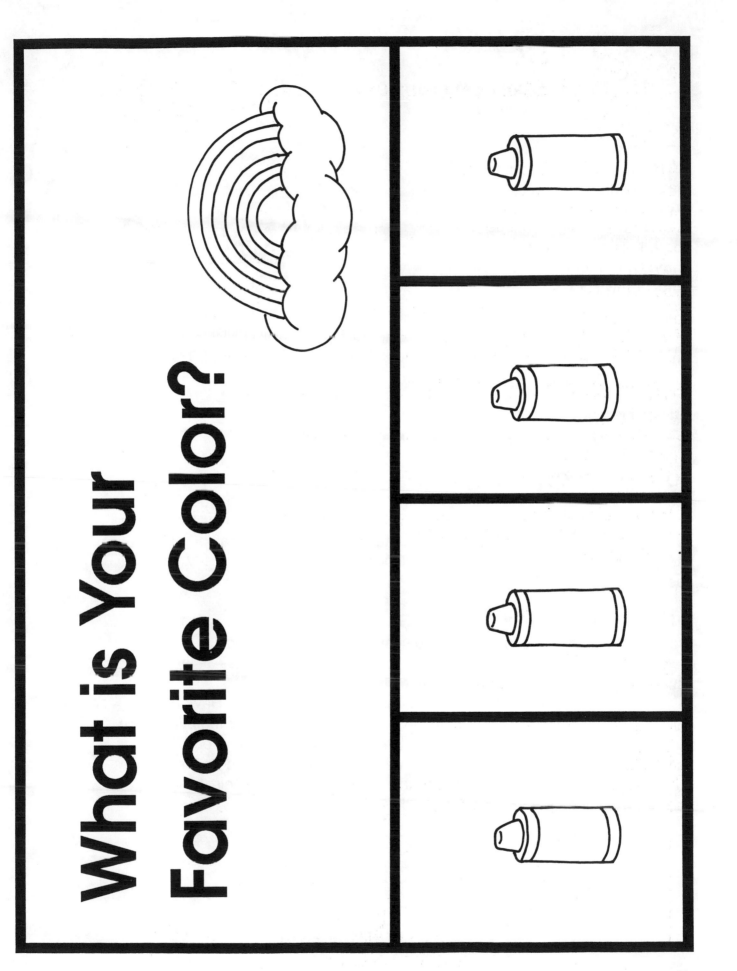

What is Your Favorite Color?

Cc
Science Connection

CAMELS

Class: Mammal
Group: Herd
Habitat: Deserts, grasslands
Food: Leaves, hay, grass, grains, dates
Baby: Calf or foal
Color: Brown or tan

People have ridden camels and used them to carry heavy loads across the desert for thousands of years. These animals' bodies are well suited to hot, dry land. They have special eyelids and nostrils to keep out blowing sand. Their humps store fat to use when food is scarce.

READ MORE ABOUT CAMELS

Camels, Ships of the Desert by John F. Water (Crowell, 1974).

DO AND DISCOVER

Let the children discover how a camel's two-toed dinner plate-sized foot keeps it from sinking into the desert sand. First, have the children push a pencil into some sand. Then have them put a quarter under the pencil and push again. Encourage the class to notice how the coin keeps the pencil from digging into the sand so easily.

WRITE A BOOK ABOUT CAMELS

Brainstorm all the things the children remember about camels from their study. Make a list of the food camels eat. Talk about their habitat. Discuss all the interesting things the children learned about camels.

Put three pages together with a cover for a book for each child. Have the children draw a picture of a camel on the cover and write a title for the book. (See "Listen and Draw A Camel.") On the first page, have them draw the food that camels eat. On the second, let them draw the camel's habitat, and on the third draw a picture of something interesting that they know about camels. Have the children write or copy a sentence about the picture on each page.

Cc
Science Connection

COLOR

Begin by discussing the children's favorite colors. Make a class graph labeled "What Is Your Favorite Color?"

Show the children how they can make all the colors of the rainbow using only three colors—red, blue, and yellow. Cover a table with newspaper. Set out foam egg cartons (lids removed) and fill each section half full of water. Give the children watercolor paints in the three primary colors. Show them how to put water on a cake of paint with a brush, stirring it to create a colored liquid, then add drops of it to one of the egg carton cups of water. Provide a container of water to wash out brushes in between color additions. Have the children mix two different primary colors in each egg carton cup. Talk about the colors they create.

CRYSTALS

Grow your own crystals in the classroom by making crystal gardens. These will mainly be observation activities for the children, since the ammonia, bluing, and hot water needed for the experiments should be handled only by adults.

Crystal Garden

1. Put one tablespoon ammonia in a bowl. Add three tablespoons salt, three tablespoons bluing, and three tablespoons water. Stir.
2. Put some charcoal into a shallow pan. Pour the mixture over the charcoal.
3. Drip food coloring onto the charcoal. Let the children observe.

Alum Crystal Garden

1. Put hot steamy water into a clear cup.
2. Dissolve powdered alum into the water one spoonful at a time until no more will dissolve.
3. Tie a length of string to a pencil so that the string hangs down into the cup when the pencil is laid across the top. Knot the end so that the string almost touches the bottom.
4. Set the cup where it won't get bumped. Have the class observe it later.

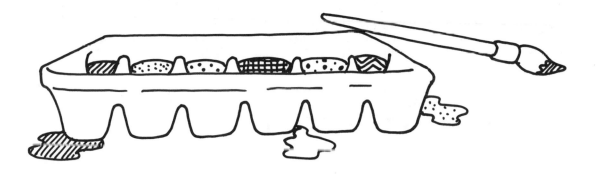

45

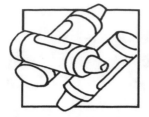

Cc
Arts and Crafts Connection

CRAZY CRAYONS

Materials:
Old crayons (peeled), old muffin tins, paper muffin
tin liners, oven

Procedure:
1. Place the paper liners into the muffin tins.
2. Turn the oven on to warm.
3. Have the children break the old crayons into short, stubby pieces and put them into the lined muffin cups. (Help the children select compatible colors to mix.)
4. Put the muffin tins into the warm oven and turn it off.
5. When the crayons become squishy but not liquid, take them out of the oven and put them into the freezer.
6. Have the children peel the paper from their crazy crayons and try them out. The crayons are great for all kinds of art projects.

COLORFUL COLLAGES

Materials:
Collage bases (matte boards, paper plates, box
lids, meat trays, etc.), glue, brushes, collage
materials (colored tissue paper, colored
cellophane, gift wrap and ties, foil, colored
construction paper, confetti, fabric scraps,
rickrack, lace trim, ribbon, yarn, Easter grass,
Christmas tinsel, etc.), containers

Procedure:
1. Cut or tear the various papers into pieces. Arrange all the materials in separate containers within easy reach of the children.
2. Give each child a container of glue, a brush, and a base.
3. Show the children how to brush glue onto their base and stick the collage materials on in interesting designs.
4. Explain that they can create a different effect by gluing some of the materials on top of each other.

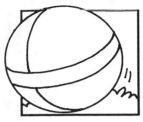

Cc
Movement Connection

COLOR CALL

Have the children form a circle and have one child who is "It" stand in the middle with a playground ball. The play begins when "It" shouts the name of a color and tosses the ball straight up into the air. All the children who are wearing that color run into the circle and try to catch the ball. The child who catches it becomes the new "It."

For a variation, try letting each child pick a favorite color and pin a paper square of that color on his or her clothing to play the game.

CROSS OVER

Divide the class into two groups, each of which stands on a designated goal line 30 to 40 feet apart. (Long jump ropes can serve as goal lines.) A "Catcher" is in the center between the two lines. He or she faces one of the lines and calls out the name of one of the players. That player calls out the name of someone in the other line. The two players named must try to change goal lines while the "Catcher" tries to tag one of them. The player that is tagged becomes the next "Catcher."

CROSSING THE CREEK

Mark off a creek on the play yard by drawing two parallel lines beginning about two feet apart and gradually increasing to about four feet apart. Divide the players into groups of five or six and have each group take turns running to the creek and jumping across, trying not to get their feet wet. Have them start at the point where the lines are closest together. Those who succeed turn around and jump back across with a standing jump instead of a running one. On either of these jumps, players who don't make it across the creek and get their feet wet must run home to get dry socks before joining the group again. "Home" can be a bench not too far from play, but far enough away to take a little time to get there and return.

After all the groups have taken their turn, lead them to points where the creek is wider and wider, until the widest part. At that point most players will have to run home for dry socks.

47

Cc

HOMEWORK

Name _____

Date Due _____

Put a √ by the activity you have chosen to do.

☐ **C**ook something with **c**arrots in it. Ask a grownup to help. Write about **c**ooking the **c**arrots, and bring the story to school.

☐ Play **c**atch with someone. Draw a picture and write how many times you **c**aught the ball. Bring the picture to school.

☐ **C**ollect some aluminum **c**ans to recycle. Tell the **c**lass how many **c**ans you collected.

_____
Signature of grown up helper

CAMEL CAL'S CARROT CUPCAKE

Ingredients (serves 1)
  carrot   egg
  brown sugar   raisins
  cooking oil   flour mixture
  chopped nuts
Flour mixture for 4
1 cup flour   1/4 tsp. salt
1 tsp. cinnamon
1/2 tsp. baking powder
1/2 tsp. baking soda

1. Put 1 packed T. of brown sugar into a bowl.

2. Add 2 tsp. egg.

3. Add 2 tsp. oil.

4. Stir in 1 1/2 T. of the flour mixture.

5. Add 1 1/2 T. grated carrot. Add 6 raisins and 1 tsp. chopped nuts.

6. Stir. Pour into a muffin cup. Bake at 350° for 15-20 minutes. (You need a helping hand.)

RAP WITH DINOSAUR DAWN

Sign Language **D**

D is for dinosaur, Dinosaur Dawn.
D /d/ /d/ /d/ /d/ /d/ /d/
Dancing, dollies, daffodils.
D /d/ /d/ /d/ /d/ /d/ /d/
Daddy, dentist, ding-dong, door.
D /d/ /d/ /d/ /d/ /d/ /d/
(Repeat the first two lines.)

Dinosaur Dawn

DETECTIVES

To introduce Dinosaur Dawn and her letter D, tell the children to pretend that they're detectives. Then give clues about things that begin with /d/ (for example, "It's round with a hole in the middle, and it tastes good"). After several objects that begin with the /d/ sound have been identified, let the "detectives" figure out what letter they will be learning about and who their new alphabet animal friend will be.

DOLL DAY

Celebrate the letter D by designating a day at school as "Doll Day." Provide a special place to display dolls that the children bring in, and make time that day for everyone to hear about the dolls from their owners.

Have scraps of fabric, ribbon, lace, beads, and buttons available for the children to make clothing for their dolls (or for playhouse corner inhabitants). Fabric glue will hold seams together, but be sure garments are dry before dolls are dressed.

The children may also make paper dolls and string them together for room decorations. They'll also have fun decorating delicious doll-size cookies (vanilla wafers) to enjoy on "Doll Day."

DINOSAUR DAWN'S Dd BOOK

Brainstorm with the class words that begin with the same sound as Dinosaur Dawn. Distribute paper and let the children each choose a word to illustrate. Have them copy the following sentence frame onto the page and write their word in the blank space. Put the pages together to make a class book.

Dinosaur Dawn delights in devouring _____.

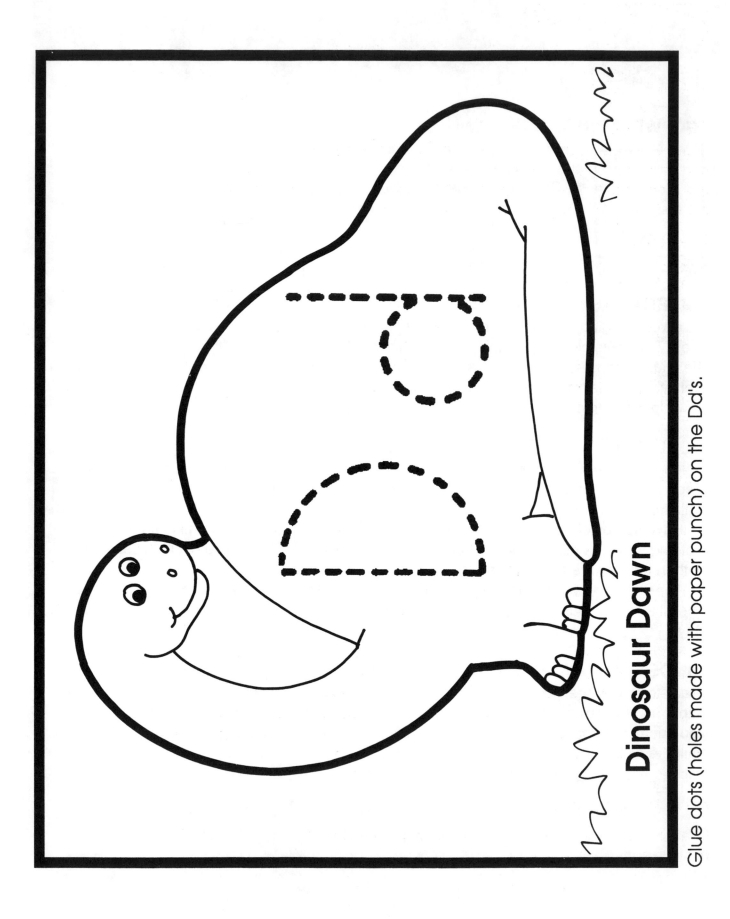

Dinosaur Dawn

Glue dots (holes made with paper punch) on the Dd's.

50

Dd
Literature Connection

READ A BOOK

If the Dinosaurs Came Back by Bernard Most (Harcourt, 1978). This creative book explores what it would be like if the dinosaurs came back to live with us in this modern day. There is lots of food for thought in the book, as well as brightly colored dinosaur pictures.

Presentation

Talk with the class about dinosaurs, finding out what the children know. Discuss what it was like on earth when the dinosaurs were here. Just before reading the book to the children, ask the question, "What If the dinosaurs came back?"

Additional Books

Dandelion by Don Freeman (Penguin, 1964); *Make Way for Ducklings* by Robert McCloskey (Puffin, 1941); *Doctor DeSoto* by William Steig (Scholastic, 1982); *Patrick's Dinosaur* by Donald Carrick (Clarion, 1983); *Whatever Happened to Patrick's Dinosaur* by Donald Carrick (Clarion, 1986); *Danny and the Dinosaur* by Syd Hoff (Harper, 1958).

RELATED ACTIVITY

A Class Dinosaur Book

Make a class book using *If the Dinosaurs Came Back* as a springboard. Have the children brainstorm ideas about what might happen if the dinosaurs really did come back. Record their responses.

Discuss the illustrations the class book will have. Talk about what the "background" of an illustration is, and how it is done with black lines in the book you read.

Provide each child with a piece of brightly colored construction paper, scissors, and a black crayon for the project. Have the children outline and detail a dinosaur on their construction paper, and then cut it out. Next, using only black crayon, show the children how to create a background scene on white construction paper that depicts their idea of what might happen if the dinosaurs came back. Have the children paste their dinosaur cutout on the background, and then finish the page with this completed sentence frame:

If the dinosaurs came back, they would _____.

Bind the pages together, and enjoy reading all the creative ideas. Display the book where others can read it.

Listen and Draw a Dinosaur

Give the children oral directions as you draw each step with them.

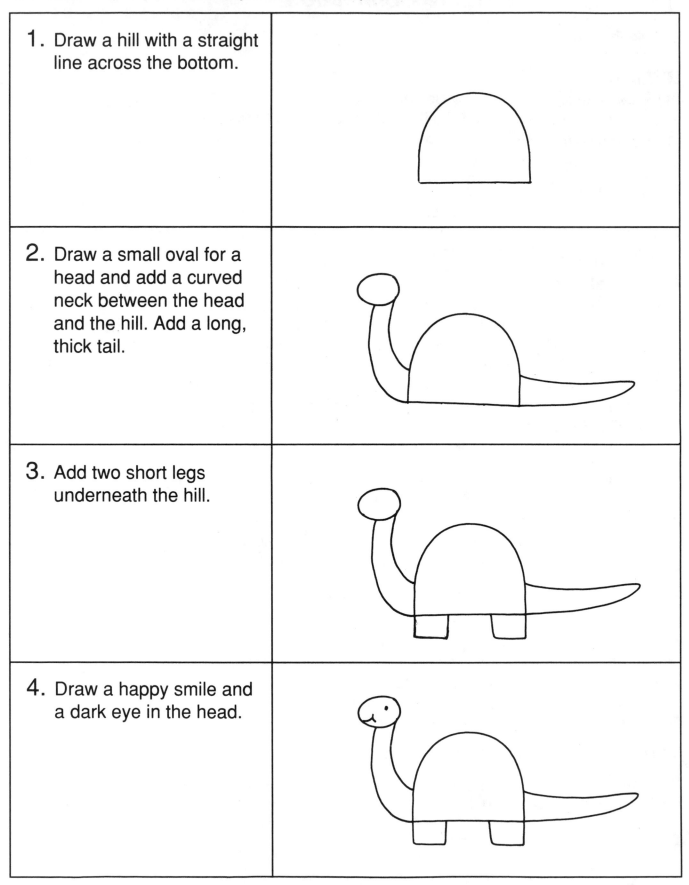

1. Draw a hill with a straight line across the bottom.

2. Draw a small oval for a head and add a curved neck between the head and the hill. Add a long, thick tail.

3. Add two short legs underneath the hill.

4. Draw a happy smile and a dark eye in the head.

Dd
Phonics Connection

AT SCHOOL

Copy the game board and the set of sound picture cards for Dinosaur Dawn's "D" Game onto oaktag for the children to color. Have them cut the cards out. Glue an envelope onto the back of the game board to store the picture cards and the directions for play.

Show the children how to play the game. Include the "At Home" directions when the game goes home.

AT HOME

Materials:

Dinosaur Dawn's "D" Game game board and set of sound picture cards; a small marker for each player

Directions:

1. Place the cards face down in a pile between the players.
2. Take turns drawing from the pile. If the picture on the card begins with the sound of "d," move the marker forward one space. If the picture begins with a letter sound other than "d," no move is made. If a player is lucky enough to draw Dinosaur Dawn's card, the marker may be moved forward two spaces.
3. Reshuffle the cards each time they have all been drawn, and continue playing until someone reaches the finish line. The player who finishes first is the winner.

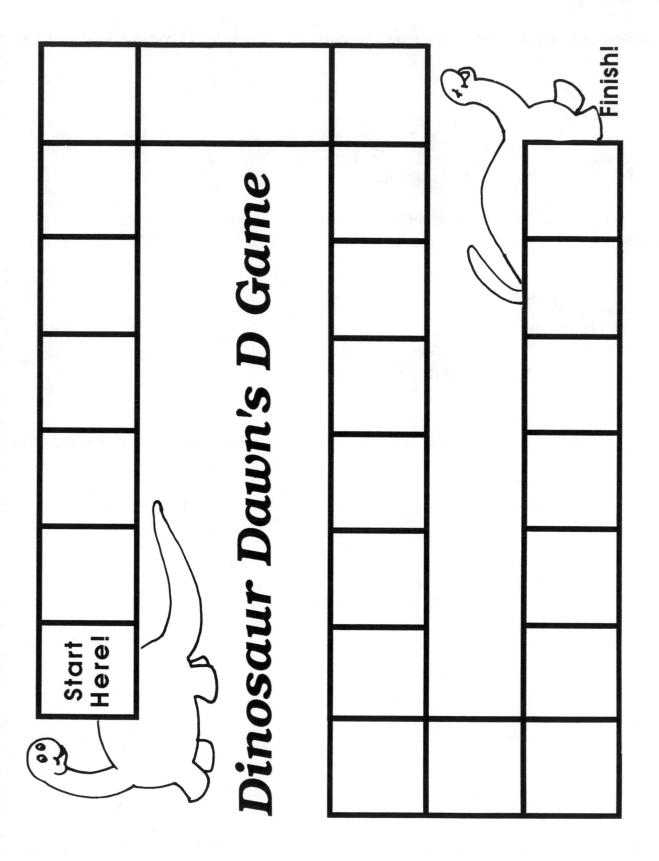

Dinosaur Dawn's D Game

Start Here!

Finish!

 ## Dd
Math Connection

DRIP, DROP MATH

Show the children a large jar and ask them how full they think it will be after collecting drips from the faucet for an hour. Have them indicate their estimates by drawing lines on the jar with a waterproof pen. Put the jar under a faucet set to a slow drip and have the children check it in an hour.

DELICIOUS DOUGH NUMERALS

Make a very stiff cookie dough (add ½ to ¾ cup more flour than the recipe calls for) and have the children roll out snakes, then form their favorite numerals. These could be their ages, part of their phone numbers, etc. Bake the numbers in a toaster oven and let the children enjoy them.

WHICH DINOSAUR IS YOUR FAVORITE?

(a graphing activity)

Ask the children to tell what they know about dinosaurs. Show them some pictures and ask, "Which dinosaur is your favorite?" Reproduce the graphing symbols on the next page and have each child select and color the one that represents his or her favorite.

Make a four-column graph (see the directions in the Introduction). Label the columns: Brontosaurus; Stegosaurus; Triceratops; Tyrannosaurus. Have the children tape the picture symbols they chose and colored onto the appropriate columns.

When everyone has recorded a choice, discuss the finished graph together. Begin the discussion by asking the children what they notice about it. At the end of the discussion, write an experience story together about the graph. Put a copy of the story into an experience story book and place it in the classroom library.

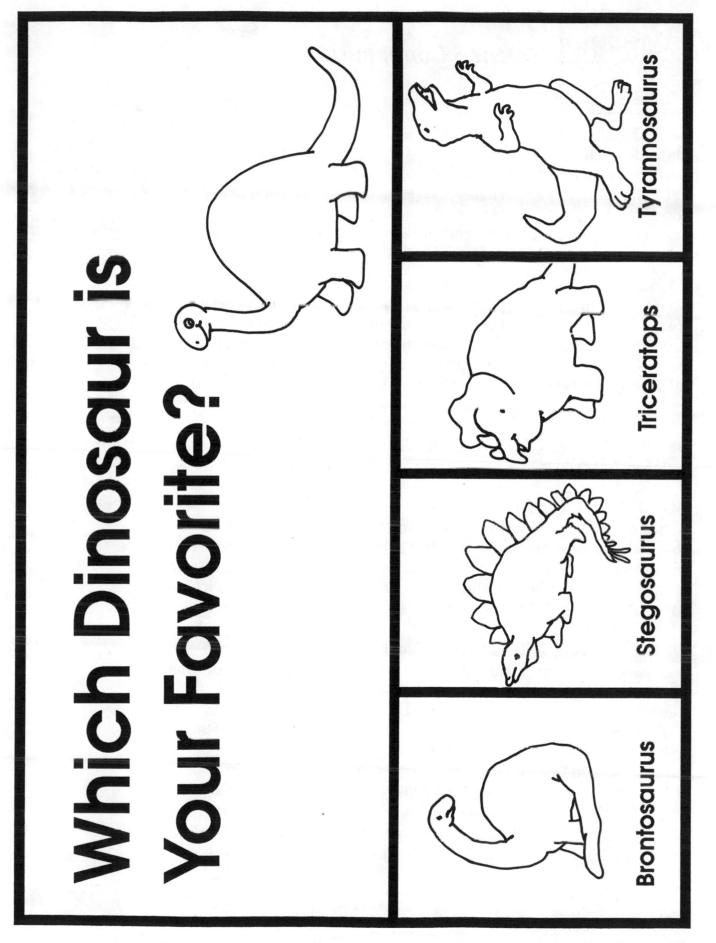

Which Dinosaur is Your Favorite?

Tyrannosaurus

Triceratops

Stegosaurus

Brontosaurus

Dd
Science Connection

DINOSAURS

Class: Reptile
Group: Some in herds
Habitat: Forests, swamps, deserts, lakes
Food: Leaves, plants, berries, small animals
Color: Unknown, but probably colored like
      reptiles of today

Scientists are discovering new things about dinosaurs all the time. Much has been learned in a relatively short time since the first dinosaur fossils were discovered only 150 years ago. Scientists call the time in which dinosaurs lived on the earth "the age of reptiles," even though dinosaurs were not much like reptiles of today. Dinosaurs stood on straight legs that were positioned under their bodies, whereas most of today's reptiles stand on bent legs that are positioned on their bodies' sides.

READ MORE ABOUT DINOSAURS

A Dozen Dinosaurs by Richard Armour (Scholastic, 1974).

DO AND DISCOVER

Let the children discover the comparative sizes of some of the dinosaurs by going out to a large area such as a field or playground. Using yarn or string, pace off the length of the children's favorite dinosaurs: Stegosaurus and Triceratops, 30 ft.; Brontosaurus (Apatosaurus), 70 ft.; Tyrannosaurus, 40 ft.; Brachiosaurus, 90 ft.; Ultrasaurus, 100 ft.; Seismosaurus (newly discovered),120 ft.

WRITE A BOOK ABOUT DINOSAURS

Brainstorm all the things the children remember about dinosaurs from their study. Make a list of the food dinosaurs ate. Talk about their habitat. Discuss all the interesting things the children learned about dinosaurs.

    Put three pages together with a cover for a book for each child. Have the children draw a picture of a dinosaur on the cover and write a title for the book. (See "Listen and Draw A Dinosaur.") On the first page, have them draw the food that dinosaurs ate. On the second, let them draw the dinosaur's habitat, and on the third draw a picture of something interesting that they know about dinosaurs. Have the children write or copy a sentence about the picture on each page.

Dd
Science Connection

DIRT

Take the children to a vacant lot, a non-grassy spot under a tree, or any other area that may have soil rich with "discoveries." Explain that the children will be doing some scientific observations, but will be leaving the area as they found it.

Using a gardener's trowel, scoop up some dirt for the children to investigate. Have them spread the dirt on white paper for their observation. Let them use old sieves or strainers to sift out the larger particles. Supply magnifying glasses for a close-up view of interesting bits and pieces. As the children explore the dirt, ask questions like, "Do you see any living things in the dirt?" "What colors do you see?" "Have you found any interesting shapes in the dirt?"

Have some magnets on hand for the children to run through the dirt. Ask them to tell you what the magnet attracts. Let the children put some of the dirt in a cup and add water, then observe the change that takes place.

When the children return to the classroom, make a list of all of their observations. Ask them why they think dirt is important to our lives. Have the children each create and illustrate a poster about dirt.

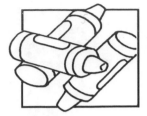

Dd
Arts and Crafts Connection

DOT DOODLES

Materials:
Hole punches; colored construction paper, including black; white glue; scissors; brushes

Procedure:
1. Cut the colored construction paper into strips about 2" wide.
2. Show the children how to use the paper punch. Then have them choose two or three colors of paper and punch out lots of dots.
3. Have the children each take a sheet of black construction paper. On the paper, have them "draw" the outline of a picture or design with white glue. Then encourage them to carefully arrange their colorful dots on the glue.
4. If the children wish to fill in the spaces of their design with dots, let them brush the glue onto one section of their picture at a time, then place the dots.

DIP AND DYE DESIGNS

Materials:
Food coloring, water, paper towels, paper napkins, coffee filters, paper tablecloths, white tissue paper, bowls

Procedure:
1. Make three or four different colored mixtures of food coloring and water and place each in a bowl. The more food coloring added, the more brilliant the color.
2. Let the children experiment with small pieces of paper towel first. Have them dip corners of small pieces into the color mixtures and watch the design that's created by the soaking action.
3. Show the children how to accordion-fold a long strip of paper towel or napkin. Then have them dip and dye corners and edges of their folded papers into the mixtures. When they unfold their papers, they will delight in the designs they have made.
4. The children can also use the procedure to make gifts and other artwork. They can dip and dye large pieces of white tissue paper to create gift wrapping paper; dip and dye inexpensive white paper napkins to make napkin sets for their families; and use eyedroppers to squirt food coloring mixtures onto a paper tablecloth (spread on newspaper on the floor) to make a table covering for a class party or the playhouse.

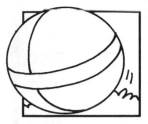

Dd
Movement Connection

DODGE BALL

Divide the children into two groups. One group forms a circle; the other group stands inside it. Have the circle players throw a small rubber playground ball into the center to try to hit one of the "insiders." Show the children how to throw the ball low so that no one is hit above the waist, since this is a "foul." When one of the "insiders" is hit with the ball, he or she joins the outside circle and tries to hit other "insiders."

Continue play until a specified number of children are left in the center. Then have those "insiders" who remain form a new circle, while the former "outsiders" go into the center. Resume play and continue until the same specified number of children is left inside the circle.

DROP THE HANDKERCHIEF

Have the children join hands and form a circle. Choose one child to be "It." "It" walks around the outside of the circle carrying an adult-sized handkerchief. While walking, he or she drops the handkerchief behind one of the children and continues walking around the circle, this time very quickly. The child behind whom the handkerchief was dropped walks quickly in the opposite direction, trying to return to the place where the handkerchief is before "It" does. The player to pick up the handkerchief first gets to be "It" next.

Dd

HOMEWORK

Name _____

Date Due _____

Put a √ by the activity you have chosen to do.

☐ Make a **d**rum and play it while someone **d**oes a **d**ance. Bring your **d**rum to school.

☐ **D**raw your favorite **d**inosaur. Tell a story about it and have someone write it **d**own. Bring the story and picture to school.

☐ **D**o some **d**ot-to-**d**ot **d**rawings. Bring them to school.

_____
Signature of grown up helper

DINOSAUR DAWN'S DATE DELIGHTS

Ingredients (serves 1)
  dates
  cream cheese
  wheat germ
  honey
  walnut halves

1. Put 1 T. cream cheese in a bowl.

2. Sprinkle 1/2 tsp. wheat germ over it.

3. Add 1/4 tsp. honey.

4. Stir.

5. Cut 4 dates open.

6. Stuff the dates with the cheese mixture.

7. Put a walnut half in each date.

Ee

RAP WITH ELEPHANT ED

Sign Language **E**

E is for elephant, Elephant Ed.
E /e/ /e/ /e/ /e/ /e/ /e/
Every, extra, energy.
E /e/ /e/ /e/ /e/ /e/ /e/
Empty, echoes, exercise.
E /e/ /e/ /e/ /e/ /e/ /e/
(Repeat the first two lines.)

Elephant Ed

EXCITING EGGS

Put pictures of things that begin with the short sound of e into plastic eggs and display the eggs as an introduction. Leave one of the eggs empty. Choose several children to open the eggs one at a time and name the objects pictured inside. Ask everyone to guess what animal begins with the same sound as the pictures. Be sure to talk about the empty egg and why it's included with the eggs that hold pictures.

EGG-STRAVAGANZA

Celebrate the letter E with an "Egg-stravaganza." Read the story of Humpty Dumpty and encourage the children to think of ways to keep an egg from breaking when it's dropped. Try some of the ideas. Then, even if it isn't Easter time, dye some eggs in class and have an egg roll or an egg hunt. Read *Green Eggs and Ham* by Dr. Seuss, and make some to eat. Make a "Before and After" graph, asking the questions, "Do you think you will like green eggs?" and "Did you?" Use the eggshells from the cooking project to make eggshell mosaics. Dye bits of shell with food coloring and rubbing alcohol and let the children glue the pieces onto simple designs they've made on pastel construction paper.

ELEPHANT ED'S Ee BOOK

Brainstorm with the class words that begin with the same sound as Elephant Ed. Distribute paper and let the children each choose a word to illustrate. Have them copy the following sentence frame onto the page and write their word in the blank space. Put the pages together to make a class book.

Elephant Ed enjoys every _____.

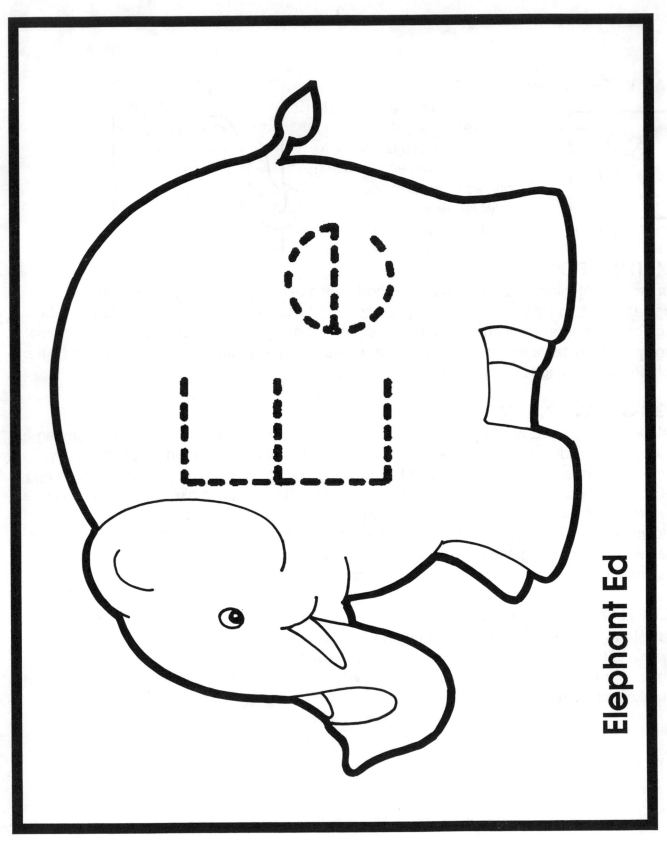

Elephant Ed

Glue crushed eggshells on the Ee's.

Ee
Literature Connection

READ A BOOK

Green Eggs and Ham by Dr. Seuss (Random House, 1960). This nonsense book written in rhyme is incredibly appealing to young children. Sam insists throughout the story that he does not like green eggs and ham, even though they are offered with many enticements. Finally he tries them, finding that he likes them after all.

Presentation

Ask the children what color eggs are. Ask about ham and its color. Then tell the class you are going to read a story about eggs and ham that are green.

Additional Books

The Emperor's New Clothes, retold by Ruth Belov Gross (Scholastic, 1977); *Uncle Elephant* by Arnold Lobel (Scholastic, 1981); *Chickens Aren't the Only Ones* by Ruth Heller (Grosset and Dunlap, 1981); *The Shoemaker and the Elves,* retold by Freya Littledale (Scholastic, 1975); *The Little Engine That Could,* retold by Watty Piper (Platt and Munk, 1976).

RELATED ACTIVITY

Green Eggs and Ham Book

After reading the story, give each child a page with one of the following sentence frames to complete:

I like green eggs and ham! I do! I like it, (child's name) **I am.**

Or

I do not like green eggs and ham! I do not like it, (child's name) **I am.**

Then have each child draw a picture of himself or herself on the page. Bind the pages together into a book for the classroom library.

Listen and Draw an Elephant

Give the children oral directions as you draw each step with them.

1. Draw a large egg-shaped body. Make an ear by drawing half an oval on the side of the egg shape.

2. Add a head and trunk to the body.

3. Draw one eye and two sharp tusks on the head. Add smile lines around one tusk.

4. Put a tail on your elephant. Add two stubby legs.

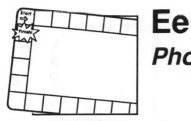

Ee
Phonics Connection

AT SCHOOL

Copy the game board and the set of sound picture cards for The "E" Game onto oaktag for the children to color. Have them cut the cards out. Glue an envelope onto the back of the game board to store the cards and the directions for play.

Show the children how to play the game. Include the "At Home" directions when the game goes home.

- -

AT HOME

Materials:
The "E" Game game board and set of sound picture cards; a small marker for each player

Directions:
1. Place the cards face down in a pile between the players.
2. Take turns drawing from the pile. If the picture on the card begins with the long or short sound of "e," move the marker forward one space. If the picture begins with another letter sound, no move is made. If a player is lucky enough to draw Elephant Ed's card, the marker may be moved forward two spaces.
3. Reshuffle the cards each time they have all been drawn, and continue playing until someone reaches the finish line. The player who finishes first is the winner.

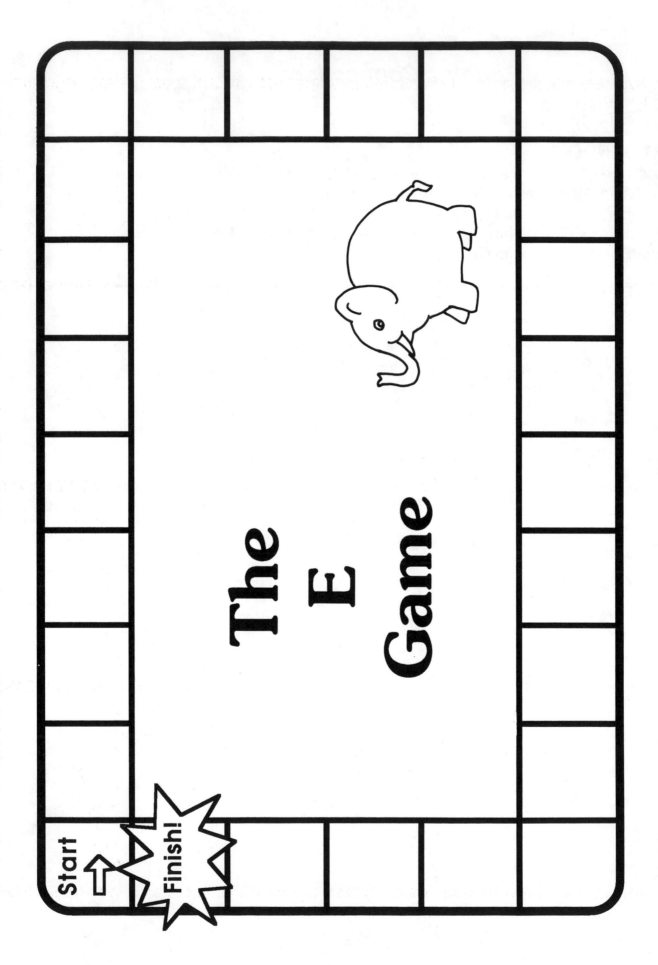

The
E
Game

Start

Finish!

Elephant Ed

Egret Eve

69 ©1993 Monday Morning Books, Inc.

Ee
Math Connection

ESTIMATION EXERCISES

Have the children practice estimating. Ask questions like, "How many girls (boys) are in our class?" "How many beads (blocks, pencils) are in this container?" "How many chairs are there in the room?" "How many books are on our library shelf?" Caution the children against counting before they make their estimates.

EASTER EGG MATH

Make ten egg-shaped tag board cards for each child to decorate like Easter eggs. Write one numeral from one to ten on each egg and have the children practice putting their eggs into numerical sequence. "Scramble" the eggs between practice sessions.

HOW DO YOU LIKE YOUR EGGS?

(a graphing activity)

Brainstorm with the class all the different ways that eggs can be prepared. Then ask the question, "How do you like your eggs?" Reproduce the graphing symbols on the next page and have each child select and color the one that represents his or her favorite.

Cut a large egg shape from white poster board. Divide the egg into three sections by drawing jagged lines across it with black felt pen, making it appear as though it's cracked. Label one section "Fried," another "Scrambled," and the other "Boiled."

Have the children tape their chosen symbols onto the appropriate egg sections. When everyone has recorded a choice, discuss the finished graph together. Begin by asking the children what they see.

Write an experience story together on egg-shaped chart paper about the graph. Put a copy of the story into an experience story book and place it in the classroom library.

How Do You Like Your Eggs?

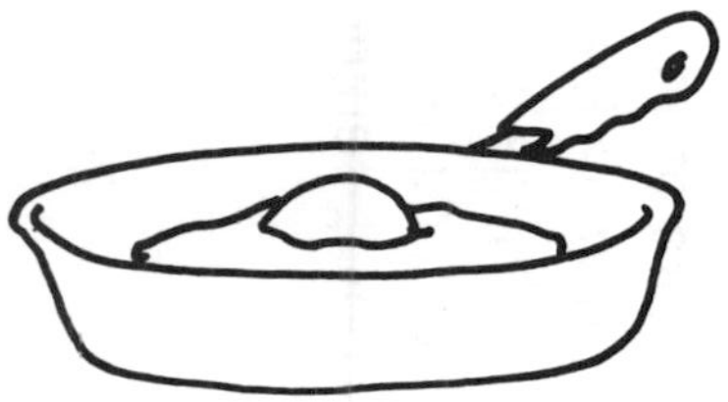

Boiled

Scrambled

Fried

71

Ee
Science Connection

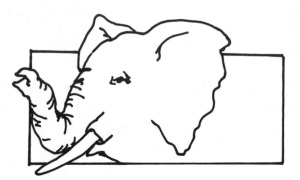

ELEPHANTS

Class: Mammal
Group: Herd
Habitat: Forests, grasslands, deserts
Food: Leaves, bark, roots, grass
Baby: Calf
Color: Gray or brown

Elephants have large ears that they use to keep themselves cool, to signal to their babies, and to scare away enemies. Their trunk is for breathing and smelling, but is also used to suck up hard-to-reach water, to give themselves showers, and as an extra "hand" to pick up, move, and carry things.

READ MORE ABOUT ELEPHANTS

Elephants by John Bonnett Wexco (Creative Education, 1989).
Elephant Baby by Ann McGovern (Scholastic, 1982).

DO AND DISCOVER

Let the children discover how elephants use their trunk to pick up and hold objects by having them grasp pencils between their upper lips and noses. The bottom of an elephant's trunk is an elongated upper lip with lots of muscles that allow fine movements.

WRITE A BOOK ABOUT ELEPHANTS

Brainstorm all the things the children remember about elephants from their study. Make a list of the food elephants eat. Talk about their habitat. Discuss all the interesting things the children learned about elephants.

Put three pages together with a cover for a book for each child. Have the children draw a picture of an elephant on the cover and write a title for the book. (See "Listen and Draw An Elephant.") On the first page, have them draw the food that elephants eat. On the second, let them draw the elephant's habitat, and on the third draw something interesting that they know about elephants. Have the children write or copy a sentence about the picture on each page.

Ee
Science Connection

EGGS

Show the children an egg, and ask them what it is. Tell them that eggs are neat little packages in which nature wraps some babies to keep them warm, to protect them, and to provide them with food and water. Explain that not all babies are born alive from their mothers' bodies like human babies are.

Tell the children that the egg that you showed them is a chicken egg. If some children fear that they are eating baby chicks when they eat eggs, explain that babies need both a mother and a father to start life. Tell them that the eggs in the store never had a father. Also explain that many animals beside chickens lay eggs. Challenge the children to name other animals whose babies are born in eggs. Make a list, adding to it throughout the study.

Organize the children into small groups to make observations about eggs. Give each group a raw egg to crack open. Ask them why they think the egg has a hard shell. Have them name the various parts of the egg. Point out that the yellow yolk would have been food for the developing chick. The clear, thick liquid that we call the egg white would have furnished water and a little more food. Show each group the white ropes in the egg that hold the yolk in place. Tell the children that there is air space in the egg that allows the chick to breathe just before it hatches.

Have the children pretend to be chicks inside an egg. Count to 21 (for the 21 days it takes chicks to hatch) and then have the children "pip," or break out of their eggs.

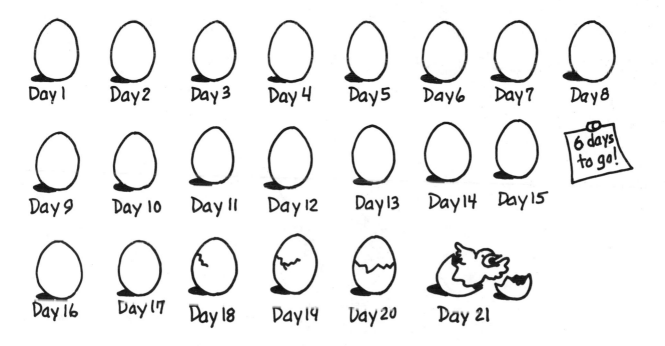

73   ©1993 Monday Morning Books, Inc.

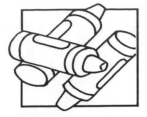

Ee
Arts and Crafts Connection

EXPLODED SHAPES

Materials:
Cardboard shape patterns for tracing (circle, triangle, rectangle, square, oval), pencils, scissors, glue, colored construction paper

Procedure:
1. Have the children choose two or three shape patterns to trace onto colored construction paper and cut out.
2. Working with one shape at a time, show the children how to cut the shapes into several pieces (see the illustration) and arrange them on a piece of construction paper of a contrasting color. Have the children keep the original shape of the pattern but separate the pieces.
3. Have the children glue down the shapes in their "exploded" positions.
4. The children may frame their work by backing the picture with a larger piece of construction paper the same color as the shape.

EMBOSSING

Materials:
Newspaper, white drawing paper, paintbrush handles, peeled crayons

Procedure:
1. Put a pad of newspaper (about ½" thick) on the table.
2. Lay a piece of drawing paper on top of the newspaper and show the children how to draw with the blunt end of a paintbrush handle. Draw so that the handle makes an indented line on the paper but doesn't tear it.
3. Have the children "draw" simple pictures or designs with the brush handles.
4. Using the sides of peeled crayons, encourage the children to lightly color over their embossed designs, letting the crayon glide over the indentations. The designs will remain white.

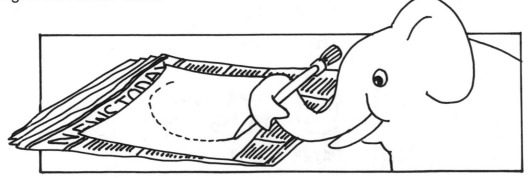

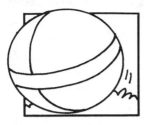

Ee
Movement Connection

EXERCISES

Warm-ups

1. Have the children lie on their back, arms and legs flat, toes pulled toward them and heels pushed away. Tell them to inhale and stretch their arms up over their heads, then exhale as they continue to stretch. Then have them lift one arm at a time and drop it down at their side. Have them repeat this stretch five times.

2. This time, have the children lie on their back with their arms down and their knees bent. Have them press their stomach in as they lift their head and gently bump their right knee against their forehead. Have them lower their head and right knee to the floor and repeat the same exercise with their head and left knee. Have them repeat this exercise three times.

3. Tell the children to lie on their back and hug their knees. Then have them lift their head, tuck their chin under, and rock forward. Have them continue hugging their knees and roll back onto their shoulders (*not* onto their neck), then come forward again. Have them repeat this exercise five times.

Toe Touches

Have the children stand with their feet apart and their arms stretched out to the sides, shoulder high. Give the directions "Turn, touch toes, and up." The children respond by twisting at the waist, touching their left toes with their right hand, and returning to an erect position. With the next command they touch their right toes with their left hand. Have them repeat this exercise five times on each side.

Lunges

Have the children stand with one foot in front of the other, toes pointed straight ahead. Keeping the heel of their back foot on the ground, have them bend the knee in front forward with both hands on it. Count to 10, then have the children relax, change foot positions, and repeat the lunge with the other foot in front. Have them do the entire exercise three times.

Running in Place

Show the children how to feel their heart beat, then have them run in place for 30 seconds and stop to feel their heart beat again. Repeat.

Cool Down

Have the children sit down with their legs crossed (knees bent) in front of them. Tell them to close their eyes and rest their chin on their chest. Have them inhale slowly through their nose, lifting their head as they do. Then have them blow the air out through their mouth as they lower their chin to their chest again. Have them do this complete exercise two times, then slowly rotate their head to the right, down to the chest, and to the left several times.

Ee

HOMEWORK

Name _____

Date Due _____

Put a √ by the activity you have chosen to do.

☐ Cook some **e**ggs with a grownup. Make a picture of what you did and bring it to school to tell about.

☐ Draw some **e**legant **E**aster **e**ggs. Bring your picture to school to share.

☐ Do some **e**xercises. Teach the class to do your favorite.

_____
Signature of grown up helper

ELEPHANT ED'S EGGNOG

Ingredients (serves 1)
egg
sugar
vanilla extract
milk
cinnamon or nutmeg

1. Break an egg into a bowl.

2. Beat the egg.

3. Add 1 T. sugar.

4. Add 1/4 tsp. vanilla extract.

5. Add 1 cup milk.

6. Beat it well. Pour it into a cup or glass.

7. Sprinkle nutmeg or cinnamon on top.

Ff

RAP WITH FENTON FOX

Sign Language **F**

F is for fox, Fenton Fox.
F /f/ /f/ /f/ /f/ /f/ /f/
Fiddle-faddle, five fat frogs.
F /f/ /f/ /f/ /f/ /f/ /f/
Fancy fishes, food, and fun,
F /f/ /f/ /f/ /f/ /f/ /f/
(Repeat the first two lines.)

Fenton Fox

FISHBOWL FUN

Introduce Fenton Fox and his letter F with a fishbowl filled with things that begin with his letter sound. (Examples: a feather, fan, flag, frying pan, football, flower, fork, flashlight, funnel.) Choose some children to take the objects out one at a time and name them. Ask everyone to guess what alphabet animal friend begins with the same sound as all the things in the fishbowl.

FRIENDSHIP FAIR

Celebrate the letter F by having a "Friendship Fair." Have the children play partner games. Let them draw a cooperative picture with a friend, and create funny paper plate and scrap material masks for a friend to wear. Have each child choose a new friend for each activity by picking a name out of the fishbowl. Read with the children books about friends: *We Are Best Friends* by Aliki, and *Will I Have a Friend* and *Best Friends* by Miriam Cohen.

FENTON FOX'S Ff BOOK

Brainstorm with the class words that begin with the same sound as Fenton Fox. Distribute paper and let the children each choose a word to illustrate. Have them copy the following sentence frame onto the page and write their word in the blank space. Put the pages together to make a class book.

Fenton Fox is funny. He is fond of _____.

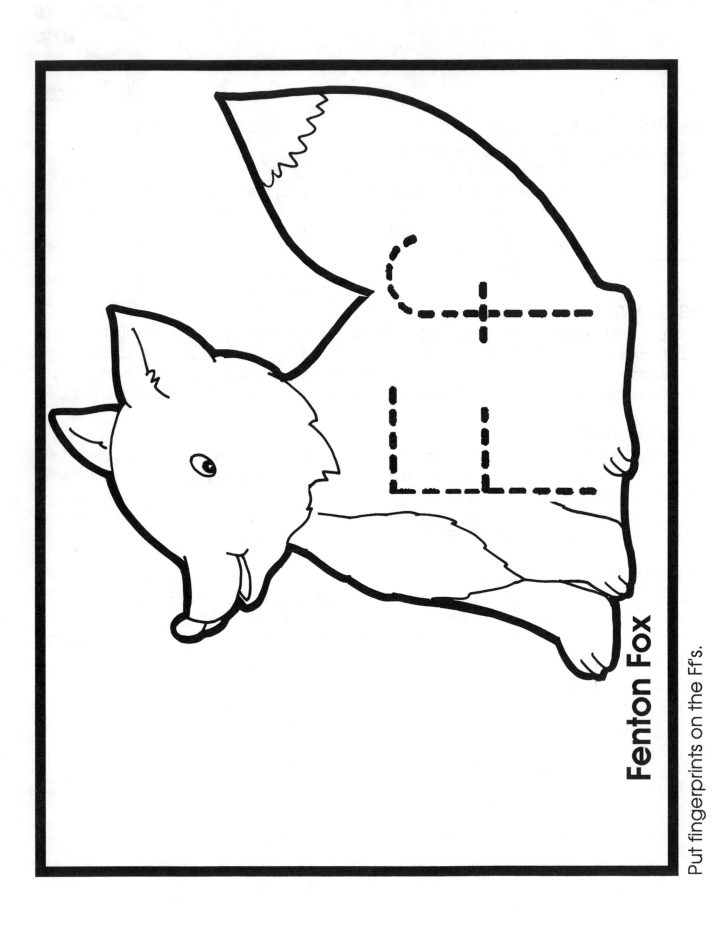

Fenton Fox

Put fingerprints on the Ff's.

Ff
Literature Connection

READ A BOOK
Frederick by Leo Lionni (Pantheon, 1973). Frederick is a sophisticated little mouse who belongs to a hard-working family of mice. As all the other family members gather food and prepare for winter, Frederick spends his time observing nature and asking questions about what he sees.

Presentation
Open a discussion about cleanup time. Ask what things the children do. Ask how they would feel if one of their classmates didn't help. Tell them that the book *Frederick* is about a family of mice getting ready for winter who think that one mouse, Frederick, is not helping. But the family finds out that there are many ways to help.

Additional Books
Hattie and the Fox by Mem Fox (Bradbury, 1986); *Friends* by Helme Heine (McElderry, 1982); *Best Friends* by Miriam Cohen (Macmillan, 1971); *Frog and Toad Are Friends* by Arnold Lobel (Harper, 1970); *One Fine Day* by Nonny Hogrogian (Collier, 1971).

RELATED ACTIVITY

Seasons Poster
After reading the book and discussing the four seasons, give each child a large sheet of paper divided into four sections. Have them label the top left-hand section as winter; the top right, spring; the bottom left, summer; and the bottom right, fall. Give each child a copy of Frederick's poem about the seasons to paste in the middle of the poster. Show the children how to make a fabric Frederick by cutting a small half circle from gray felt, adding a yarn tail, and drawing in ears and eyes with crayons. Have them make four mice and glue one in each of the poster's sections.

Show the children how to create a scene around Frederick for each of the seasons: glitter raindrops, cotton clouds, and an umbrella for spring; a construction paper sun and crushed tissue paper flowers for summer; colored paper pumpkins and a sprig of real wild wheat for fall; and a decorated paper snowman and cotton ball or paper snow for winter.

Listen and Draw a Fox

Give the children oral directions as you draw each step with them.

1. Draw a round head. Add a triangle body.	
2. Make two triangle ears. Add a triangle nose.	
3. Draw a curved back leg with a foot on one side. Make a curved foot on the other side.	
4. Put one eye in the middle of the head and a dark circle at the end of the nose. Add a bushy tail to the body.	

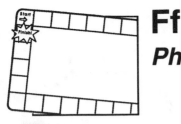

Ff
Phonics Connection

AT SCHOOL

Materials:

One 8" wooden stick (wooden chopstick) per player, string, paper clips, fish-shaped beginning sound picture cards, blue construction paper, oaktag, crayons, hole punch, scissors

To make the fishing poles: Have the players tie an 8" to 10" length of string to the end of each stick. Help them tie a small paper clip bent into a hook shape to the other end of the string.

To make the pond: Round the corners of a 9" by 12" sheet of blue construction paper.

To make the fish: Copy the fish-shaped beginning sound picture cards onto oaktag for the children to color and cut out. Punch a hole at the end of each card.

Show the children how to play the game. Include the "At Home" directions when the game goes home.

AT HOME

Materials:

Set of fish-shaped beginning sound picture cards; one fishing pole for each player; the pond

Directions:

1. Shuffle the cards and scatter them face down on the pond.
2. Take turns drawing cards. If a picture is drawn that begins with the sound of "f," the card is hooked onto the fishing pole and kept. If the card begins with another letter sound, it should be "thrown back" into the pond face up.
3. The winner is the person with the most fish when only face up fish are left in the pond.

 **Ff**
Math Connection

FRESH FRUIT SALAD

Bring a variety of fresh fruits to class. Discuss the attributes of each, such as smooth, bumpy, little, long, round, soft, orange, etc. Help the children develop general category names for the attributes (size, color, shape) and have them sort the fruit in various ways. Make a fine fruit salad as a grand finale.

WHAT'S YOUR FAVORITE FRUIT?

(a graphing activity)

During a class brainstorming session, make a list of all the different kinds of fruit the children can think of. Ask each child to bring a piece of his or her favorite kind of fruit to school the next day.

Lay out a large four-column graph grid on the floor (see the directions for making one in the Introduction). Label three columns according to the three most popular fruits. Label the last column "Others" and explain that this is the place to put all the other kinds of fruit that are not named in the first three columns.

Have the children put their pieces of fruit in the appropriate columns on the graph. Then discuss the finished graph together. Ask the children to tell you everything they can about the graph.

Write an experience story together about the graph after the discussion. Put a copy of the story into an experience story book for the classroom library.

Ff
Science Connection

FOXES
Class: Mammal
Group: Skulk
Habitat: Forests, deserts, meadowlands
Food: Rodents, insects, birds, fruit, berries
Baby: Pup, kit, or cub
Color: Often reddish with white chest, brown, white

Since foxes sleep during the daytime, they curl their tails over their eyes to keep out the sunlight. They hunt for food at night. Their big ears help them hear well. Some foxes live where it snows, and their fur changes to white for the winter.

READ MORE ABOUT FOXES
Animal Life Stories-The Fox by Angela Royston (Ideals, 1988).

DO AND DISCOVER
Discover why foxes have a wet nose by having the children fan their own face gently. Then have them put some water on their nose with a wet cotton ball or cloth and fan again. Help them to see that the fox's wet nose helps him feel the direction of the wind. Then he knows which way to face to catch the scent of food or to escape danger.

WRITE A BOOK ABOUT FOXES
Brainstorm all the things the children remember about foxes from their study. Make a list of the food foxes eat. Talk about their habitat. Discuss all the interesting things the children learned about foxes.

Put three pages together with a cover for a book for each child. Have the children draw a picture of a fox on the cover and write a title for the book. (See "Listen and Draw A Fox.") On the first page, have them draw the food that foxes eat. On the second, let them draw the fox's habitat, and on the third draw something interesting that they know about foxes. Have the children write or copy a sentence about the picture on each page.

Ff
Science Connection

FEATHERS

Give the children magnifying glasses and an assortment of feathers to investigate. Ask questions such as, "What animals have feathers?" "Do all the feathers look alike?" "Do all feathers feel the same?" "What are some words that describe how feathers feel?" (stiff and soft). Tell the children that soft feathers help keep birds warm, and stiff ones protect them and help them fly. Have the children run their fingers along the shaft of stiff contour feathers to separate the barbs, then have them "zip" tho feathers back together.

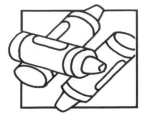

Ff
Arts and Crafts Connection

FINGER PAINTING

Materials:
Finger paints (see the recipes below, or use liquid
starch and tempera paint), glossy freezer wrap or
finger painting paper, smooth, non-absorbent
table top, white drawing paper

Procedure:
1. Make finger paint using one of the recipes and give some to each child, or
simply pour a puddle of liquid starch onto glossy paper or directly onto the table
top and add dry or liquid tempera paint.
2. Have the children smooth their puddle of paint over the work surface. Show
them how to use their fingers, hands, fingernails, fists, and forearms to achieve
different design effects in their paint. Encourage them to use a variety of movements as well. Try letting them paint to music.
3. If the children have finger painted directly on the table top, a monoprint can be
made by laying a piece of white drawing paper gently on top of the painting and
smoothing it evenly over the design. Have the children peel the paper off the
table top. They will have a print of their finger painted artwork to take home.

Finger Paint Recipe #1 (for 20 to 30 children)
1. Mix half a box of cornstarch into cold water to make a thin paste.
2. Use a wire whisk to stir in three quarts of boiling water.
3. Cook over medium heat, stirring constantly.
4. Cool, and add dry or liquid tempera for color.

Finger Paint Recipe #2 (for one child)
1. Mix three tablespoons cornstarch with three tablespoons cold water.
2. Add one cup of boiling water and stir.
3. Add a squirt of liquid detergent.
4. Add dry or liquid tempera for color.

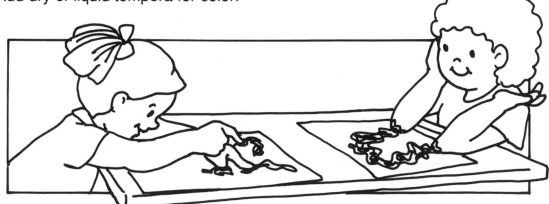

Ff
Movement Connection

FLYTRAPS

Divide the children into two groups. One group will be scattered around the designated playing area. They will be sitting on the ground and will be the "Traps." They are not allowed to move from their spots. The other group will be the "Flies."

When play begins, the "Flies" buzz in and out among the children sitting on the ground. They must freeze at the sound of the whistle. If any "Trap" can touch a frozen "Fly" from his or her sitting position, the two trade places, with the "Fly" sitting in the "Trap's" place. The "Trap" becomes a "Fly" and play continues.

FROGGIE, FROGGIE

Before playing the game, teach the children how to do the "frog jump." Have them squat down with their hands on the floor about a shoulder's width apart. Their feet should be placed together between their hands. Show them how to jump forward with their hands and feet leaving the floor at the same time. Give them time to practice.

The Game:

Have the children sit in a circle. Choose one child to be the "Frog." The "Frog" jumps around the circle, saying, "Froggie, Froggie, how's your friend?" The "Frog" taps another child who then becomes the new "Frog," and says, "I don't know, but I'll go see." The new "Frog" jumps around the circle, repeating the question. Another child is tapped, and play continues. Each child who is tapped is replaced in the circle by the previous "Frog."

Ff
HOMEWORK

Name _____

Date Due _____

Put a √ by the activity you have chosen to do.

☐ Make a frisbee from a paper plate. Practice flying it. Bring it to school to fly with a friend.

☐ Count how many footsteps it is from your room to other places in your house. Tell about it at school.

☐ Draw a picture of your family. Tell a story about the picture and ask someone to write it down. Bring it to school.

_____
Signature of grown up helper

FENTON FOX'S FRUIT FACE

Ingredients (serves 1)
    orange slice
    seedless grape
    pineapple cube
    apple wedge
    alfalfa sprouts

1. Put an orange slice on a plate.

2. Cut a grape in half.

3. Put the grape halves on for eyes.

4. Put a pineapple piece on for a nose.

5. Put an apple wedge on for a mouth.

6. Add alfalfa sprouts for hair.

Gg

RAP WITH GERTIE GOOSE

Sign Language **G**

G is for goose, Gertie Goose.
G /g/ /g/ /g/ /g/ /g/ /g/
Gooey garbage, giggling girls.
G /g/ /g/ /g/ /g/ /g/ /g/
Goosey, gander, Goldilocks.
G /g/ /g/ /g/ /g/ /g/ /g/
(Repeat the first two lines.)

Gertie Goose

GERTIE'S GIFT

Wrap objects that begin with the hard sound of g and put them in a gift box with a card saying the gift is for the children from Gertie Goose. Read the card out loud before opening the box, and have the children guess what might be inside. Choose a different child to unwrap each gift. When all the objects have been named, discuss the fact that they all begin with the same sound as Gertie Goose.

GRANDPARENTS DAY

Let the children decorate invitations to their grandparents, asking them to come to school on a special day. Plan a program of songs and recitations. Make Gorp (a mixture of raisins, peanuts, Cheerios, and chocolate chips) to serve with grape punch. Give tours of the classroom and the school.

GERTIE GOOSE'S Gg BOOK

Brainstorm with the class words that begin with the same sound as Gertie Goose. Distribute paper and let the children each choose a word to illustrate. Have them copy the following sentence frame onto the page and write their word in the blank space. Put the pages together to make a class book.

If I were Gertie Goose, I'd give _____ to girls.

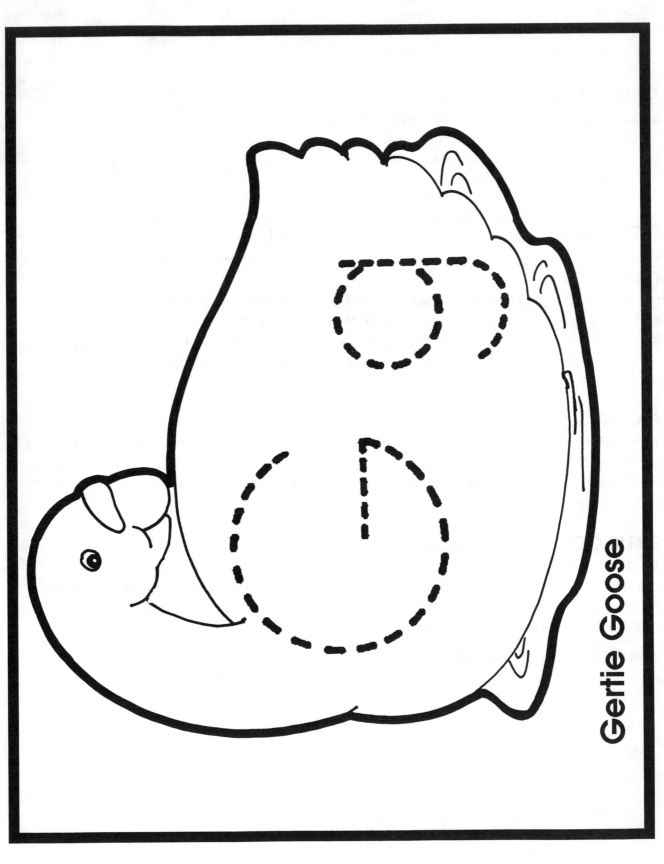

Gertie Goose

Glue gold glitter on the Gg's.

Gg
Literature Connection

READ A BOOK

The Three Billy Goats Gruff by Paul Galdone (Clarion, 1973). Children enjoy hearing this classic tale about three billy goats and an ugly troll over and over again.

Presentation

Tell the children that you would like them to help you read the story of the three Billy Goats Gruff. Tell them that each time one of the goats goes over the bridge, they should say, "Trip, trap, trip, trap, trip, trap," just the way the goat would sound (softly for the little goat, a little louder for the middle-sized goat, and very loudly for the great big billy goat).

Additional Books

Goggles by Ezra Jack Keats (Aladdin, 1969); *Goodnight Moon* by Margaret Wise Brown (Harper, 1947); *The Three Billy Goats Gruff* by Marcia Brown (Harcourt, 1985).

RELATED ACTIVITIES

Dramatization

Ask the children if anyone has ever been to the theater. Discuss the difference between a live production and a movie. Introduce the vocabulary of drama: play, stage, actors, parts, sound effects, props, etc. Be sure to discuss the importance of the audience—its role and what it does to show its appreciation at the end of a play.

Have the children take turns acting out *The Three Billy Goats Gruff.* An elaborate set isn't necessary. With just a table serving as a bridge, the children's imaginations will be enough to bring the characters alive. Have them use rhythm instruments to make the sound of the billy goats' feet clip-clopping across the bridge—a triangle for the sound of the littlest billy goat's feet, a wooden tapping block for the middle-size goat, and a drum for the largest billy goat.

Narrate the action, allowing selected children to join in on their respective speaking parts. Let the audience join in on the "Clip clop, clip clop" chant.

A Troll Book

Ask the children what they think trolls are—where they live, what they eat, how they dress, what they do all day, their size and color, etc. Discuss their ideas. Then provide crayons, paint, and paper and encourage the children to use their imaginations to create their own versions of trolls. Use the pictures as illustrations for a class book. Have each child dictate or write a sentence caption (or a story) to accompany his or her picture.

Listen and Draw a Goose

Give the children oral directions as you draw each step with them.

1. Draw a large oval for the body. Add a triangle tail.

2. Draw a small circle for the head. Add a curved neck between the head and the body. Make a pie-shaped bill on the head.

3. Add a band across the bill. Make a curved wing in the middle of the body.

4. Make one eye on the head. Draw two webbed feet.

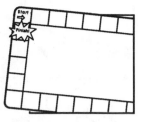

Gg
Phonics Connection

AT SCHOOL

Materials:
One paper-fiber egg carton cut in half the short way, Popsicle sticks, 6" by 2" green construction paper strips, glue, tape, crayons, oaktag, scissors, flower-shaped beginning sound picture cards

To make the gardens: Give the children some green construction paper strips to glue around the egg cartons like fringe. Cut slits in the bottoms of the egg carton cups that will accommodate Popsicle stick flowers. Make two gardens for each game.

To make the flowers: Copy the flower-shaped beginning sound picture cards onto oaktag for the children to color and cut out. Tape a Popsicle stick stem onto each.

Show the children how to play the game. Include the "At Home" directions when the game goes home.

- -

AT HOME

Materials:
A set of flower-shaped beginning sound picture cards; an egg carton garden for each player

Directions:
1. Shuffle the cards and scatter them face down between the players.
2. Take turns drawing cards. If a card is drawn with a picture that begins with the sound of "g," the card is planted in the garden. If it begins with another letter sound, the card is put in a discard pile.
3. The winner is the person with the most planted flowers after all the cards have been drawn.

Gg
Math Connection

GUMDROP GUESS-TIMATIONS

Fill a jar with gumdrops and ask the children to guess how many there are. Record their "guess-timations" and then count the candy. Have the children sort the estimates according to the categories "Too Few," "Just Right," and "Too Many." At another time have the children estimate and later count how many of each color gumdrop there are in the jar.

GORP GRAPHING

(a graphing activity)

Make Gorp, a mixture of raisins, peanuts, chocolate chips, and Cheerios, and give the children each half a cupful in a small plastic bag. Have them make individual graphs by sorting their Gorp into separate ingredient columns on a prepared grid (duplicate the graphing form on this page). Discuss their findings with questions like, "How many people have more (name an ingredient) than anything else?" "Was there anyone who didn't have any (name an ingredient), and how does that look on your graph?"

Write an experience story together about the graph findings. Put a copy of the story into an experience story book and place it in the classroom library.

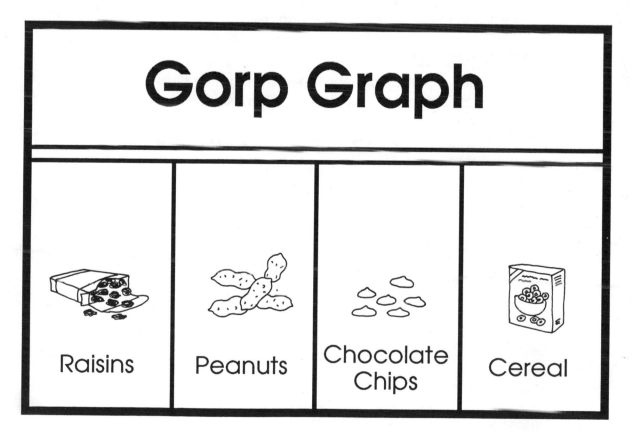

Gg
Science Connection

GEESE

Class: Bird
Group: Flock and gaggle
Habitat: Swamps, lakes, ponds
Food: Grass, seeds, plants
Baby: Gosling
Color: White, black, brown, or gray

Many geese migrate, or move from one place to another during parts of the year. When they migrate, some fly in a V-shaped pattern. In that way the leader pushes the air and makes a path for the others to follow. After a female lays eggs, she plucks special soft feathers from her breast to line her nest.

READ MORE ABOUT GEESE

Ducks, Geese, and Swans by John Wexco (Creative Education, 1989).

DO AND DISCOVER

Let the children discover how much energy it takes for geese to migrate. Have the children flap their arms like wings for at least one minute. As they tire, explain that geese can fly as far as 1,000 miles without stopping to rest!

WRITE A BOOK ABOUT GEESE

Brainstorm all the things the children remember about geese from their study. Make a list of the food geese eat. Talk about their habitat. Discuss all the interesting things the children learned about geese.

Put three pages together with a cover for a book for each child. Have the children draw a picture of a goose on the cover and write a title for the book. (See "Listen and Draw A Goose.") On the first page, have them draw the food that geese eat. On the second, let them draw the goose's habitat, and on the third draw something interesting that they know about geese. Have the children write or copy a sentence about the picture on each page.

Gg
Science Connection

GARBAGE GARDEN

Ask the children to bring to class the parts of vegetables and fruits that are often thrown into the garbage as the vegetables are being prepared. Place the cut-off tops of carrots, radishes, beets, turnips, and the like in a shallow pan that has been spread with a half-inch layer of soil. Cover them all around with pebbles. Keep them well watered. Have the children observe what happens.

The class can also grow sweet potatoes or yams by inserting three toothpicks around the midsection of each and putting them into glasses full of water, with the toothpicks resting on the rims. Avocado seeds can be started in the same way, with the pointed end of the seed going down into the water. Keep the glasses filled with water.

Try growing beans using ordinary planting techniques. Citrus seeds can be planted as soon as they come from the fruit; apple seeds need a cold moist period of two months before planting.

GRAVITY

Ask the children to recall some things they have studied that they cannot see but that are real, such as air and static electricity. Explain that they will be discovering another real thing that cannot be seen—gravity.

Ask the children to jump as high as they can. Then ask them to jump up and stay up until you tell them to come down. They will delight in trying to stay up! Ask them why they didn't wait for your signal. Ask, "What made you come down?" "Does everything come down?"

Have the children take turns dropping various objects, such as blocks, pencils, toys, paper, etc., from atop a big building block placed in the center of a circle of the children. Use the word "gravity" and explain that this is a force that cannot be seen but can be felt. Gravity is strong enough to keep things on the ground, or at least close to the earth.

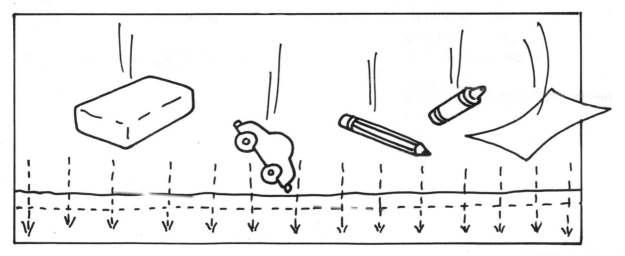

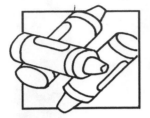

Gg
Arts and Crafts Connection

GONFALONS

A gonfalon is a flag that hangs from a crosspiece rather than from an upright staff.

Materials:
Newsprint, tempera paint, 12" by 14" pieces of burlap, brushes, sticks or dowels, colored felt pens, masking tape, yarn and blunt needles

Procedure:
1. Discuss what gonfalons are with the children.
2. Have them draw several pictures on newsprint, and select one to use on their gonfalon.
3. Show them how to paint their design onto the burlap.
4. When the paintings are thoroughly dry, show the children how to pull strings across the bottom and two sides of the burlap to make a narrow fringe.

5. Fold over the top of the gonfalon about two inches to form a tube. Secure with masking tape, and show the children how to use some yarn and the blunt needle to sew across the top about 1" to 1½" from the fold.
6. Show the children how to slip the dowel through the tube and tie a piece of yarn to each edge of the dowel. Remove the masking tape and the gonfalon is ready to hang.

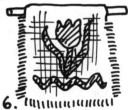

GLUE DESIGNS

Materials:
White drawing paper, watercolor paints, white glue, soft paintbrushes, art fixative

Procedure:
1. Have the children "draw" a simple design on the white drawing paper with white glue. Let the designs dry thoroughly.
2. Show the children how to drip and dab watercolor paints onto their design with a soft brush.
3. Spray the dry paintings with any glossy art fixative.

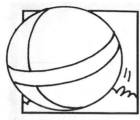

Gg
Movement Connection

GALLOPING HORSES

Before playing the game, teach the children how to gallop. Have them move slowly in a circle, putting one foot in front and pulling the other up behind it, rather than in front as in normal walking. Let them practice slowly at first, then suggest that they try "galloping" faster.

The Game:

Play this game on a large grassy area. Designate two goals about 30 to 40 feet apart. They are the "fences." (Mark them with jump ropes.) One child will be the "Cowhand" who stands in the middle and shouts, "Gallop, Horses!" The other children are the "Horses" and stand behind one of the fences. When they hear the signal from the "Cowhand" they gallop toward the other fence, and the "Cowhand" tries to touch as many of them as possible. Tagged "Horses" become "Cowhands." The game continues until all the children are tagged.

GHOST

Have the children sit on the floor in a circle. Choose someone to lie down in the center of the circle and be the "Ghost." Cover the "Ghost" with a sheet and instruct him or her to hold up a body part for the children to try to identify. If the "Ghost" hears the wrong answer, he or she wails loudly, "NO-O-O-O-O-O-O." If the answer is right, the "Ghost" responds in an equally eerie voice, "YE-E-E-E-E-E-S." After a specified number of the "Ghost's" body parts have been identified, another "Ghost" is chosen.

Gg

HOMEWORK

Name _____

Date Due _____

Put a √ by the activity you have chosen to do.

☐ Tell a story about your **g**randparents. Have someone write it down for you. Make a picture and bring the story and the picture to school.

☐ Make a **g**ift for someone at school. (Some ideas are: a card, bookmark, or picture.) Bring the **g**ift to school to **g**ive to the person.

☐ Plant a **g**arden. Bring a picture of it to school. Tell the class what you planted in your **g**arden.

_____
Signature of grown up helper

GERTIE GOOSE'S GRANOLA

Ingredients (serves 1)
uncooked oatmeal
wheat germ
nuts
sunflower seeds
honey
cooking oil

1. Put 1 T. oatmeal into a bowl.

2. Add 1/2 tsp. nuts.

3. Add 1/2 tsp. wheat germ.

4. Add 1/2 tsp. sunflower seeds.

5. Add 1/2 tsp. honey.

6. Add 1/2 tsp. oil, and stir.

7. Put into paper-lined muffin cup and bake at 350° for 5-10 minutes. (You need a helping hand.)

RAP WITH HIPPO HAL

Sign Language **H**

H is for hippo, Hippo Hal.
H /h/ /h/ /h/ /h/ /h/ /h/
Hopping, hiccups, Hula-Hoops.
H /h/ /h/ /h/ /h/ /h/ /h/
Happy homes and Halloween.
H /h/ /h/ /h/ /h/ /h/ /h/
(Repeat the first two lines.)

Hippo Hal

HIDE A HAT

To introduce Hippo Hal and his letter H, hide a hat full of things that begin with /h/ before the children arrive at school. Tell them there is something different in the classroom, and appoint a small committee to look for what it is. When the hat is found, choose other children to remove the objects one at a time and name them. Ask all the children who they think is the alphabet animal friend who hid the hat in the classroom.

HAPPY HAT HOLIDAY

Have a "Happy Hat Holiday" to celebrate the letter H. Invite the children to wear special hats to school on that day. Give an award for each hat, for example, the funniest, the biggest, the smallest, the fanciest, the most beautiful, the most original, the craziest. Dance the Mexican Hat Dance. Eat hot dogs. Read *Who Took The Farmer's Hat?* by Joan L. Nodset. Take pictures of the children in their hats and make a class book about the holiday.

HIPPO HAL'S Hh BOOK

Brainstorm with the class words that begin with the same sound as Hippo Hal. Distribute paper and let the children each choose a word to illustrate. Have them copy the following sentence frame onto the page and write their word in the blank space. Put the pages together to make a class book.

Hippo Hal is happy to have his _____.

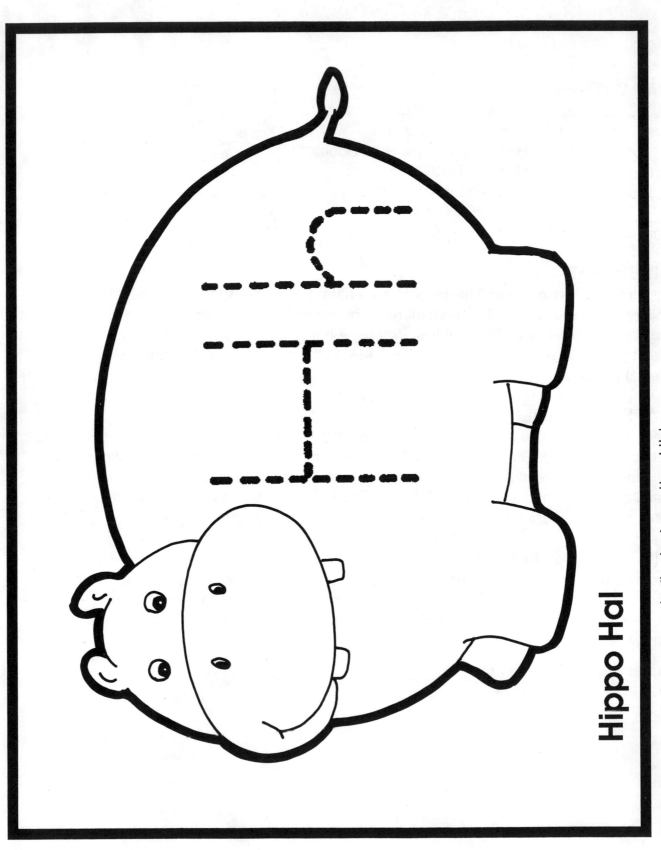

Hippo Hal

Glue paper reinforcements (holes) on the Hh's.

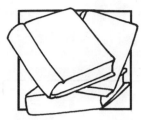

Hh
Literature Connection

READ A BOOK
Who Took The Farmer's Hat? by Joan L. Nodset (D. C. Heath, 1963). This is a book about a farmer who lost his old brown hat. The children will delight in all the funny things the farm animals imagine the farmer's hat to be. The values of giving and caring are gently modeled in the sensitive ending.

Presentation
Ask the children if they've ever lost anything, and, if they did, how they looked for it. Tell them that in this story the farmer loses his old brown hat, and asks the animals if they have seen it.

Additional Books
A House Is a House for Me by Mary Ann Hoberman (Viking, 1978); *Harold and the Purple Crayon* by Crockett Johnson (Harper, 1955); *The Little Red Hen* by Paul Galdone (Clarion, 1973); *Harry, the Dirty Dog* by Gene Zion (Harper, 1956); *Henny Penny* by Werner Zimmermann (Scholastic, 1989); *The Little House* by Virginia L. Burton (Houghton, 1942).

RELATED ACTIVITY

Hat Big Book
After reading the story, talk about the farmer's hat and all the things the animals imagined it to be. Give each child a large piece of paper with the following sentence frame on it, inserting the child's name in the first blank:

_____, have you seen my old brown hat?

Then have the children draw a picture based on the discussion, incorporating a cutout brown construction paper hat into it. Bind the pages into a book for the library corner.

Listen and Draw a Hippo

Give the children oral directions as you draw each step with them.

1. Draw a bean-shaped muzzle. Put a round bump on the top.

2. Make a big oval body. Add two tiny ears to the hippo's head.

3. Draw a tail. Add two short legs under the body.

4. Make two dark eyes on the hippo's head. Make two small circle nostrils on the muzzle.

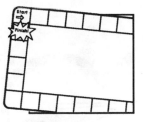

Hh
Phonics Connection

AT SCHOOL

Materials:
Paper cups, construction paper circles 2" larger in diameter than the open end of the paper cups, scissors, crayons, oaktag, tape, pencils, heart-shaped beginning sound picture cards

To make the hats: Have two children trace the open end of a paper cup in the center of a construction paper circle and cut it out. With their cups upside down, have them bring their circle down over the bottom and tape it into place around the open end of the cup. Make two hats for each game.

To make the hearts: Copy the heart-shaped beginning sound picture cards onto oaktag for the children to color and cut out.

Show the children how to play the game. Include the "At Home" directions when the game goes home.

AT HOME

Materials:
One paper cup hat for each player; one set of heart-shaped beginning sound picture cards

Directions:
1. Shuffle the cards and scatter them face down in front of the players.
2. Take turns drawing cards. If a picture is drawn that begins with the sound of "h," it is put in the hat. If a picture begins with another letter sound, it is put in a discard pile.
3. The winner is the person whose hat holds the most cards after all the cards have been drawn.

Hh
Math Connection

HANDS FULL OF HEARTS

Fill a bowl with candy hearts and ask the children to estimate how many they can hold in one hand. Have them trace and cut out their handprint, then record their estimate on one side. Then have them each take a handful of hearts from the bowl, count them, and record the actual count on the other side of their handprint. Lead a discussion about the results.

WHAT'S YOUR FAVORITE HOLIDAY?

(a graphing activity)

Make a list with the children of all the holidays they can think of. Ask the question, "What is your favorite holiday?" Give each child a 2" by 2" piece of drawing paper and have all the children draw a picture of something that represents the holiday they like the most. Some symbols might be a decorated egg for Easter, an ornament for Christmas, a heart for Valentine's Day, a jack-o'-lantern for Halloween, and a Star of David for Channukah. Write the name of the holiday on each child's picture.

Make a four-column graphing grid (see the directions in the Introduction). Label three columns according to the three most popular holidays. Label the last column "Others," explaining that this is where holiday symbols should go if they don't represent one of the named holidays on the graph. Have the children tape their picture symbols onto the appropriate columns.

When everyone has recorded a choice, ask the children to tell you as many things as they can about the graph. Then write an experience story together about the graph, put it in an experience story book, and place it in the classroom library.

Hh
Science Connection

HIPPOPOTAMUSES

Class: Mammal
Group: Herd or school
Habitat: Lakes, rivers
Food: Grass, water plants, leaves, fruit, grain
Baby: Calf
Color: Brown or gray

"Hippo" means "water horse," but a hippo is more like a pig. A mother often "piggybacks" her baby around in the water. When it gets dry, the hippo's skin secretes a pink fluid called "blood sweat." Hippos can walk along river bottoms completely under water for as long as 10 minutes.

READ MORE ABOUT HIPPOS

Jane Goodall's Animal World: Hippos by Miriam Schlein (Byron Preiss, 1989).

DO AND DISCOVER

Let the children discover the difference between the lengths of time people and hippos can hold their breath. Use a timer and have the children hold their breath three different times. What was their longest time? Hippos can hold their breath for over 10 minutes!

WRITE A BOOK ABOUT HIPPOS

Brainstorm all the things the children remember about hippos from their study. Make a list of the food hippos eat. Talk about their habitat. Discuss all the interesting things the children learned about hippos.

Put three pages together with a cover for a book for each child. Have the children draw a picture of a hippo on the cover and write a title for the book. (See "Listen and Draw A Hippo.") On the first page, have them draw the food that hippos eat. On the second, let them draw the hippo's habitat, and on the third draw something interesting that they know about hippos. Have the children write or copy a sentence about the picture on each page.

Hh
Science Connection

HEART

Ask the children to do what you do as long as they can. Hold up your fist and open it, then squeeze it shut. Repeat these actions over and over. As the children tire, stop and explain that there is a muscle in their bodies that is much stronger than their hand muscles. It is so strong that it can pump all the time and never get tired. Ask the children if they can guess which muscle it is. If they don't guess it, tell them that it is their heart muscle.

Explain that a living heart is not shaped like a valentine heart; it is more the shape of a pear or a fist. Its job is to pump blood through the body. Tell them their heart fills with blood, then It squeezes itself together and sends the blood out through tubes called arteries all through their body. When their heart stops squeezing, it opens and more blood comes into it through other tubes called veins. Sometimes people can see their veins on the back of their hand. Ask the children to look for veins on their hands.

Give the children cardboard tubes such as paper towel or toilet tissue tubes. Have them listen to a partner's heart by placing one end of the tube in the middle of their friend's chest and the other against their own ear. Have the child whose heart is being listened to run in place for 30 seconds, then have the other child listen again. Ask, "What happened to the heartbeats?"

HEAVY/LIGHT

Make a simple balance scale from a coat hanger, two paper cups, and some string. Punch four holes around the top of each cup. Attach the cups to the hanger with string, moving them back and forth on the hanger until the cups balance. Hook the hanger over a yardstick suspended between two chairs.

Show the children how the balance works. Have them choose one of the objects you've collected, such as shells, paper clips, rocks, coins, corks, chalk, crayons, blocks, erasers, and scissors. Then have them sort the other objects according to which are heavier than the chosen object and which are lighter. Discuss the results. Ask, "Is the heavier object bigger?" "Which of these things is the heaviest?" "How can we find out?"

Hh
Arts and Crafts Connection

HOLIDAY HATS

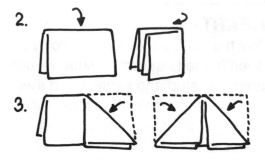

Materials:

Newsprint or butcher paper, tape, 14" squares of colored construction paper, patterns for holiday symbols and other decorating materials for 3 or 4 of the children's favorite holidays

Procedure:

1. Encourage the children to choose a construction paper square that is a color appropriate to their favorite holiday.
2. Show them how to fold their paper in half and in half again, as pictured in the first illustration.
3. Have them open their paper once. Using the second fold line as a guide to the midpoint, have the children fold the corners at the top (fold) of the paper to the middle of the bottom of the paper (open). (See the second illustration.)
4. Show the children how to tape the two ends in place.
5. Have them decorate the resulting hat with appropriate materials and symbols of their favorite holiday.

HAND IN HAND

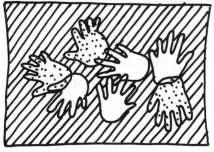

Materials:

12" by 18" pieces of white paper, handprint patterns (optional), crayons, watercolors and water, brushes, wallpaper or fabric samples

Procedure:

1. Have the children trace around their own hand, a friend's hand, a hand pattern, or all three on a piece of white paper. Encourage them to fill up most of the paper with hand shapes; shapes may overlap. They will need to press down hard with their crayons.
2. Show the children samples of patterned wallpaper or fabric, and point out how the design on each repeats itself over and over until it fills up the whole piece. Have the children fill in each of their hand shapes with a different pattern (polka dots, stripes, squiggles, spirals, etc.), continuing to press down hard with their crayons.
3. Show the children how to put a watercolor wash over their entire picture. The crayon will resist the watercolors and show through, enhancing the "Hand in Hand" designs.

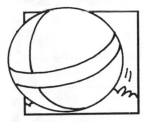

Hh
Movement Connection

HOME, SWEET HOME

Designate a "home" for each child, marking it with a circle of rope or yarn. Arrange the "homes" in a big circle. Give the children some commands to familiarize them with their "homes," such as, "Jump into your home," "Sit cross-legged in your home," "Put one foot inside and one foot outside your home," etc.

When the children are familiar with their "homes," have them stand in them with their left hand extended into the center of the circle. One child is chosen to be "It," and walks around the inside of the circle. While walking, "It" selects another child to walk with by taking that child's extended left hand in his or her right hand.

The line grows as each new walker takes the left hand of another child still waiting at "home." When about three fourths of the children are holding hands and walking in line, "It" (or the teacher) shouts, "Home, sweet home!" and the children must drop hands and return to their own "homes" before the count of 10. Play continues with a new person chosen to be "It."

HIDE THE HAMBURGER

Have the children sit in a circle. Choose a child to stand in the center of the circle and hide his or her eyes. Give a beanbag, which represents the hamburger, to a child sitting in the circle to hide in his or her lap. When the "hamburger" is hidden, "It" uncovers his or her eyes and begins to walk within the circle while the other players clap to help "It" find the "hamburger." The children should clap louder and faster when "It" gets close to the player with the "hamburger," and softer and slower as he or she moves away. Give "It" three guesses to find the player with the "hamburger." Then that player becomes "It," and the previous "It" gets to choose the player who hides the "hamburger."

Hh

HOMEWORK

Name _____

Date Due _____

Put a √ by the activity you have chosen to do.

☐ Trace the **h**and of each person in your family.
Whose **h**and is the largest? Whose is the smallest?
Show your pictures to the class, and tell about them.

☐ Pick up a **h**andful of small things, such as Cheerios,
peanuts, or raisins.

☐ Find out how many you can **h**old in your **h**and. **H**ave
a grownup write the number down. Tell about it at
school.

_____
Signature of grown up helper

HIPPO HAL'S HOT DOG

Ingredients (serves 1)
hot dog
refrigerator biscuit
cheese strip
mustard, catsup, etc.

1. Cut a slit down the middle of the hot dog.

2. Put a strip of cheese in the slit.

3. Flatten the biscuit.

4. Wrap the biscuit around the hot dog. Pinch the edges.

5. Put the prepared hot dog on a cookie sheet.

6. Bake at 350° for 8-10 minutes. (You need a helping hand.)

RAP WITH ICHABOD INDRI

Sign Language I

I is for indri, Ichabod Indri.
I /i/ /i/ /i/ /i/ /i/ /i/
Icky, insects, injuries.
I /i/ /i/ /i/ /i/ /i/ /i/
Imitating instruments.
I /i/ /i /i/ /i/ /i/ /i/
(Repeat the first two lines.)

Ichabod Indri

INTRODUCING THE INDRI

Introduce the letter I by telling the children about the interesting animal called the indri (in´-dri). The indri is a large lemur, a primate that lives only on the island of Madagascar off the eastern coast of Africa. It is an endangered species because its habitat, the rain forest, is being destroyed.

Show the children pictures as you talk about the indri. The National Geographic Society is a good source for animal photographs, and more information about the animal can be found in the *World Book Encyclopedia.*

ICE CREAM SOCIAL

Invite the children to an interesting "Ice Cream Social" to celebrate the letter I. Make ice cream at school, if possible, and have the children bring their favorite toppings to share. During the party, talk about things that interest people. Ask the children to tell about their own interests. Make a class book called "Things That Interest Us."

ICHABOD INDRI'S Ii BOOK

Brainstorm with the class words that begin with the same sound as Ichabod Indri. Distribute paper and let the children each choose a word to illustrate. Have them copy the following sentence frame onto the page and write their word in the blank space. Put the pages together to make a class book.

Ichabod Indri is interested in _____.

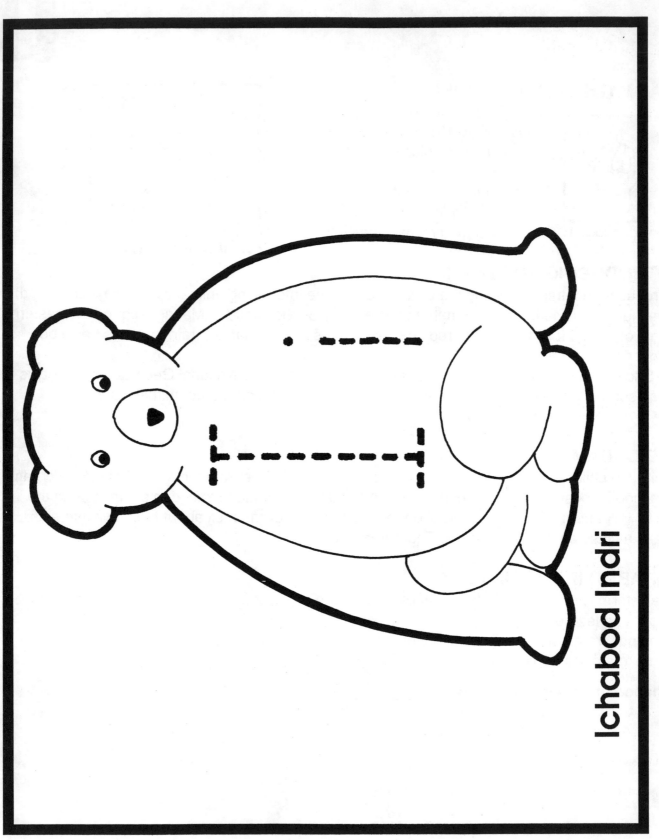

Ichabod Indri

Trace the Ii's with ink.

114

Ii
Literature Connection

READ A BOOK

Inch By Inch by Leo Lionni (Astor-Honor, 1960). This is the story of a little inch-worm who loves to measure things until the day he is threatened by a bird who says he's going to eat him.

Presentation

Explain to the children that one way we measure things is by counting how many inches long they are. Show them the approximate size of an inch with your fingers. Tell them that the story *Inch By Inch* is about a little worm that is just about one inch long.

Additional Books

Ira Sleeps Over by Bernard Waber (Houghton, 1972); *The Important Book* by Margaret Wise Brown (Harper, 1949); *Imogene's Antlers* by David Small (Crown, 1985).

RELATED ACTIVITIES

Movement

Have the children lie on their tummy and scoot their knees up under their chest. Then, keeping their knees still, have them push their arms ahead of them across the floor, flattening out again. Explain that this is the way an inchworm moves. Let the children pretend they are inchworms and try to move their bodies across the room.

Measurement Books

Give each child a 12" strip of card stock with inch marks on it. Make a 1" long inchworm out of green construction paper to go with each ruler. Show the children how to lay the ruler on an object and measure it by counting the number of times their inchworm can be laid end to end on it.

Encourage the children to measure several things around the room before choosing one to illustrate. Have them glue their inchworm on their page and incorporate it into a drawing of the chosen object. Have them complete the following sentence frame on the page:

I measured a _____. It was _____ inches long.

Bind the pages together for everyone to enjoy.

Listen and Draw an Indri

Give the children oral directions as you draw each step with them.

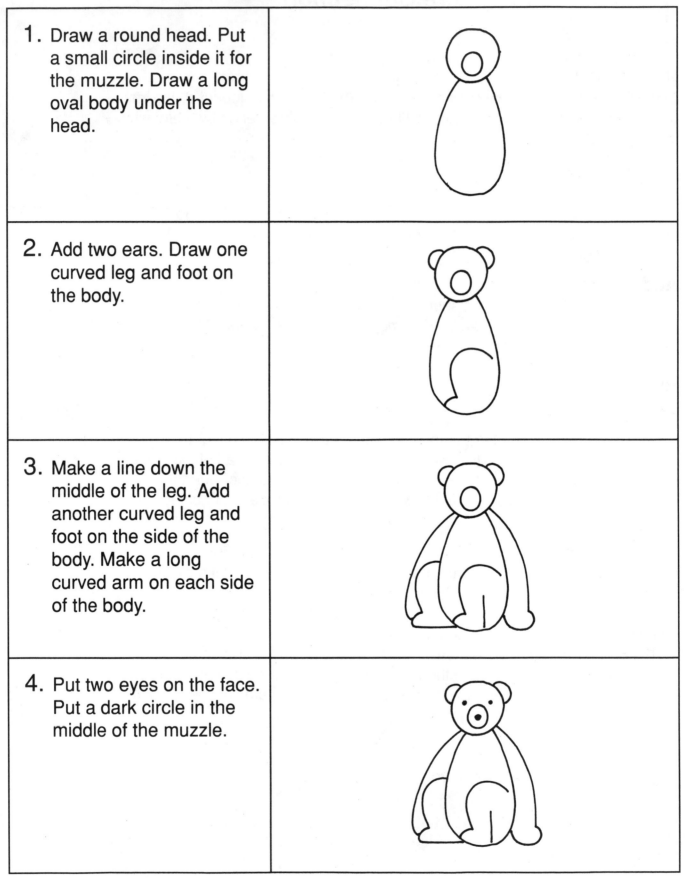

1. Draw a round head. Put a small circle inside it for the muzzle. Draw a long oval body under the head.

2. Add two ears. Draw one curved leg and foot on the body.

3. Make a line down the middle of the leg. Add another curved leg and foot on the side of the body. Make a long curved arm on each side of the body.

4. Put two eyes on the face. Put a dark circle in the middle of the muzzle.

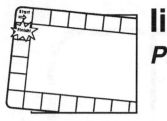 **Ii**

Phonics Connection

AT SCHOOL

Copy the game board and the set of sound picture cards for The "I" Game onto oaktag for the children to color. Have them cut the cards out. Glue an envelope onto the back of the game board to store the cards and the directions for play.

Show the children how to play the game. Include the "At Home" directions when the game goes home.

- -

AT HOME

Materials:
The "I" Game game board and set of sound picture cards; a small marker for each player

Directions:
1. Place the cards face down in a pile between the players.
2. Take turns drawing from the pile. If the picture on the card begins with the long or short sound of "i," move the marker forward one space. If the picture begins with another letter sound, no move is made. If a player is lucky enough to draw Ichabod Indri's card, the marker may be moved forward two spaces.
3. Reshuffle the cards each time they have all been drawn, and continue playing until someone reaches the finish line. The player who finishes first is the winner.

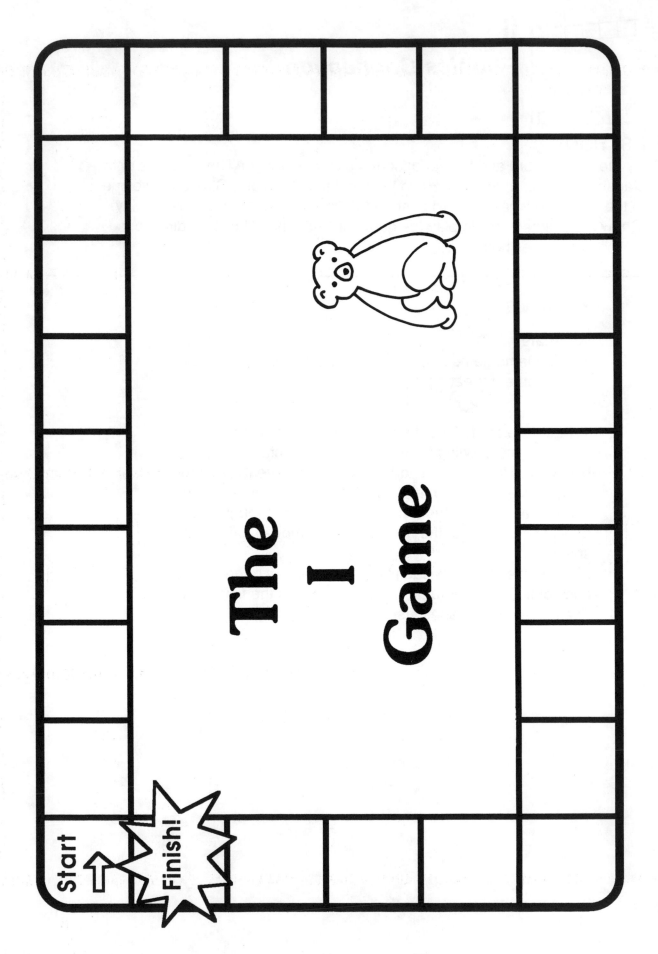

The
I
Game

Start

Finish!

Ichabod Indri

Ibex Ike

Ii

Math Connection

INCH
WORM

INCH BY INCH

Explain that the inchworm got its name because it seemed to be measuring leaves as it crawled along them. Cut out inch-long green construction paper inchworm shapes, and have the children use them to measure the length of familiar classroom objects such as books, erasers, and puzzles.

WHAT FLAVOR ICE CREAM DO YOU LIKE BEST?

(a graphing activity)

Brainstorm with the children all the flavors of ice cream they can think of. Make a list on the chalkboard or a chart. Reproduce the ice cream cone graphing symbols on the next page and have each child choose and color one that represents his or her favorite flavor.

Make a five-column graphing grid (see the directions in the Introduction). Label each column with one of the ice cream cone graphing symbols on which you've written the name of one of the four most popular ice cream flavors. Mark the fifth graphing symbol "Others" and put it at the head of the fifth column. Have the children tape their symbols onto the appropriate columns.

When all the children have recorded their choices, discuss the finished graph with them. Begin the discussion by asking the children what they see on the graph.

Then write an experience story together about the graph. Put a copy of the story into an experience story book and place it in the classroom library.

What Flavor Ice Ice Cream Do You Like Best?

Ii
Science Connection

INDRIS
Class: Mammal
Group: Troop
Habitat: Treetops of tropical forests
Food: Leaves, birds, insects
Color: Black and white

The indri is the largest of the lemurs though it looks much like an ape. The females get to eat first. If a male gets tired of waiting and starts to eat before his turn, the female may hit him. The indri uses sound to scare away enemies and to call its young. Every morning and evening the whole troop gathers to "sing."

READ MORE ABOUT INDRIS
"Madagascar's Lemurs—On the Edge of Survival" by Alison Jolly (National Geographic, August, 1988).
The Illustrated Encyclopedia of the Animal Kingdom (vol. 1, p. 19; vol. 5, pp. 32, 42; vol. 20, p. 51), ed. by Herbert Kondo (Danbury, 1972).

DO AND DISCOVER
Let the children discover how a troop of indris can make their call, or "song," last for a long time. Teach the children a simple song that can be sung in rounds. Time how long it takes to sing it through one time. Then sing it in rounds, with each child entering separately. Compare how long the song lasts in rounds to singing it together one time.

WRITE A BOOK ABOUT INDRIS
Brainstorm all the things the children remember about indris from their study. Make a list of the food indris eat. Talk about their habitat. Discuss all the interesting things the children learned about indris.

Put three pages together with a cover for a book for each child. Have the children draw a picture of an indri on the cover and write a title for the book. (See "Listen and Draw an Indri.") On the first page, have them draw the food that indris eat. On the second, let them draw the indri's habitat, and on the third draw something interesting that they know about indris. Have the children write or copy a sentence about the picture on each page.

Ii
Science Connection

INCLINED PLANES

Present the children with a pull toy, and ask if they can think of a way it could be pulled or pushed to the top of the table easily and without lifting it up. Challenge them to think of something they can use that is in the room. (Have some large building blocks and a long board within easy access.) Accept any ideas the children come up with.

When several techniques have been tried and discussed, ask which way the class thinks is the easiest. If someone has not created an inclined plane, show the children how to make one, stating what it's called several times. Ask the children why they think the inclined plane is the easiest way to get the toy to the top of the table.

Encourage the children to create their own inclined planes with small blocks.

INSECTS

Give the children pencils and drawing paper. Tell them that they are going to learn about a kind of animal that starts with the letter i by drawing one with you step by step.
1. Draw an oval in the middle of the paper.
2. Add another oval at the top and one on the bottom. Pause to explain that this kind of animal has three body parts.
3. Explain as you draw that the animal has six jointed legs—three on each side of the middle body part.
4. Draw two antennae on the head (the oval on the top). Use the term "antennae" as you draw.
5. Say that sometimes the animal has wings on the middle body part (the thorax) and that sometimes it has a stinger on the bottom body part (the abdomen).

Ask the children to look at their drawings and tell you what kind of an animal they think it is. If they don't know, tell them that it is an insect.

Take the children on a science walk outdoors armed with magnifying glasses to see how many insects they can find. Have them make a picture list of their discoveries.

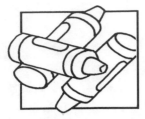

Ii
Arts and Crafts Connection

INK BLOTS

Materials:
Paper, containers of liquid tempera, eyedroppers

Procedure:
1. Have the children fold their paper in half either crosswise or lengthwise.
2. Show them how to use an eyedropper to squirt very thin liquid tempera onto the inside fold or one side of the paper.
3. Have them refold their paper and press gently. Then let them unfold their paper to see the symmetrical design that they have created.

INVISIBLE INITIAL INSIGNIAS

Materials:
4" squares of white construction paper, white crayons, watercolors and water, brushes, badge patterns, scissors, pencils, scrap paper, safety pins

Procedure:
1. First explain to the children that their initials are the first letters of their names. The maturity level of the children will determine whether you use one, two, or all three initials.
2. Have the children practice writing their initials on scrap paper.
3. Furnish each child with a square of white paper and a white crayon. Explain that their writing will be invisible at first. Have them press firmly as they write their initials on the white paper with the white crayon.
4. Show them how to cover their "invisible initials" with a badge pattern and trace around it.
5. Have the children brush a watercolor wash over their traced badges. The crayon should resist the wash, so that the previously invisible initials appear suddenly.
6. When the wash dries, let the children cut out their "Initial Insignias" and pin them on to wear with pride.

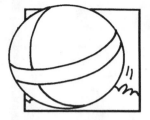

Ii
Movement Connection

IN AND OUT THE WINDOWS

Before beginning the game, teach the children the song:

    Go in and out the windows,
    Go in and out the windows,
    Go in and out the windows,
    As you have done before.

    Now stand and face your partner,
    Now stand and face your partner,
    Now stand and face your partner,
    And bow before you go.

Have the children form a large circle and join hands. Choose someone to be "It." The children raise their joined hands and sing the song as "It" moves "in and out the windows" around the circle. When the song says "Now stand and face your partner," tell "It" to stop and face one of the children in the circle. When the song says to bow, the partners do so and join hands to go in and out the windows together.

The song is sung again. On the second verse, the partners drop hands and choose new partners. The game continues with the two sets of partners moving in and out the windows. Play can continue until up to five sets of partners are going around the circle. You may then wish to stop play, reform the circle, and begin the game again with a new "It."

INCHWORMS

Have the children bend at the waist, placing their hands palms down on the floor with their feet between their hands. Their knees should be bent slightly. Tell the children to pretend that their feet are frozen in place and cannot move. Then have them move their hands forward in tiny "inchworm steps." Let them move their hands forward as far as they can while still keeping good balance. Next, tell them to "freeze" their hands in place, and move their feet forward in tiny "inchworm steps" to meet their hands.

125

Ii HOMEWORK

Put a √ by the activity you have chosen to do.

☐ Invent and make a musical instrument. Play it at school.

☐ Make an insect cage. Catch an insect to put in it and bring it to school. Tell what you learned as you inspected your insect.

☐ Interview each person in your family. Find out each person's favorite flavor of ice cream. Make a list to bring to school.

_____
Signature of grown up helper

ICHABOD INDRI'S ICKY BUN

Ingredients (serves 1)
refrigerator biscuit
margarine
brown sugar
raisins
walnut half

1. Put 1 tsp. margarine into a foil muffin cup.

2. Add 1 tsp. brown sugar.

3. Add 5 raisins

4. Break the walnut half into pieces. Add to the muffin cup.

5. Shape the biscuit into a ball.

6. Place the dough ball into the muffin cup.

7. Bake at 350° for 10-12 minutes. (You need a helping hand.)

8. Invert onto a plate and remove the foil cup.

Jj

RAP WITH JAGUAR JAN

Sign Language **J**

J is for jaguar, Jaguar Jan.
J /j/ /j/ /j/ /j/ /j/ /j/
Jingle-jangle, jumping jacks.
J /j/ /j/ /j/ /j/ /j/ /j/
Jam and jelly, Jack and Jill.
J /j/ /j/ /j/ /j/ /j/ /j/
(Repeat the first two lines.)

Jaguar Jan

JELLY BEAN JAR

Display a jar of jelly beans to introduce Jaguar Jan and her letter J. Ask the children what alphabet animal friend might have left the jelly beans for them. Give each child some jelly beans when someone guesses the jaguar.

JUMPING J PARTY

Celebrate the letter J with a party. Have the children jump rope, substituting "Jaguar Jan, Jaguar Jan" for "Teddy Bear, Teddy Bear" in the traditional jump rope rhyme. Lead the children in some jumping jacks. For refreshments, have the class make Jelly Bean Jello (fold different-colored jelly beans into the jello just as it begins to thicken). Read together the book *Jelly Beans for Breakfast* by Miriam Young.

JAGUAR JAN'S Jj BOOK

Brainstorm with the class words that begin with the same sound as Jaguar Jan. Distribute paper and let the children each choose a word to illustrate. Have them copy the following sentence frame onto the page and write their word in the blank space. Put the pages together to make a class book.

Jaguar Jan joyfully jumps over _____.

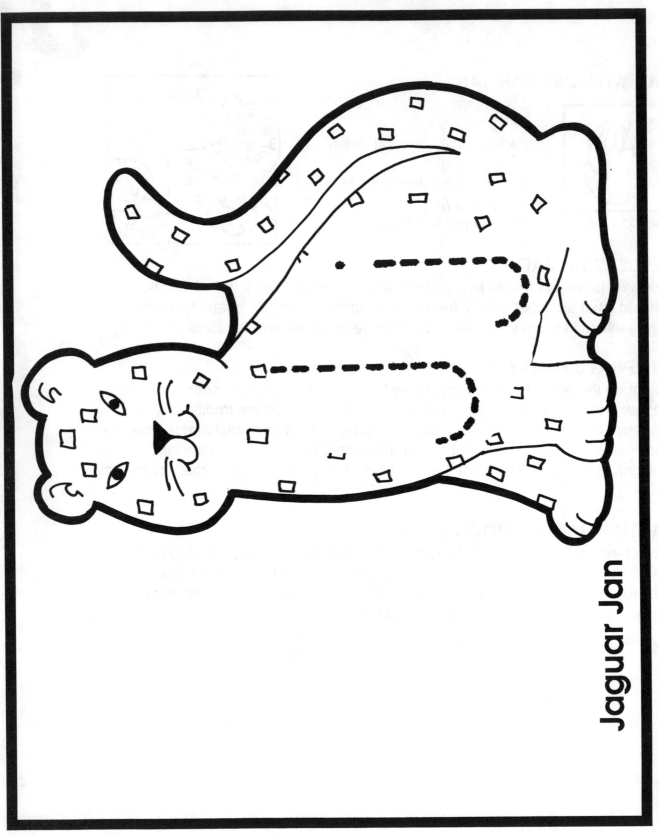

Jaguar Jan

Glue small jelly beans on the Jj's.

Jj
Literature Connection

READ A BOOK
Jamberry by Bruce Degen (Harper, 1983). This book is the joyous celebration of a boy and a bear in search of berries for jam. It is full of delightfully happy pictures, and the children will be able to chant and sing the charming verses after only a few readings.

Presentation
Ask the children to name their favorite kind of jam or jelly and their favorite berries. Read *Jamberry* at least twice, encouraging the children to join in on the rhyming lines they remember.

Additional Books
Jump Frog Jump by Robert Kalan (Scholastic, 1981); *Jesse Bear, What Will You Wear?* by Nancy Carlstrom (Macmillan, 1986); *Journey Cake* by Ruth Sawyer (Puffin, 1953); *Jelly Beans for Breakfast* by Miriam Young (Random House, 1968).

RELATED ACTIVITIES

Make a Berry Book
Talk about the illustrations in *Jamberry* and how they made you laugh. Ask the children to think of silly pictures with lots of berries in them. Remind them of the canoe pictured in the book that was full of blueberries, and the picture full of strawberries and animals dancing in the meadow with ribbons and an umbrella. Provide paper and crayons for the children to make their own pictures for a class *Jamberry* book.

Movement
Remind the children of the picture in *Jamberry* of the bear and the boy dancing with the animals in the field. Show them Degen's illustration, and demonstrate how to wave your arms in a swaying motion. Then give each child a paper streamer to dance with as you play light, happy music.

Listen and Draw a Jaguar

Give the children oral directions as you draw each step with them.

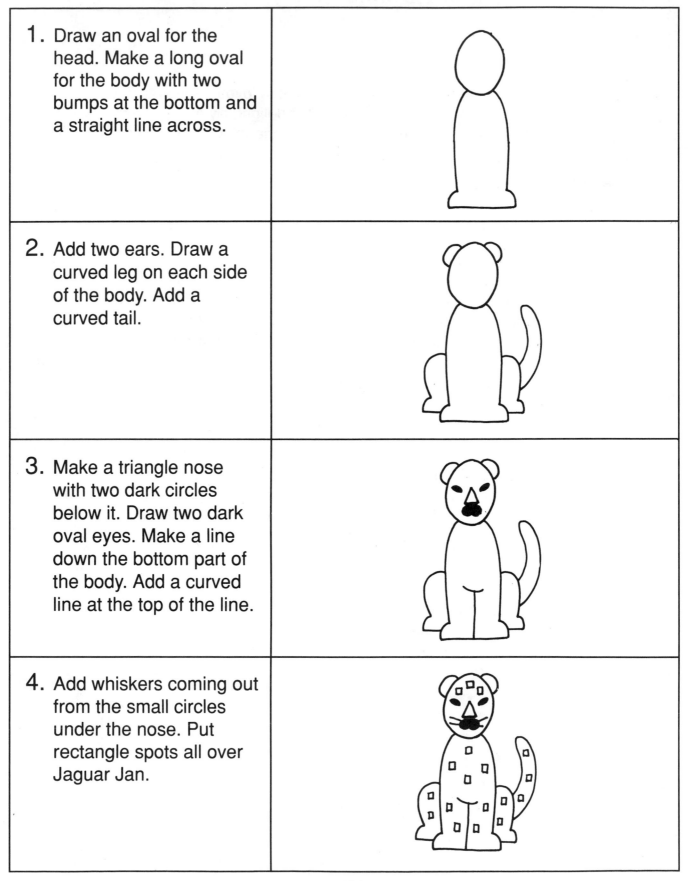

1. Draw an oval for the head. Make a long oval for the body with two bumps at the bottom and a straight line across.

2. Add two ears. Draw a curved leg on each side of the body. Add a curved tail.

3. Make a triangle nose with two dark circles below it. Draw two dark oval eyes. Make a line down the bottom part of the body. Add a curved line at the top of the line.

4. Add whiskers coming out from the small circles under the nose. Put rectangle spots all over Jaguar Jan.

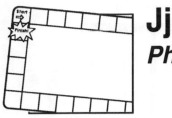 # Jj
Phonics Connection

AT SCHOOL
Copy the game board and the set of sound picture cards for the "J" game onto oaktag for the children to color. Have them cut the cards out. Glue an envelope onto the back of the game board to store the cards and directions for play.

Show the children how to play the game. Include the "At Home" directions when the game goes home.

- -

AT HOME

Materials: Jaguar Jan's game board and set of sound picture cards; a small marker for each player

Directions:
1. Place the cards face down in a pile between the players.
2. Take turns drawing from the pile. If the picture on the card begins with the sound of "j," move the marker forward one space. If the picture begins with another letter sound, no move is made. If a player is lucky enough to draw Jaguar Jan's card, the marker may be moved forward two spaces.
3. Reshuffle the cards each time they have all been drawn, and continue playing until someone reaches the finish line. The player who finishes first is the winner.

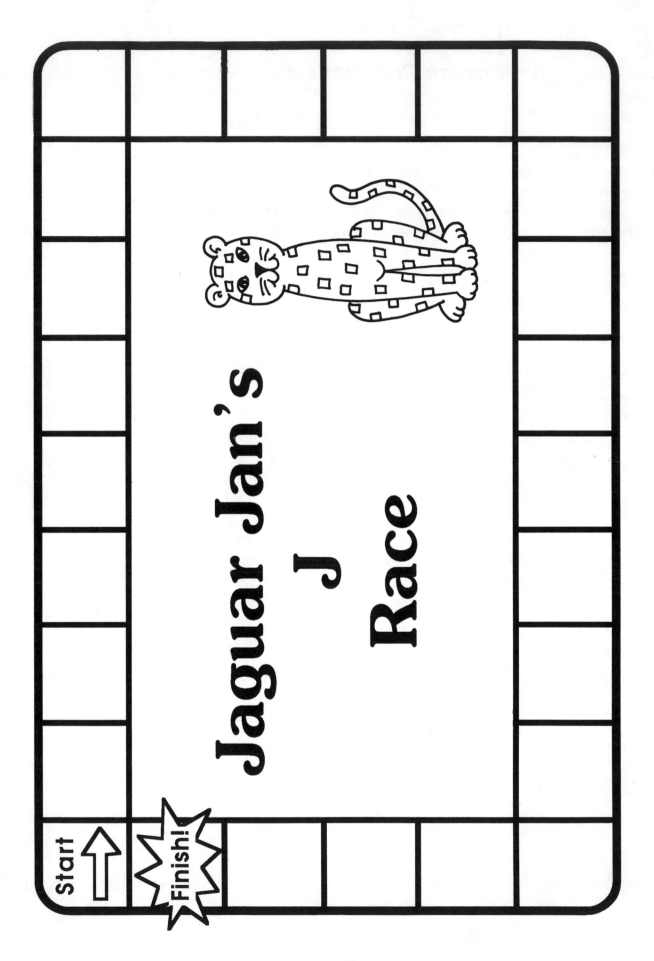

Jaguar Jan's
J
Race

Start

Finish!

Jj
Math Connection

JUMP AND COUNT

Take a long jump rope outside and have someone help you turn it while the children jump, one at a time, for as long as they can. Have the children who are waiting their turn help you count each jumper's jumps. Record the numbers on chart paper, but don't record the children's names.

When everyone has had a turn to jump, discuss the chart together, making observations about the "greatest" number of jumps, the number that "most" children jumped, and the "least" number of jumps.

WHAT KIND OF JUICE DO YOU LIKE?

(a graphing activity)

Bring to class some paper cups and enough of four different kinds of juice (perhaps orange, apple, grape, and tomato) for everyone to have a cup. Choose a somewhat isolated area of the playground and mark off a four-column grid with chalk. Designate a column on the graphing grid for each kind of juice available. Have each child write his or her name on a cup and fill it with his or her favorite kind of juice. Allow the children to drink their juice and record their choice by putting their empty cup in the appropriate column.

When all the cups are on the graph, have the children tell you as much as they can about the graph. Then write an experience story together about the graph. Put a copy of the story into an experience story book and place it in the classroom library.

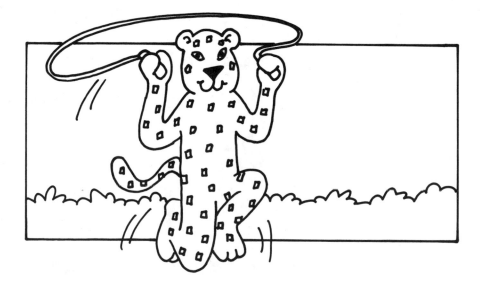

What Kind of Juice Do You Like?

Grape Juice

Tomato Juice

Apple Juice

Orange Juice

Jj
Science Connection

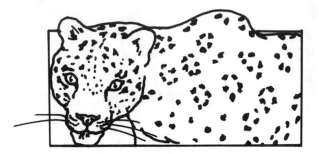

JAGUARS

Class: Mammal
Group: Solitary
Habitat: Jungle
Food: Turtles, fish, alligators, rodents,
    small mammals
Baby: Cub
Color: Brown with black spots

Jaguars are one of the few kinds of cats that likes to swim. They have a clever way to catch fish. They stand very still and drool into the water. A curious fish comes up to the surface to see what caused the drops, and the jaguar catches it.

READ MORE ABOUT JAGUARS

The Jaguar by Lynn Stone (Rourke, 1989).

DO AND DISCOVER

Let the children discover why a jaguar's coat is colored and patterned the way it is. Take the children outside on a sunny day to an area where the sun shines through trees and casts dappled shadows on the ground. Place two large pieces of construction paper in the shadows—one bright colored (red, pink, etc.) and the other brown with black rectangles drawn on it. Tell the children to stand way back and compare which piece of paper can be seen more easily. Ask them why. Then ask them if a jaguar would want to be seen or not seen.

WRITE A BOOK ABOUT JAGUARS

Brainstorm all the things the children remember about jaguars from their study. Make a list of the food jaguars eat. Talk about their habitat. Discuss all the interesting things that the children learned about jaguars.

Put three pages together with a cover for a book for each child. Have the children draw a picture of a jaguar on the cover and write a title for the book. (See "Listen and Draw A Jaguar.") On the first page, have them draw the food that jaguars eat. On the second, let them draw the jaguar's habitat, and on the third draw something interesting that they know about jaguars. Have the children write or copy a sentence about the picture on each page.

Jj
Science Connection

JET PROPULSION

Begin by asking the children if any of them has taken a trip on an airplane. Ask them if they know another name for airplane (jet). Tell them to watch the science experiment that you are going to do to learn how jets work.

Thread a straw onto a five-foot length of string. Tape the long side of an oblong balloon along the length of the straw, leaving the balloon opening open. Position two chairs across from each other and tie one end of the string to each chair. Blow the balloon partially full and hold the end to keep the air in. Ask the children what you just put into the balloon (air). Then let go of the end of the balloon, and ask where the air in the balloon went. Ask, "Which way did the air go?" "Which way did the straw go?" Explain that a jet engine works much the same way as the balloon; it blows air out the back of a plane and moves the plane through the air in the opposite direction, just as the straw was moved. Jet boats operate the same way, except that their engines blow water out the back of the boat and move it forward through the water.

Tell the children to remember that jet action occurs when one thing goes one way making something else go the opposite way.

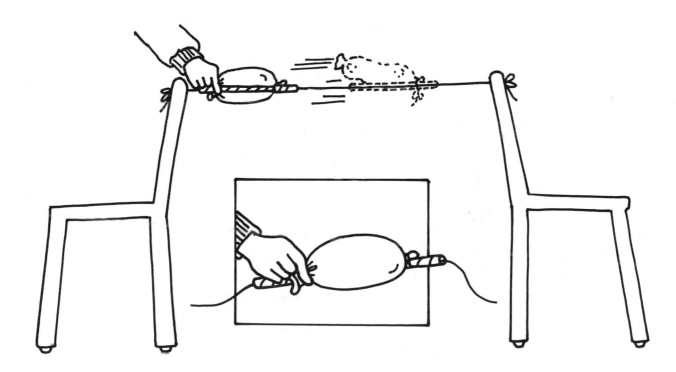

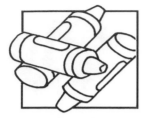

Jj
Arts and Crafts Connection

JEWELS

Materials:
Squeeze bottles of white glue, felt pens, aluminum foil, yarn, lightweight cardboard, stapler

Procedure:
1. Have the children squeeze small, round blobs of white glue onto aluminum foil.
2. When the blobs are thoroughly dry (they will be nearly transparent), let the children transform them into jewels by adding color to them with felt pens.
3. Have the children peel their jewels off the foil, and glue them onto strips of lightweight cardboard which they have decorated with felt pen designs and stapled to form rings and bracelets.

JUNK SCULPTURE

Materials:
An assortment of "junk" (jar lids, bottle caps, old puzzle pieces, bread bag tags, bits of scrap wood, old jewelry, corks, spools, etc.), cardboard, glue

Procedure:
1. Place the "junk" on the table and let the children choose what they would like to use.
2. Give them each a piece of cardboard to use as a sculpture base. Then let them create, gluing bits and pieces together. They will need little help except to be reminded to use a puddle of glue to secure heavier objects, and to hold an object in place until the glue has set a bit.

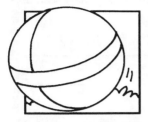

Jj
Movement Connection

JACK BE NIMBLE JUMPING

Have the children find a place where they will not bump into anyone or anything and get ready to do some jumping. Explain that jumping means taking off and landing on both feet at once—both feet must leave the ground at the same time.

Ask the children to bend their knees and go down, then come back up and stretch up high, higher, higher. Have them try it again, this time making their feet leave the floor. Give them time to practice jumping.

Then chant the rhyme:

> Jack be nimble,
> Jack be quick.
> Jack jump over the candlestick.

Each time you say the word "jump," have the children pretend they are jumping over the candlestick. Let them take turns. Use the children's names instead of Jack's.

JUMP ROPE

Give the children individual jump ropes. Challenge them to hold both ends of their rope in one hand and turn it so the loop hits the ground near their feet. Let them practice for awhile, then have them change hands and repeat the activity.

Ask them to do the same thing again, but this time when the loop hits the ground next to their feet tell them to jump. Give them time to practice this step before going on.

Next, have the children hold the rope with both hands and jump as they swing it back and forth under their feet—not over their head. This is known as "Blue Bells." Encourage them to try jumping rope the standard way, turning it over their head and under their feet, only when they feel confident with the other activities.

Jj

HOMEWORK

Name _____

Date Due _____

Put a √ by the activity you have chosen to do.

☐ Practice **j**umping rope. Count how many times you can **j**ump without missing. Write the number down. Make a picture next to the number and bring the picture to school.

☐ Learn a **j**oke to tell at school.

☐ Make some **j**ewelry to wear at school.

_____
Signature of grown up helper

JAGUAR JAN'S JELL-O JEWELS

Ingredients (serves 1)
Jell-O mix
boiling water
unflavored gelatin
cold water
lemon juice

1. Put 1 T. Jell-O into a bowl.

2. Add 3 T. boiling water.

3. Stir.

4. Put 1 tsp. gelatin into another bowl.

5. Add 1 T. cold water and stir.

6. Add 1/2 T. lemon juice.

7. Stir both mixtures. Freeze for 15 minutes. Cut into shapes. (You need a helping hand.)

Kk

RAP WITH KATY KANGAROO

Sign Language **K**

K is for kangaroo, Katy Kangaroo.
K /k/ /k/ /k/ /k/ /k/ /k/
Kindergarten, kids, and keys
K /k/ /k/ /k/ /k/ /k/ /k/
Kittens, kisses, kindly kings.
K /k/ /k/ /k/ /k/ /k/ /k/
(Repeat the first two lines.)

Katy Kangaroo

K SONGS

Introduce Katy Kangaroo and her letter K by singing songs like "Polly, Put the Kettle On," "Old King Cole," and "K K K Katy." Ask the children what alphabet animal begins with the same sound as kettle, king, and Katy.

KING FOR A DAY

Celebrate the letter K with a "King for a Day" party. Have the children make kingly crowns to wear in a royal procession. Show them how to play the kazoo by wrapping a comb in waxed paper and holding it against the lips while humming. Let the children make fruit kabobs (chunks of fruit threaded on toothpicks or longer skewers) for refreshments.

KATY KANGAROO'S Kk BOOK

Brainstorm with the class words that begin with the same sound as Katy Kangaroo. Distribute paper and let the children each choose a word to illustrate. Have them copy the following sentence frame onto the page and write their word in the blank space. Put the pages together to make a class book.

Kindly Katy Kangaroo likes _____ , and kids too.

Katy Kangaroo

Glue (popcorn) kernels on the Kk's.

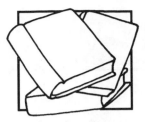

Kk
Literature Connection

READ A BOOK
Katy No Pocket by Emmy Payne (Houghton, 1972). Katy Kangaroo is a mother kangaroo who has no pocket in which to carry her baby. She tries the suggestions of many animals but with no success, until a carpenter comes to her rescue.

Presentation
Discuss with the children what pockets in clothing are for. Brainstorm things that people put in their pockets. Explain that in the story *Katy No Pocket* they'll learn of a mother who needs a pocket for carrying her baby.

Additional Books
Little Koala by Suzanne Noguere and Tony Chen (Random House, 1979); *Katy and the Big Snow* by Virginia L. Burton (Houghton, 1943); *Sloppy Kisses* by Elizabeth Winthrop (Puffin, 1983); *A Kiss for Little Bear* by Else Holmelund Minarik (Harper, 1968); *Koala Lou* by Mem Fox (Ian Drakeford, 1988).

RELATED ACTIVITY

Pocket Book
Make a class book about pockets. Give each child a page with the following sentence frame on it:

I keep a _____ in my pocket.

Have the children create a pocket from colored construction paper (4" by 6"), put glue along two sides and the bottom (leaving the top open), and glue it on the sentence frame page. Give the children plain 3" by 5" cards and let them draw a picture of what they would like to keep in their pocket. Have each child label the picture and put it in the paper pocket. Bind the pages together into a class book. When the children read the book they may pull out the different cards to see what's in the pockets.

Listen and Draw a Kangaroo

Give the children oral directions as you draw each step with them.

1. Draw a circle for the head. Put in a triangle nose. Add a long oval body. Draw a curved line across the middle of the body for the pocket.

2. Add two ears. Draw a curved leg and foot on each side of the body.

3. Add a fat tail.

4. Make two dark eyes in the head. Add two curved arms.

Kk
Phonics Connection

AT SCHOOL

Copy the game board and the set of sound picture cards for Katy Kangaroo's "K" Game onto oaktag for the children to color. Have them cut out the cards. Glue an envelope onto the back of the game board to store the cards and the directions for play.

Show the children how to play the game. Include the "At Home" directions when the game goes home.

AT HOME

Materials: Katy Kangaroo's game board and set of sound picture cards; a small marker for each player

Directions:
1. Place the cards face down in a pile between the players.
2. Take turns drawing from the pile. If the picture on the card begins with the sound of "k," move the marker forward one space. If the picture begins with another letter sound, no move is made. If a player is lucky enough to draw Katy Kangaroo's card, the marker may be moved forward two spaces.
3. Reshuffle the cards each time they have all been drawn, and continue playing until someone reaches the finish line. The player who finishes first is the winner.

Katy Kangaroo's
K Game

Start
Here!

Finish!

Kk
Math Connection

KEYS OF ALL KINDS

Give the children lots of opportunities to explore a collection of old keys. (Locksmiths often give away their rejects.) Then introduce the children to this sorting activity by asking, "What can you tell me about the keys in our collection?" Choose one of the more obvious visual attributes, perhaps color, mentioned by the children, and encourage them to help you find all the keys with that attribute. Then mix up the keys and ask if the children can think of another way to sort them.

HAVE YOU EVER FLOWN A KITE?

(a graphing activity)

Talk about kites with the children, discussing different kinds and the different ways people get kites to fly. Ask the children how they think kites stay up in the air. Then ask them the graphing question: "Have you ever flown a kite?" Make a two-column graph (see the directions in the Introduction). Label one column "Yes" and the other column "No." Reproduce the kite graphing patterns on the following page. Give one to each child to color and then tape onto the graph column that answers if they've ever flown a kite.

When everyone has taped on a pattern, discuss the finished graph together. Ask the children to tell you as many things as they can about what they see. After the discussion, write an experience story together about the graph. Include the children's observations. Put a copy of the story into an experience story book and place it in the classroom library.

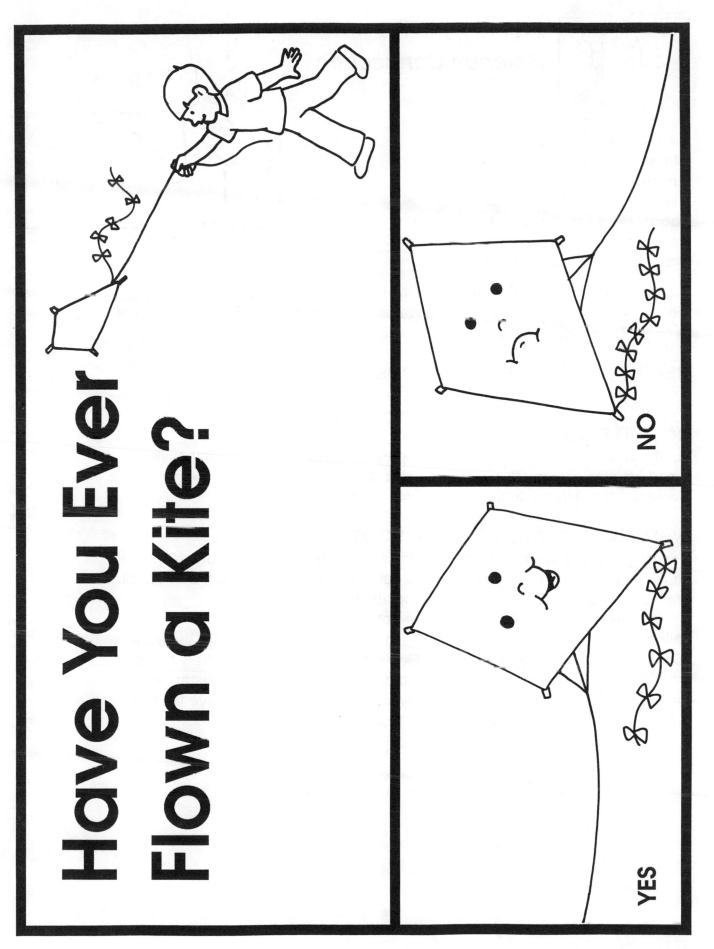

Have You Ever Flown a Kite?

NO

YES

149

Kk
Science Connection

KANGAROOS

Class: Mammal
Group: Mob or troop
Habitat: Deserts, woodlands
Food: Grass
Baby: Joey
Color: Reddish brown or gray

A baby kangaroo is smaller than your little finger when it's born. It lives in its mother's pouch for almost a year. Kangaroos like to nap most of the day, and eat at night. They keep cool by licking their saliva over their bodies.

READ MORE ABOUT KANGAROOS
Animal Days by David Sharp (Bay, 1984).

DO AND DISCOVER
Let the children discover what good jumpers kangaroos are. Engage them in a broad-jumping contest. Record the farthest distance the children can jump. Compare that distance to the 30-foot jump a kangaroo can make.

WRITE A BOOK ABOUT KANGAROOS
Brainstorm all the things the children remember about kangaroos from their study. Make a list of the food kangaroos eat. Talk about their habitat. Discuss all the interesting things the children learned about kangaroos.

Put three pages together with a cover for a book for each child. Have the children draw a picture of a kangaroo on the cover and write a title for the book. (See "Listen and Draw A Kangaroo.") On the first page, have them draw the food that kangaroos eat. On the second, let them draw the kangaroo's habitat, and on the third draw something interesting they know about kangaroos. Have the children write or copy a sentence about the picture on each page.

Kk
Science Connection

KITES

Have the children run across the playground and back. Next, have them take turns running with a large piece of lightweight cardboard held in front of them. Ask them which way running was easier. Ask if they could feel the air pushing against the cardboard as they ran. Tell them that they are going to make something that will fly when air pushes on it—a kite.

For each kite you will need two drinking straws, a piece of plastic garbage bag (see the illustration), masking tape (at least 1½" wide), and string. Follow these steps.

1. Have the children lay each of their straws on a 12" strip of masking tape.
2. Have them press each straw and tape onto the garbage bag piece as shown.
3. Let the children put a small piece of masking tape on both sides of both points of the garbage bag piece and punch a hole through each.
4. Give each child a 20" length of string. Have the children tie the ends of the string through the holes; there will be slack in the middle.
5. Have them tie a long length of string to the center of the shorter length of string; this will be the string with which they will fly the kite.
6. Give each child two 1" by 24" strips of plastic garbage bag to tape to their kite for tails. Have them tape each tail to the same end of the straws (see the illustration).

To fly the kite, have the children run into the wind holding the string, slowly letting it out as the kite begins to lift. Once the kite is in the air it will fly on its own. If it begins to come down, tell the children to pull on the string and it will go up again.

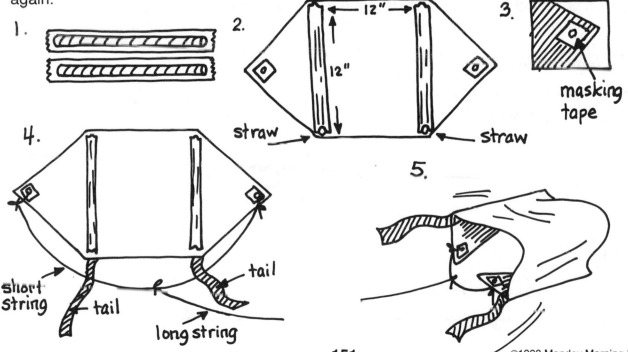

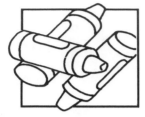

Kk
Arts and Crafts Connection

KITCHEN ART

Materials:
A variety of everyday kitchen utensils and gadgets (potato mashers, cookie cutters, corks, bottle caps, slotted spatulas, forks, scouring pads, wire whisks, etc.), liquid tempera paint, water, sponges, paper plates, paper

Procedure:
1. Thin the tempera paint to the consistency of cream and pour some onto a sponge that has been put on a paper plate.
2. Show the children how to press one of the kitchen gadgets lightly into the paint and then onto a piece of paper.
3. Encourage them to repeat the process with other utensils and other colors until they are pleased with their designs.

KITES

Materials:
Paper lunch bags, different colored felt pens, tape, string

Procedure:
1. Help the children fold back the open edges of their bags about 1½".
2. Provide felt pens and let the children decorate all the surfaces of their bags.
3. Tape a five-inch piece of string to each corner of each bag, and join the four strings together with a knot.
4. Attach a five-foot-long string to each knot, and let the children fly their kites.

(These kites will not fly the way traditional ones do, but will stay aloft as long as the children run with them.)

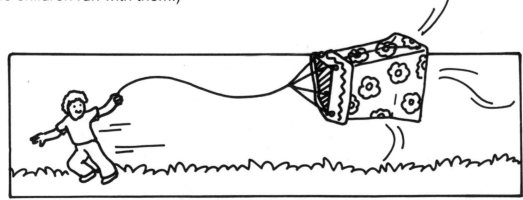

Kk
Movement Connection

KING AND QUEEN

One boy and one girl are chosen to be "King" and "Queen." Each is "crowned" with a beanbag. The rest of the children become the "court" and sit in two long rows facing each other—the boys in one row, the girls in the other. The "King" and "Queen" stand together at one end of the two rows between the lines. At a given signal they walk as quickly as they can without dropping their "crowns" down through the rows and back up the outside. They cannot touch the beanbags with their hands while they are walking. If one of them loses his or her "crown," he or she may pick it up, replace it, and continue walking. The first child back to the top of the rows gets another turn. The other child chooses someone from the "court" to be "crowned" the new "King" or "Queen."

KICK AND RUN

Pair the children off. Give each pair a kickball, and have the partners line up side by side facing a goal line. One child will be the "Kicker" and the other the "Runner." At a given signal, the "Kicker" kicks the ball and the "Runner" takes off. The object of the game is to see if the ball or the "Runner" will reach the goal first.

Have the partners take turns being "Kicker" and "Runner." Keep the goal distance reasonable for the children's skill level.

Kk

HOMEWORK

Name _____

Date Due _____

Put a √ by the activity you have chosen to do.

☐ How far can you **k**ick a ball? Have someone measure the distance. Bring a picture to school that shows how far.

☐ Fly a **k**ite. Make a picture about it to bring to school. Tell how to fly a **k**ite.

☐ Pretend you are a **k**ing. Draw a picture to bring to school. Tell a story.

_____

KATY KANGAROO'S KABOB

Ingredients (serves 1)
cocktail sausage
cherry tomato
pineapple chunk
soy sauce

1. Put a sausage on a dampened wooden skewer.

2. Add a cherry tomato.

3. Add a pineapple chunk.

4. Brush the kabob with soy sauce.

5. Grill or broil the kabob for 2-3 minutes on each side. (You need a helping hand.)

6. Remove the kabob from the skewer.

RAP WITH LION LOU

Sign Language **L**

L is for lion, Lion Lou.
L /l/ /l/ /l/ /l/ /l/ /l/
Licking lemon lollipops.
L /l/ /l/ /l/ /l/ /l/ /l/
Letters, love, and ladybugs.
L /l/ /l/ /l/ /l/ /l/ /l/
(Repeat the first two lines.)

Lion Lou

LION LOU'S LETTER

Write a letter introducing Lion Lou and his letter L and put it in the library for the children to discover. Follow up with a letter for each day of the study of the letter L, telling about that day's lesson.

LEAVE NO LITTER DAY

Celebrate the letter L with Lion Lou's "Leave No Litter Day." Have the children decorate grocery bags with pictures of Lion Lou and collect litter from around the school or neighborhood. Have lemonade ready for the children after their work.

Talk about what can be done to prevent litter buildup. Ask the children what would happen to the school or neighborhood if all the people just threw their garbage on the ground. Have them make signs that say "Leave No Litter!" and post them around the school.

LION LOU'S Ll BOOK

Brainstorm with the class words that begin with the same sound as Lion Lou. Distribute paper and let the children each choose a word to illustrate. Have them copy the following sentence frame onto the page and write their word in the blank space. Put the pages together to make a class book.

Lion Lou loves _____, and you, too.

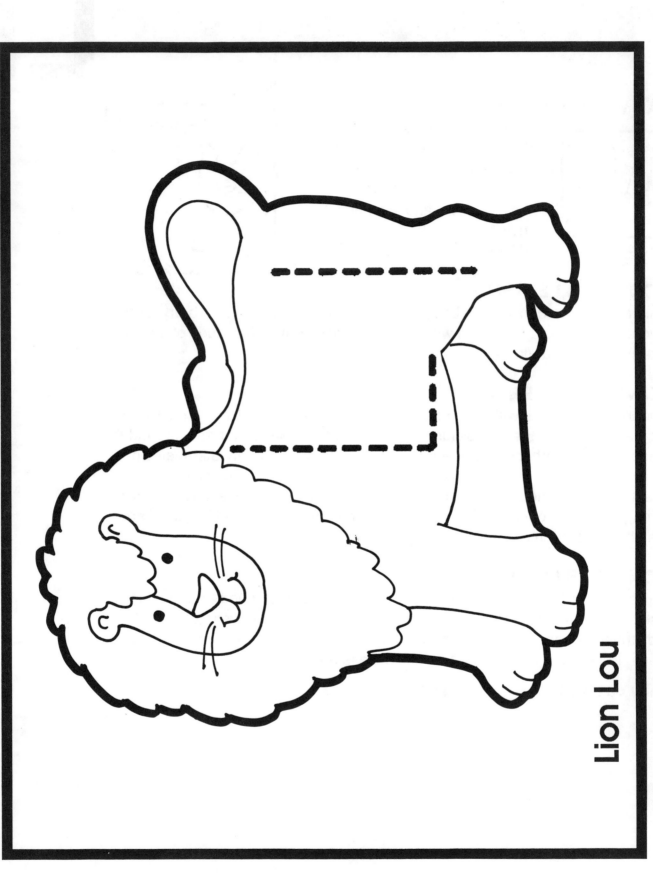

Lion Lou

Glue small leaves on the Ll's.

156

LI
Literature Connection

READ A BOOK

Leo the Late Bloomer by Robert Kraus (Simon & Schuster, 1971). This is a sensitive book about a lion named Leo who cannot seem to do the same things others do. Then one day he can. The story teaches valuable lessons about acceptance and patience during the process of growing up.

Presentation

Discuss growing up with the children. Help them to realize how many more things they can do now than they could when they were younger. Explain that people start to do things like walking, talking, and losing teeth at different times. Tell them that Leo is a little lion who is worried because he can't do what his friends can do.

Additional Books

The Grouchy Ladybug by Eric Carle (Crowell, 1977); *Leaves* by Fulvio Testa (Peter Bedrick, 1980); *Lost* by David McPhail (Little, Brown, 1990); *The Happy Lion* by Louise Fatio (McGraw, 1954).

RELATED ACTIVITY

Make a Book

After reading the book, ask the children if they can remember something that used to be hard for them to do. Talk about the way that made them feel. Discuss how everyone learns to do things at different times, and that some people take longer than others to grow up.

Have the children make a book about how they have grown. Put the following sentence frame on a page for each child to complete (take dictation for the "late bloomers"):

When I was little I couldn't _____. But now I can!

Have the children illustrate their answer on the page. Then bind all the pages together for a class book.

Listen and Draw a Lion

Give the children oral directions as you draw each step with them.

1. Draw a circle for the head. Make a jagged mane around the head.

2. Add two round ears to the head. Draw a long oval body with two bumps at the bottom and a straight line across the bottom. Make a curved leg and foot on each side of the body. Add a tail.

3. Make a triangle nose with two circles below it.

4. Give the head two dark eyes. Make whiskers coming out from the circles below the nose. Make a fuzzy end on the tail.

Ll

Phonics Connection

AT SCHOOL

Materials:
Brown paper lunch bags, sandwich-shaped sound picture cards, crayons, oaktag, scissors

To make the lunch bags: Have the children decorate brown paper lunch bags with pictures of Lion Lou and his letter "L." Make two lunch bags for each game.

To make the sandwiches: Copy the sandwich-shaped beginning sound picture cards onto oaktag for the children to color and cut out.

Show the children how to play the game. Include the "At Home" directions when the game goes home.

AT HOME

Materials:
A set of sandwich-shaped sound picture cards; a decorated lunch bag for each player

Directions:
1. Shuffle the cards and scatter them face down in a pile between the players.
2. Take turns drawing cards. If a picture is drawn that begins with the sound of "l," put it in the lunch bag. If the picture begins with another letter sound, put it in a discard pile.
3. The winner is the person whose lunch bag holds the most sandwiches after all the cards have been played.

LI
Math Connection

LEMON DROP MATH

Bring a small plastic jar filled with lemon drops to class, and ask the children to estimate how many candies are in the jar. Record their responses in a scattered array on the chalkboard. Then have the children help you count 10 lemon drops at a time into small cups. When all the lemon drops are portioned out, have the children count by tens to find out how many there were in the jar. As the counting is going along, cross out the numbers on the board that are lower than the actual amount.

MORE LEMON DROP MATH

Copy the lemon pattern below onto a piece of lightweight cardboard. Have each child trace the shape onto a piece of yellow construction paper and cut it out. Next have the children estimate how many real lemon drops they think will cover the surface of their paper lemon, and write the number on one side of the lemon. Have them cover their paper lemon with candies, and then record that number on the blank side of the shape. Ask the children to compare the two numbers and to discuss their findings while they enjoy a tasty lemon drop treat.

HAVE YOU EVER RECEIVED A LETTER IN THE MAIL?

(a graphing activity)

Ask the children if any of them has ever gotten a letter in the mail. After a brief discussion, have the children who have received a letter get in one line and those who haven't get in another parallel line. Have the children hold the hand of the child opposite them. Then have them drop hands and stand still. Tell them that their two lines are two columns of a graph, and ask them to tell you everything that they can about what they see.

Write an experience story together after the discussion. Encourage someone to draw a picture of the graphing activity. Put the story and the drawing into an experience story book and place it in the classroom library.

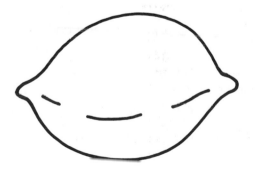

LI
Science Connection

LIONS

Class: Mammal
Group: Pride (the only cat that likes to live in a group)
Habitat: Grasslands, forests
Food: Meat—zebra, gazelle, antelope
Baby: Cub
Color: Tan or tawny

Male lions have manes that protect their necks during a fight and help to scare enemies away; their manes make them seem bigger than they really are. Females do the hunting. Their cubs follow them and learn how to hunt too. Females let the cubs play with the animals they kill. Once the cubs taste the meat, they learn to like it. All lions spend most of their time sleeping—as many as 20 hours a day!

READ MORE ABOUT LIONS

Finding Out About Lions and Tigers by Kate Petty (Willowisp, 1989).

DO AND DISCOVER

Let the children discover why lions have retractable claws. Show them a picture of a lion's paw print. Have them tell you what they notice (no claws). If any of the children have dogs at home, have those children describe the sound dogs make as they walk on hard-surfaced floors (scratching sounds). Compare the sound cats make when they walk on hard floors (almost no sound). Explain that lions are not as fast as some of the animals they must catch. Ask how walking quietly helps lions catch their prey.

WRITE A BOOK ABOUT LIONS

Brainstorm all the things the children remember about lions from their study. Make a list of the food lions eat. Talk about their habitat. Discuss the interesting things the children learned about lions.

   Put three pages together with a cover for a book for each child. Have the children draw a picture of a lion on the cover and write a title for the book. (See "Listen and Draw A Lion.") On the first page, have them draw the food that lions eat. On the second, let them draw the lion's habitat, and on the third draw something interesting they know about lions. Have the children write or copy a sentence about the picture on each page.

LI
Science Connection

LIGHT

Talk about light with the children. Ask them to tell you where light comes from (the sun, flashlights, candles, lamps, light bulbs, etc.). Make a picture list of all their ideas. Then tell them that they are going to do scientific experiments that will tell them two things that light can do.

Provide a glass of water for every two children. Have the partners take turns placing the following objects into the water, one at a time: a pencil, a crayon, and a long, fairly straight stick. Ask them if the object looks the same or different in the water. Ask if it looks broken. (The object will look broken at the water level.) Have the children take the object out of the water, and ask them if it is truly broken. Explain that the object only looks broken because the light bends when it goes from the air to the water.

Next, give every two children a small mirror, and have them reflect a spot of sunlight onto the walls or ceiling. As they do this, explain that light reflects, or bounces off, some things and goes in another direction. Let the children try reflecting light with various materials, such as foil, metal, and paper. Have them cut small foil shapes and glue them to black paper squares. They will be able to create light patterns on the wall as the light reflects off the shiny surfaces.

LIQUIDS

Gather together various containers of assorted shapes and sizes. Provide plastic dishpans and containers of water. Let the children work together in small groups, pouring the water from one container to another. After everyone has had a chance to try out the activity, discuss what they observed. Ask questions such as, "What did you do to make the water go from one container to another?" "Did you spill any?" "Did the spill have the same shape as the container the water had been in?"

Tell the children that water is a liquid; liquids are things that can be poured. Explain that liquids take on the shape of the container they are in, so a liquid cannot stand up by itself like a glass or a bottle does. When liquids are not in a container, they simply spread out in the form of a puddle.

There are many different kinds of liquids. Brainstorm with the children names of liquids that they know. Bring in old magazines for the children to look through for pictures of liquids. Make a class collage of the pictures.

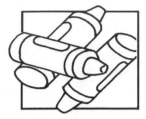

LI
Arts and Crafts Connection

LEAF PRINTS

Materials:
Orange, yellow, and red liquid tempera; brushes; dark brown and other colors of construction paper; fresh leaves (not dry); brayers (from art store); newspaper; glue

Procedure:
1. Show the children how to brush paint onto the underside (vein side) of the leaves, using a different color for each one.
2. Have them arrange the leaves into a pleasing design, paint side up, on a pad of newspaper that is about the same size as the dark brown construction paper.
3. Help the children lay their piece of construction paper on top of the leaves and carefully roll the brayer all over the paper.
4. Lift the paper and let the children see their beautiful leaf prints.
5. Mount the leaf print designs onto a slightly larger piece of construction paper of a complementary color, such as yellow or orange. This is a great autumn art project.

Variation:
If brayers are not available, the children can lay a painted leaf onto a piece of dark brown construction paper, lay a piece of newsprint over it, and gently press down with their hand. Have them lift the paper and the leaf and repeat the step with different colors and different shaped leaves until they have a design that pleases them.

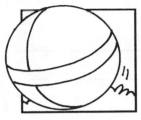

LI
Movement Connection

LOG ROLLING

If you don't have access to tumbling mats, take the children out to a grassy area. Have them lie on their stomach with their arms extended in front of them, palms touching, and their legs together. Explain that their legs and arms must be kept as straight as possible while they roll their bodies like logs over and over across the grass (or mats).

LONDON BRIDGE

Teach the children the song "London Bridge" before playing the game. There are many more verses to the song than are listed here, but this seems to be an adequate number for young children to use in their game.

1. London Bridge is falling down,
   Falling down, falling down.
   London Bridge is falling down,
   My fair lady.
2. Build it up with iron bars, etc.
3. Iron bars will bend and break, etc.
4. Build it up with pins and needles, etc.
5. Pins and needles will rust and bend, etc.
6. Build it up with silver and gold, etc.
7. Gold and silver I have not, etc.

Choose two children to be the bridge. Tell them to decide secretly on two objects, such as silver and gold, ice cream and cake, sun and moon, etc. Have each child choose one of the objects. Then have those two children form the bridge by facing each other and holding their hands up in an arch for the other children to pass under.

Tell the other children to form a line and march under the "bridge" as everyone sings the song. On the words "My fair lady" the "bridge" makers should drop their arms to capture a player. The child who is caught is asked (out of the other players' hearing) which secret object he or she prefers, and then stands behind the player whose object he or she chose. Play continues until all the children have been caught. Then hold a tug of war.

Ll

HOMEWORK

Name _____

Date Due _____

Put a √ by the activity you have chosen to do.

☐ Write a letter to someone at school. Bring it to school to give to that person.

☐ Go to the library and check out a book. Bring it to school to tell about.

☐ Make a list of things you love. Bring it to school to share.

_____
Signature of grown up helper

LION LOU'S LEMONADE

Ingredients (serves 1)
lemon half
sugar
water
ice

1. Squeeze the lemon half into a cup or glass.

2. Add 2 tsp. sugar.

3. Add 1 cup water.

4. Put in some ice.

5. Stir.

Mm

RAP WITH MOE MONKEY

Sign Language **M**

M is for monkey, monkey Moe.
M /m/ /m/ /m/ /m/ /m/ /m/
Magic, mittens, marbles, me.
M /m/ /m/ /m/ /m/ /m/ /m/
Macaroni, mud, and milk.
M /m/ /m/ /m/ /m/ /m/ /m/
(Repeat the first two lines.)

Moe Monkey

MAGIC MIRROR

Introduce Moe Monkey and his letter M by pretending you see things that begin with /m/ in a magic mirror. Peer into a hand mirror and name things that begin with /m/. Then ask the children if they can guess who the alphabet friend is that gave you the magic mirror.

MERRY MASQUERADE

To celebrate the letter M, hold a "Merry Masquerade." Have the children make masks out of paper plates and scrap materials. Ask them to wear the masks on a merry march around the room or the school. Lead the children in singing "Here We Go 'Round the Mulberry Bush" and "The Muffin Man." Help the children make muffins, and serve them with milk. Read together the book *If You Give a Moose a Muffin* by Laura Joffe Numeroff.

MOE MONKEY'S Mm BOOK

Brainstorm with the class words that begin with the same sound as Moe Monkey. Distribute paper and let the children each choose a word to illustrate. Have them copy the following sentence frame onto the page and write their word in the blank space. Put the pages together to make a class book.

Moe Monkey makes marvelous _____.

Moe Monkey

Glue macaroni on the Mm's.

Mm
Literature Connection

READ A BOOK
The Mitten by Jan Brett (Putnam, 1989). *The Mitten* is an adaptation of an old Ukrainian folk tale about a little boy who loses his mitten in the snow. One by one, animals from the forest creep into it to get out of the cold. The mitten soon becomes very crowded, but it doesn't explode, as it does in other versions, until something quite unusual happens.

Dramatization
This is a wonderful story to act out. And, because of the large number of characters, lots of children can be involved. Puppets work well, even without a puppet theater. Or you can have the children make different animal masks for the production. Provide the narration while the children speak the different animal parts.

Additional Books
Mike Mulligan and His Steam Shovel by Virginia L. Burton (Houghton, 1939); *Mouse Paint* by Ellen Stoll Walsh (Harcourt, 1989); *Mouse Count* by Ellen Stoll Walsh (Harcourt, 1991); *If You Give a Moose a Muffin* by Laura Joffe Numeroff (HarperCollins, 1991); *Mooncakes* by Frank Asch (Prentice Hall, 1983); *If You Give a Mouse a Cookie* by Laura Joffe Numeroff (Harper, 1985); *Are You My Mother?* by P. D. Eastman (Random House, 1960).

RELATED ACTIVITIES

Mitten Shape Book
Give the children mitten-shaped pieces of paper on which to draw an animal that might want to crawl into a warm mitten on a snowy day. Have the class arrange the pictures in order according to animal size, from the smallest to the largest. Bind the pages together into a class book for everyone to enjoy.

Snow Day
Choose a day and invite the children to dress in snow clothes—mittens, hats, scarves, snow boots, etc. Let the children hold a pantomime snowball fight outside and then make angels in the "snow." For a math activity, have the children sort all the mittens into a variety of categories. Let them make snowy pictures for an art project, using Q-tips and white paint on dark blue paper.

Listen and Draw a Monkey

Give the children oral directions as you draw each step with them.

1. Draw an oval muzzle. Make a bump on top for the head. Add an oval body.

2. Make a round ear on each side of the head.

3. Make a dark triangle in the top of the muzzle. Add two curved legs to the body.

4. Put two round eyes on the monkey's head. Add a curved smile on his muzzle. Draw two long curved arms.

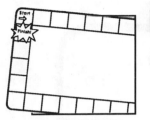

Mm
Phonics Connection

AT SCHOOL

Copy the game board and the set of sound picture cards for the "M" game onto oaktag for the children to color. Have them cut the cards apart. Glue an envelope onto the back of the game board to store the cards and directions for play.

Show the children how to play the game. Include the "At Home" directions when the game goes home.

- -

AT HOME

Materials:
Moe Monkey's game board and set of sound picture cards; a small marker for each player

Directions:
1. Place the cards face down in a pile between the players.
2. Take turns drawing from the pile. If the picture on the card begins with the sound of "m," move the marker forward one space. If the picture begins with another letter sound, no move is made. If a player is lucky enough to draw Moe Monkey's card, the marker may be moved forward two spaces.
3. Reshuffle the cards each time they have all been drawn, and continue playing until someone reaches the finish line. The player who finishes first is the winner.

Moe Monkey's M Race

Start

Finish!

172

173

Mm
Math Connection

M&M MATH

Provide each child (or pair of children) with a small package of M&M candies. Before the packages are opened, ask the children to estimate how many M&Ms are in their bag. Ask also what color they think they will have the most of and the least of.

Give each child a set of paper circles that match the basic M&M colors. Have the children sort their package's contents onto the colored circles. Encourage them to discuss the results. If the children have worked as partners, ask them if they can think of a way to divide the M&Ms equally.

DO YOU PREFER MITTENS OR GLOVES?

(a graphing activity)

Have a class discussion about winter weather and the kind of clothing that's appropriate for going out into the cold. Ask the children how people keep their hands warm outside. After several responses have been made, ask the question, "Do you prefer mittens or gloves?"

Prepare a two-column graph as described in the Introduction; label one column with a picture of a mitten and the other with a picture of a glove. Reproduce the mitten and glove graphing symbols on the following page and have each child choose the one he or she prefers. Have the children decorate their choice and tape it onto the appropriate column.

When everyone has recorded a choice, discuss the finished graph by asking the children to tell you everything they can about what they see. After the discussion, write an experience story together about the graph. Put a copy of the story into an experience story book and add a photo of the graph. Place the book in the classroom library.

Do You Prefer Mittens or Gloves?

Mm
Science Connection

MONKEYS

Class: Mammal
Group: Troop
Habitat: Trees, rocky areas
Food: Leaves, bark, fruit, grains,
       vegetables, insects
Color: Black, brown, tan, white

Monkeys are a lot like humans. Touching is very important to them; they often hug each other. Mother monkeys hold their babies a lot. The baby monkey's fingers are very strong at birth, so that it can hold tightly to its mother's fur as she climbs about. Monkeys are very curious and playful.

READ MORE ABOUT MONKEYS

A Monkey Grows Up by Rita Golden Gelman (Scholastic, 1991).

DO AND DISCOVER

Let the children discover how monkeys can use their paws much the way humans use their hands. Tape a child's fingers and thumb together. Then have him or her crack and eat a peanut. Use a timer to see how long it takes. Now, untape the child's fingers and thumb and compare how long it takes him or her to crack and eat a peanut.

Most monkeys, unlike other animals, have opposable thumbs. That means that, like humans, their thumbs can move independently of their other fingers.

WRITE A BOOK ABOUT MONKEYS

Brainstorm all the things the children remember about monkeys from their study. Make a list of the food monkeys eat. Talk about their habitat. Discuss all the interesting things the children learned about monkeys.

Put three pages together with a cover for a book for each child. Have the children draw a picture of a monkey on the cover and write a title for the book. (See "Listen and Draw A Monkey.") On the first page, have them draw the food that monkeys eat. On the second, let them draw the monkey's habitat, and on the third draw something interesting they know about monkeys. Have the children write or copy a sentence about the picture on each page.

Mm
Science Connection

MAGNETS

Gather a variety of large and small magnets and an assortment of small objects such as paper clips, bottle caps, nails, pins, coins, marbles, and leaves. Allow the children to explore the magnets. Ask questions such as, "What will the magnet pick up (attract)?" "Will it pick up everything?" "What kinds of things will it attract?" "In what ways are the objects that the magnet attracts alike?"

Have the children place some metal paper clips on a piece of construction paper or lightweight cardboard, and move the magnet under the paper. Ask what happens. Next, place some paper clips in a glass of water. Let the children move their magnet around the outside of the glass. Again, ask them what happens. Set up experiments using large and small magnets to attract the same objects. Compare the distances at which the objects are attracted.

THE MOON

Begin a study unit on the moon by asking the children to tell you all they know about it. Make a chart to refer to and to add to throughout the study.

Have the children make moon mobiles. Give each of them lumps of white plasticine clay and a six-inch piece of string that has been knotted at one end. Show them how to mold the clay around the knotted end of the string and shape it into a ball. Then explain that the moon's surface is covered with tall mountains and flat empty spaces. There are many "dents" called craters all over the moon; the craters were caused by huge rocks (meteors) that whizzed in from space and smashed into the moon. Have the children sculpt craters all over their moon's surfaces. Hang each moon on a wire clothes hanger. Let the children make other "space" things from paper to hang on the mobile, such as stars, spaceships, etc. Add to the chart the new words that have been introduced: craters and meteors.

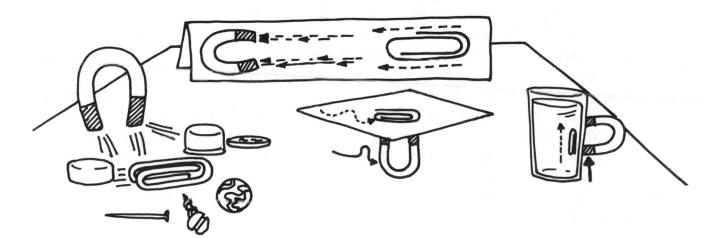

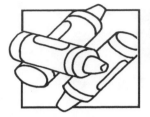

Mm
Arts and Crafts Connection

MONSTER MASKS

Materials:
Paper bags (medium and large sizes), chalk, scrap paper, scissors, felt pens, found materials (ribbons, buttons, paper grass, feathers, etc.), glue

Procedure:
1. Let the children decide whether they wish to make a "head" or a "full body" monster mask.
2. For head masks, cut medium-sized bags about 4" down from the bottom (closed) end and mark the child's eye positions with chalk. For full body masks, place a large grocery bag over the child's head and shoulders and mark the eye, nose, mouth, and arm positions with chalk.
3. Help the children cut out eye holes and, for full body masks, nose, mouth, and arm holes also.
4. Show the children how to do some paper sculpturing, such as curling, fringing, folding, and cutting, and encourage them to use some of these techniques to create features on their monster masks.
5. Also let the children use the felt pens and found materials for decorations.

MOSAICS

Materials:
Colored paper scraps, 9" by 12" pieces of construction paper, bowls of white glue, old paint-brushes or Q-tips, black felt pens, egg carton halves

Procedure:
1. Have the children tear scraps of paper into pieces the size of a thumb nail. Tell them to keep the pieces sorted as they tear by placing each color in a separate egg carton cup. This project works best if the children have an abundance of paper "mosaic" pieces available before they begin the gluing process.
2. Have the children draw a simple picture on a piece of construction paper and trace the lines with a fat felt pen.
3. Using an old brush, show the children how to paint glue onto a small portion of a picture and add mosaic pieces before the glue dries.
4. Encourage the children to cover all parts of their background paper with mosaic pieces, even outside the picture they have drawn.
5. After the glue dries, the children may go back and re-outline their design or figure with a felt pen.

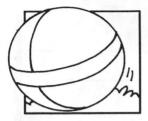

Mm
Movement Connection

MAY I?

This game can be played either inside or outside. Establish a start and a finish line, and have the players line up, toes behind the start line. Choose someone to be "It." This player stands behind the finish line and gives commands describing the number and kind of steps a child may take toward the finish line. For example, "Shirley, you may take five baby steps" or "Donald, you may take two giant steps." Some suggestions for steps the players may be asked to take are giant steps, hops, jumps, twirl steps, backward steps, and leaps.

The player to whom a command is given must respond by asking permission, using these exact words: "May I, please?" If the phrase is not repeated correctly, the child loses his or her turn. "It" responds to an appropriately asked inquiry by saying, "Yes, you may." The player must say "Thank you" before taking the action.

Play continues as "It" gives commands to all the players. The first child to reach the finish line becomes the new "It."

MAN FROM MARS

Take the children out to a grassy area that has established boundaries and a goal line. Have the children line up at the goal line. Chose a child to be the "Man from Mars" and have him or her stand in the middle of the play area.

Play begins as the children call out, "Man from Mars, can we chase you to the stars?" He or she responds with, "Yes, if you are wearing (name of a color)." All the players wearing that color chase the "Man from Mars" around the play area. They must all stay within the established boundaries. The player who tags the "Man from Mars" becomes the new "Man from Mars."

Mm

HOMEWORK

Name _____

Date Due _____

Put a √ by the activity you have chosen to do.

☐ Listen to some **m**usic. Bring your favorite **m**usic to school to share (a tape, a record, or a song to sing).

☐ **M**ake a **m**ap of your room. Bring it to school.

☐ **M**ake a picture of your **m**other. Bring it to school and tell a story about the picture.

_____
Signature of grown up helper

MOE MONKEY'S MUSHROOM MUNCHIE

Ingredients (serves 1)
mushroom
Cheddar cheese

1. Wash a mushroom and put it on a paper towel to dry.

2. Carefully take off the stem.

3. Grate some Cheddar cheese.

4. Put 1 T. cheese in the mushroom cup.

5. Put the mushroom on a cookie sheet.

6. Broil for 3-5 minutes. (You need a helping hand.)

Nn

RAP WITH NARWHAL NED

Sign Language **N**

Narwhal Ned

N is for narwhal, Narwhal Ned.
N /n/ /n/ /n/ /n/ /n/ /n/
Numbers, names, and necklaces.
N /n/ /n/ /n/ /n/ /n/ /n/
Never, naughty, nice, and new.
N /n/ /n/ /n/ /n/ /n/ /n/
(Repeat the first two lines.)

NARWHAL NEWS

Introduce Narwhal Ned and his letter N by pretending to read a newspaper article about narwhals to the children. Show them a newspaper on which you have glued a picture of a real narwhal and the following information, which you read to them: "A narwhal is an unusual sea animal that belongs to the whale family. It lives in the cold waters of the Arctic Ocean, and used to be hunted for its strange spiral tusk. Sailors claimed that the narwhal's tusks were really the horns of unicorns. People soon learned that this was not true. Then they began to call the narwhal the 'unicorn of the sea.' "

A NATURE WALK

Take a nature walk with the class to celebrate the letter N. Give the children cardboard-and-rubber band clipboards on which to draw pictures of their observations. If possible, have the children bring back leaves and bark, and show them how to make nature rubbings.

NARWHAL NED'S Nn BOOK

Brainstorm with the class words that begin with the same sound as Narwhal Ned. Distribute paper and let the children each choose a word to illustrate. Have them copy the following sentence frame onto the page and write their word in the blank space. Put the pages together to make a class book.

Narwhal Ned is nice, and so is a _____.

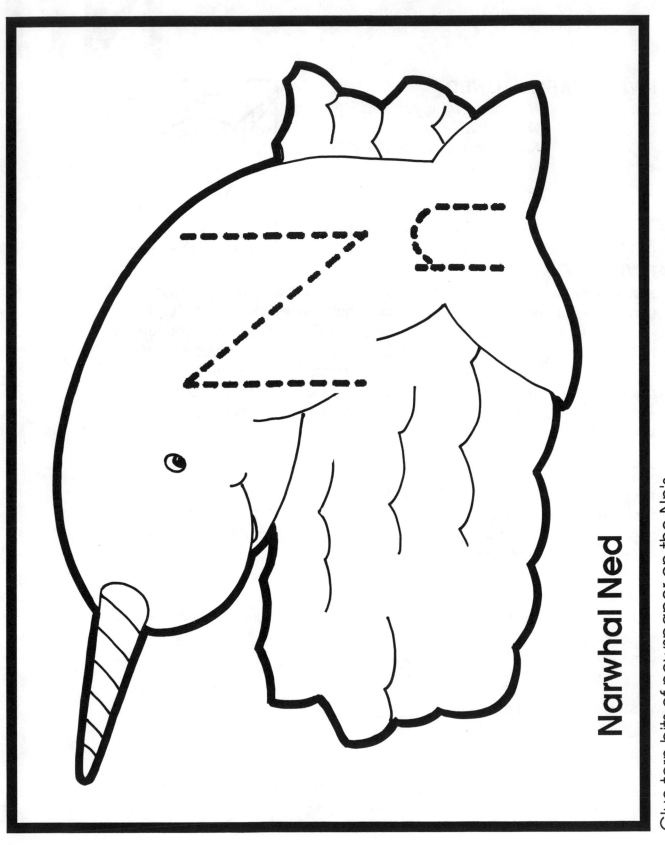

Narwhal Ned

Glue torn bits of newspaper on the Nn's.

Nn
Literature Connection

READ A BOOK
There's a Nightmare in My Closet by Mercer Mayer (Dial, 1968). Nighttime fears concern most children at one time or another. In this book, such fears are dealt with humorously, and the child in the story finds out that his nightmare monster is really afraid of him.

Presentation
Ask the children what they do when they are afraid at night. Make a list of their ideas. Show them the book and tell them to listen for the way that the boy in the story changes his fear.

Additional Books
The Napping House by Audrey Wood (Harcourt, 1984); *Too Much Noise* by Ann McGovern; *Miss Nelson is Missing* by James Marshall (Houghton, 1977); *Night in the Country* by Cynthia Rylant (Bradbury, 1986).

RELATED ACTIVITIES

Closet Doors Book
Brainstorm with the children things that are kept in closets (both real and imaginary). Make a class book titled "Behind Closet Doors." Give the children rectangular pieces of construction paper to decorate as closet doors. Have them make a hinge by making a half inch fold along one of the long sides of the door and gluing it along the narrow fold to a piece of drawing paper. Show the children how to open their "closet door" and make a picture of the things inside. There may even be some scary nightmares there. Bind the pages together as a book for the classroom library.

Crayon Resist Art
Have the children use crayons to draw nighttime pictures, filling in and pressing as hard as possible. The children might draw their bedroom as it looks to them at night, or as they imagine it does. After the drawings are finished, spread a black wash made with water and a small portion of black paint over the pictures. Have the children complete the following sentence frame on the page:

At night, sometimes, I am afraid of _____ .

Bind the pages together to make a book for the classroom library, or pin the pages up separately to create a spooky bulletin board.

Listen and Draw a Narwhal

Give the children oral directions as you draw each step with them.

1. Draw a straight line with a long low hill on top.

2. Draw a long sharp tusk at one end.

3. Make a pointed fin on the body. Add two loops for the tail at the end of the body that doesn't have the tusk.

4. Draw diagonal lines on the tusk. Add one eye and a smile at the tusk end of the narwhal.

Nn
Phonics Connection

AT SCHOOL

Materials:

Small paper bowls, brown grocery bags, scissors, glue, oaktag, crayons, set of egg-shaped beginning sound picture cards

To make the nests: Have the children cut and tear grocery bags into tiny pieces shaped like dry leaves and twigs. Have them glue the scraps onto the inside and outside of the paper bowls. Make two nests for each game.

To make the eggs: Copy the egg-shaped beginning sound picture cards onto oaktag for the children to color and cut out.

Show the children how to play the game. Include the "At Home" directions when the game goes home.

- -

AT HOME

Materials:
A set of egg-shaped beginning sound cards; a nest for each player

Directions:
1. Shuffle the cards and put them in a pile face down between the players.
2. Take turns drawing cards. If you draw a picture that begins with the sound of "n," put it in the nest. If the picture begins with another letter sound, put it in a discard pile.
3. The winner is the person whose nest holds the most eggs after all the cards have been played.

 **Nn**
Math Connection

NUTTY SORTING

Bring a bag filled with many different kinds of unshelled nuts to class. Tell the children that today they are going to sort nuts. Have the children sit in a circle on the floor. Pour the nuts out so that everyone can see them, and ask the children to tell you what they observe. As the observations are voiced, encourage others to contribute by asking, "Anything else?"

After several observations have been made, suggest that the class decide on one way the nuts can be sorted (by shape, color, hardness, texture of the shell, etc.). Guide a small group in sorting as the other children watch. When sorting is finished, ask all the children to tell you about each of the piles as you point them out.

Mix all the nuts together again and ask the children to decide on another attribute or way in which to sort them. Have a different small group of children do the sorting as the others watch.

A NUTTY GRAPH

(a graphing activity)

Have a "Nut Tasting Party." Bring four different kinds of nuts (perhaps peanuts, walnuts, pecans, and almonds), unshelled, to class, and have the children help crack them and extract the nutmeats. Leave a number of nuts of each variety unshelled. Have the children put the different meats into four separate bowls; put one of the corresponding unshelled nuts into the bowl of its meats as identification.

Prepare a four-column graphing grid according to the directions in the Introduction, and glue one of the different types of unshelled nuts to the top of each column. Save the rest of the unshelled nuts for the children to use to record their choices on the graph.

Ask the question, "What kind of nut do you like best?" Encourage the children to taste each nutmeat variety before they select their favorite. Let them glue the whole nut of their choice onto the appropriate column. When everyone has done this, discuss the completed graph, asking the children to tell you everything they can about what they see.

Write an experience story together after the discussion. Put a copy of the story into an experience story book and place it in the classroom library.

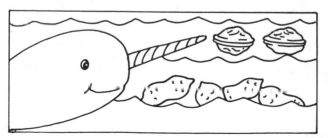

Nn
Science Connection

NARWHALS

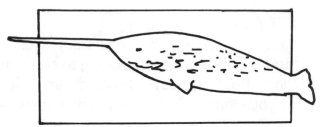

Class: Mammal
Group: Pod
Habitat: Ocean
Food: Shrimp, krill, crab, fish, squid
Baby: Calf
Color: Gray on top, white underneath,
   with dark spots all over

A narwhal has two teeth that grow straight forward from its top jaw. The male's left tooth keeps growing into a spiral, as long as nine feet. Narwhals were once hunted nearly to extinction for their teeth, which were sold as "unicorn horns." The narwhal became known as the "sea unicorn."

READ MORE ABOUT NARWHALS

Sea Full of Whales by Richard Armour (Scholastic, 1974).

DO AND DISCOVER

Let the children discover how a narwhal's sonar system works. Blindfold a child. Place a box on the floor close to or far from the child. Bounce a Ping-Pong ball on the floor, then bounce it against the box. Have the child listen to the clicking sound the ball makes on the floor and then on the box, and tell if the box was placed close to him or her or far away.

WRITE A BOOK ABOUT NARWHALS

Brainstorm all the things the children remember about narwhals from their study. Make a list of the food narwhals eat. Talk about their habitat. Discuss all the interesting things the children learned about narwhals.

   Put three pages together with a cover for a book for each child. Have the children draw a picture of a narwhal on the cover and write a title for the book. (See "Listen and Draw A Narwhal.") On the first page, have them draw the food that narwhals eat. On the second, let them draw the narwhal's habitat, and on the third draw something interesting they know about narwhals. Have the children write or copy a sentence about the picture on each page.

Nn
Science Connection

NESTS

If you have access to some abandoned birds' nests, bring them into the class-room for the children to examine. As they are looking at them, ask, "Are the nests all alike?" "How are they different?" "What are the nests made of?"

Set up an experiment to better identify some of the materials used by birds in nest building. Place one of the nests in a clear plastic bag, spray the nest with water, and fasten the bag closed. Some of the things used to build the nest will begin to sprout in about a week. Ask, "What is happening to the nest?" "Are all the parts of the nest growing?" "Can you name some parts of the nest that are not growing?"

After the children have identified the nesting materials, invite them to bring as many of these items from home as they can (cotton, string, yarn, dryer fluff, fiberfill, straw, etc.). In the spring of the year, have the children loosely fill net bags (onion bags) with the nesting materials. Hang the bags outside and watch birds take the materials for their nests.

NOSES

Have the children choose partners and take an "odor" walk in the classroom. Tell them to smell things that they might think don't have a fragrance, such as blocks, chalk, crayons, paper, tables, rugs, and paint. Hold a discussion about the things they smelled. Make a chart classifying the odors as "bad smells" and "good smells."

Prepare "smell cards" for the children. Paint a circle of watered-down white glue on the center of several 3" by 5" file cards. Sprinkle one of the following on each of the glue spots: cinnamon, garlic powder, pepper, baby powder, and scouring powder. Label each substance on the back of its card. Then tell the children that they can use only their nose to try to identify each smell. A variation of this activity is to make two cards of each substance and have the children match the cards that smell the same.

Cut a giant nose out of tagboard. Have the children look through magazines to find pictures of things with a definite smell. Have them cut the pictures out and paste them onto the nose to create a class collage. Title the collage "Our Nose Knows."

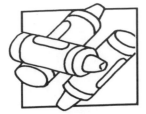

Nn
Arts and Crafts Connection

NOTEWORTHY NUMERALS

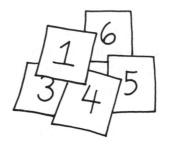

Materials:
12" by 18" pieces of white paper, pencils, erasers, liquid tempera paints (blue, violet, green, and yellow), paint containers, brushes, bag containing slips of paper with a single-digit numeral written on each one (1 per child)

Procedure:
1. Let each child reach into the numeral bag and pull out a slip of paper.
2. Have the children use pencils to draw the numeral they selected in the center of a piece of white paper. Be sure the numerals are very large.
3. Tell the children that they have drawn a "skeleton" numeral. Show them how to draw around their numeral on both sides to "fatten it up." Encourage them to keep their lines the same distance away from the skeleton all the way around.
4. Have them erase their skeleton lines.
5. Show them how to start at various points on the edges of their " fat" numerals and draw 9 or 10 lines out to the edges of their papers. Don't let them draw the lines too close together, since they will be painting within the shapes that are formed.
6. Give the children brushes and the liquid tempera, and let them paint the background shapes in "cool" colors (blue, violet, and green are called "cool" because they are the color of shadows, trees, lakes, sky, and grass).
7. Have them paint their numeral with the "warm" color, yellow (the color of the sun), and watch it appear to pop right out of the picture.

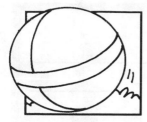

Nn
Movement Connection

NIGHTINGALES IN NESTS

For this game approximately two thirds of the children sit in pairs, facing each other with hands joined. These are the "nests." The pairs should be scattered about on the playground with considerable space between them. The other children are the "Nightingales." (Be sure the children know that nightingales are birds.) There should be a few more "Nightingales" than there are "nests."

To play the game, call out, "Fly, Nightingales, fly!" and have the "birds" flap their arms and "fly" to one of the "nests." Each time the signal is given, the "Nightingales" must leave their "nests" and find new ones. Since only one "Nightingale" at a time is allowed in a "nest" there will be some players left over after each flight, but they will have another opportunity to find a "nest" as soon as the command is given again.

After several turns, rotate the children so that every child has a chance to be a "Nightingale" as well as part of a "nest."

NAME BALL

Have the children sit in a circle. Give one of the children a 7" rubber ball. The child with the ball says his or her name and rolls the ball to another child with whom he or she has established eye contact. The child who receives the ball repeats the process, establishing eye contact with another player, calling out his or her own name, and rolling the ball to that player.

The game moves quickly enough to allow everyone a turn. It's a good "get acquainted" game and later, after the children know each other's names, the child rolling the ball can call out the name of the receiving child rather than his or her own name.

191

Nn

HOMEWORK

Name _____

Date Due _____

Put a √ by the activity you have chosen to do.

☐ Find some **n**ews in the **n**ewspaper to bring and tell about at school.

☐ Collect different kinds of **n**uts. Bring them to school to tell about. Tell which is your favorite.

☐ Write the whole **n**ame of everyone in your family. Bring the list to school.

_____
Signature of grown up helper

NARWHAL NED'S NACHOS

tortilla chips
refried beans
chopped ripe olives
Cheddar cheese

1. Put tortilla chips together on a cookie sheet.

2. Put 1 T. refried beans on top.

3. Add 2 tsp. chopped olives.

4. Grate some cheese.

5. Cover with grated cheese.

6. Broil until the cheese melts. (You need a helping hand.)

RAP WITH OLIVER OSTRICH

Sign Language **O**

O is for ostrich, Oliver.
O /o/ /o/ /o/ /o/ /o/ /o/
Octopus and operate.
O /o/ /o/ /o/ /o/ /o/ /o/
Oblong, olives, off, and on.
O /o/ /o/ /o/ /o/ /o/ /o/
(Repeat the first two lines.)

Oliver Ostrich

ODD OATMEAL

Display a large oatmeal box filled with objects or pictures of objects that begin with the long or the short sound of the letter o (for example, olive, oval, ocarina, oatmeal cookie, ostrich, opossum, ocelot, otter, octopus, and osprey). Choose children to take out one item or picture at a time and name it. Then tell the class that there is an alphabet animal friend whose letter they will be learning about. Ask them to guess who it is.

A DAY AT THE OPERA

Plan a "Day at the Opera" to celebrate the letter O. Invite a local opera singer to talk to the children about what an opera is. Have him or her talk about the singing style of the opera, and demonstrate by singing an aria.

Read the story of Hansel and Gretel and play some of the music from the opera composed by Englebert Humperdinck.

OLIVER OSTRICH'S Oo BOOK

Brainstorm with the class words that begin with the same sound as Oliver Ostrich. Distribute paper and let the children each choose a word to illustrate. Have them copy the following sentence frame onto the page and write their word in the blank space. Put the pages together to make a class book.

Oliver Ostrich is odd, and so is an _____.

Oliver Ostrich

Glue oat berries on the Oo's.

Oo
Literature Connection

READ A BOOK

Over and Over by Charlotte Zolotow (Harper, 1957). *Over and Over* is a book about a little girl who does not understand about time. As she watches the seasons and the holidays go by, she asks what comes next. On her birthday, she wishes that all that had happened would come again, and, of course, "over and over, year after year, it did."

Presentation

Ask the children their favorite special day of the year. After the discussion, tell them that the little girl in the story you are going to read finds out something very important about her favorite days.

Additional Books

Over in the Meadow by Olive Wadsworth (Penguin, 1986); *Exactly the Opposite* by Tana Hoban (Greenwillow, 1990); *Push, Pull, Empty, Full: A Book of Opposites* by Tana Hoban (Greenwillow, 1988).

RELATED ACTIVITY

Special Days Big Book

Have each child illustrate his or her favorite special day and complete this sentence frame:

What comes next? _____

Organize the pictures into sets so that all the holidays are represented in each. Help the children arrange the pictures in each set chronologically. Bind all the pictures into a class book.

Listen and Draw an Ostrich

Give the children oral directions as you draw each step with them.

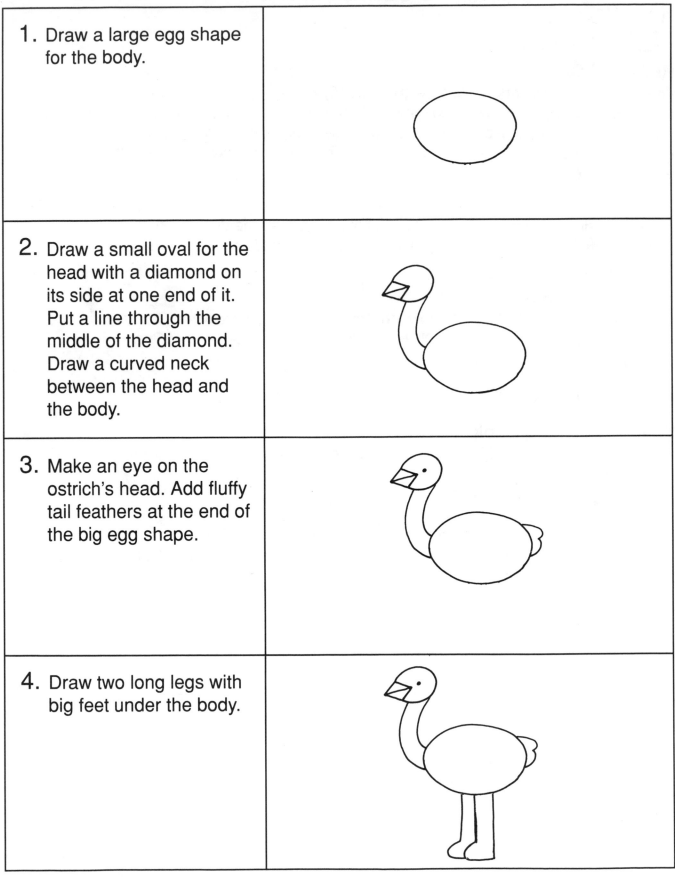

1. Draw a large egg shape for the body.

2. Draw a small oval for the head with a diamond on its side at one end of it. Put a line through the middle of the diamond. Draw a curved neck between the head and the body.

3. Make an eye on the ostrich's head. Add fluffy tail feathers at the end of the big egg shape.

4. Draw two long legs with big feet under the body.

Oo
Phonics Connection

AT SCHOOL

Copy the game board and the set of sound picture cards for The "O" Game onto oaktag for the children to color. Have them cut the cards out. Glue an envelope onto the back of the game board to store the cards and the directions for play.

Show the children how to play the game. Include the "At Home" directions when the game goes home.

AT HOME

Materials:
The "O" Game game board and set of sound picture cards; a small marker for each player

Directions:
1. Place the cards face down in a pile between the players.
2. Take turns drawing from the pile. If the picture on the card begins with the long or short sound of "o," move the marker forward one space. If the picture begins with another letter sound, no move is made. If a player is lucky enough to draw Oliver Ostrich's card, the marker may be moved forward two spaces.
3. Reshuffle the cards each time they have all been drawn, and continue playing until someone reaches the finish line. The player who finishes first is the winner.

The
O
Game

Start

Finish!

Oliver Ostrich

Olivia Opossum

Oo
Math Connection

OBSERVING OCTAGONS AND OVALS

Take the children on a walk, equipped with pencils and large sheets of paper. Have them make a pictorial "list" of as many things as they can find that are oval or octagonal.

HOW DO YOU PREFER YOUR OATS?

(a graphing activity)

Bring a box of oatmeal and another kind of oat cereal, such as Cheerios, to class. Discuss the fact that oats are a grain (like wheat) with which people make many different kinds of foods. Ask if anyone has ever eaten an oatmeal cookie. Then ask the graphing question: "How do you prefer your oats?"

Prepare a three-column graph as described in the Introduction; label the columns "Hot Oatmeal," "Cheerios," and "Oatmeal Cookies." Reproduce the oatmeal graphing symbols on the following page and have the children choose the one they prefer. Let them tape their choice on the appropriate column on the graph.

When everyone has recorded a choice, discuss the finished graph by asking the children to tell you everything they can about what they see. Record their observations on big paper "bubbles" (like those in which dialogue is found in a comic strip). Pin up the graph on the bulletin board and post the bubbles around it for a great Open House bulletin board display.

You may also want to write an experience story together about the graph after the discussion. Put a copy of the story into an experience story book and place it in the classroom library.

How Do You Prefer Your Oats?

Oo
Science Connection

OSTRICHES

Class: Bird
Group: Flock
Habitat: Grasslands, deserts
Food: Plants, lizards
Baby: Chick
Color: Male, black and white;
     female, brown

The ostrich is the biggest of all birds. It has small wings and can't fly, but its legs are very strong. It can run fast and kick hard to protect itself. It never swims or bathes, but it takes "dust baths." Both the mother and father guard and sit on the eggs.

READ MORE ABOUT OSTRICHES
Ostriches and Other Flightless Birds by Caroline Arnold (Carolrhoda, 1990).

DO AND DISCOVER
The belief that ostriches hide their heads in the sand when frightened because they don't think they can be seen is not true. Help the children discover what ostriches really do when they are frightened. Take them out to a large field. Choose one child to be the "ostrich" and go far out into the field while the other children sit down and watch. Have the "ostrich" lie down as low as possible. Point out to the children how difficult it is to see the "ostrich" in this position. A real ostrich's feather-covered body looks like a small hill when it lies down, and is even more difficult to see than a child lying down.

WRITE A BOOK ABOUT OSTRICHES
Brainstorm all the things the children remember about ostriches from their study. Make a list of the food ostriches eat. Talk about their habitat. Discuss all the interesting things the children learned about ostriches.

    Put three pages together with a cover for a book for each child. Have the children draw a picture of an ostrich on the cover and write a title for the book. (See "Listen and Draw An Ostrich.") On the first page, have them draw the food that ostriches eat. On the second, let them draw the ostrich's habitat, and on the third draw something interesting that they know about ostriches. Have the children write or copy a sentence about the picture on each page.

Oo
Science Connection

OBSERVATION

Tell the children that today they are going to pretend they are scientists. They are going to practice something that scientists find very important in their work—observation. Explain that observation means looking very closely and carefully at things. Plan with the children to make observation journals for a future project or experiment such as observing and recording the weather for a week or noting changes in a seed-sprouting activity. Tell them that before they can make a journal they must practice observing.

Choose one child to stand in front of the class. Have the children observe and then describe the child. Help them to observe the small details that help to identify this child as different from all the others. Ask questions such as, "What color is his (her) hair?" "Is it curly or straight?" "Can you see what color eyes this person has?" "What kind of clothes (shoes) is he (she) wearing?"

Next, have the children observe a flowering plant that you have brought to class. Say, "Let's observe this plant. What do you see?" Help the children notice details by asking questions such as, "What colors do you see?" "Are the leaves round or long and pointed?" "How many petals does the flower have?" "Do you see a stem?"

Have the children draw what they have observed about the plant.

OXYGEN

Tell the children you have a riddle for them: What is something you cannot see, feel, or smell but that all animals and people need to live? After taking several guesses (someone may really know), ask if anyone has heard of oxygen before. Explain that it is a gas in the air and water. Have the children take deep breaths and feel their lungs stretch to fill with air. Explain that our lungs take oxygen out of the air so that our body can use it.

To demonstrate that there is oxygen in the air, place a candle in a tall jar and light it. Put the cover on the jar. When the oxygen is used up, the candle will go out.

Bring a goldfish to class for the children to watch. Have them imitate the fish as it opens and closes its mouth. Explain that instead of lungs, fish have special parts called gills. In order to breathe, the fish opens its mouth and lets in water. The fish's gills take the oxygen from the water, just as our lungs take oxygen from the air.

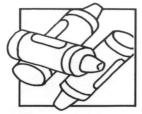

Oo
Arts and Crafts Connection

ODD OGRES

Materials:
Clay (plasticine, baker's dough [see recipe below], or modeling sand [see recipe below]), clay-working tools (large nails, Popsicle sticks, toothpicks, combs), collage materials (buttons, pipe cleaners, sticks, bottle caps, sphagnum moss, etc.), work surfaces (plastic place mats, paper plates, linoleum squares)

Procedure:
Discuss the meaning of the words "ogre" and "odd" before beginning this project.
1. Set out workable-sized portions of clay on plastic place mats, paper plates, linoleum squares, or other surfaces to protect the table top.
2. Show the children a few techniques for working with clay, such as rolling, pinching, and pressing.
3. Ask them how they think they could make an odd ogre out of clay. Do not make a model for them, but encourage them to use their imaginations.
4. Set out the collage materials for the children to use as eyes, arms, hair, beards, etc.

Baker's Dough (for 1 child)
Mix 1 cup of flour with ½ cup of water. (The children can mix their own portions for modeling. Their sculptures will air dry within 24 hours.)

Modeling Sand (for 4 to 6 children)
Mix 1 cup of cornstarch, 2 cups of sifted sand, and 1½ cups of water in an old cooking pan. Cook 5-10 minutes, stirring constantly. Turn onto a plate, cover with a damp cloth, and cool. Knead well, and use like modeling clay.

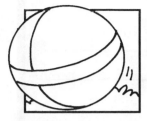

Oo
Movement Connection

OBSTACLE COURSE

An obstacle course can be set up almost anywhere—a grassy area, hard-top playground, gym, classroom, or a combination of these areas. Let the children help set it up; the setup can be as much fun as actually going through the course. Use obstacles that the children can go under, over, through, around, inside, outside, and between. Some suggestions are: chairs, tables, cardboard cartons, blocks (the big floor variety), old tires, or Hula-Hoops.

Draw a line between obstacles with colored chalk for the children to follow. Have the children decide together how each obstacle is to be met, and then form a "train" to go through the course. Each time the course is completed, the leader goes to the end of the line and the next child becomes the leader.

Once the course has become familiar to the children, let them try other ways to move from one obstacle to another, such as hopping, jumping, walking backwards, or skipping.

ODD BALL

Have the children stand in a circle. Begin the game by passing a small playground ball around the circle in one direction. Encourage the children to keep the ball moving as fast as possible. As they master a one-way pass, start another ball going in the opposite direction. This may cause some silly confusion, but continue to encourage the children to keep the balls moving.

When the balls are moving steadily, call out "Odd ball!" to signal the children to reverse the directions in which they have been passing the balls. Challenge older children by adding more balls (one at a time) to the game.

Oo

HOMEWORK

Name _____

Date Due _____

Put a √ by the activity you have chosen to do.

☐ Draw all the **o**val-shaped things you can find in your house. Bring the pictures to school.

☐ Make a picture list of **o**pposite words. (Some examples are fat/thin and hot/cold.) Bring your list to school.

☐ Set up an **o**bstacle course to go through. Bring a picture of it to school and tell about it.

_____
Signature of grown up helper

OLIVER OSTRICH'S OLIVE BALL

Ingredients (serves 1)
  cheese spread
  butter
  flour
  pitted ripe olive

1. Put 1 tsp. cheese spread into a bowl.

2. Add 1/2 tsp. butter.

3. Add 1 1/2 tsp. flour. Mix with your fingers.

4. Make a ball of dough with the olive in the middle.

5. Put the olive ball on a cookie sheet.

6. Bake at 400° for 12-15 minutes. (You need a helping hand.)

RAP WITH PENGUIN PETE

Sign Language **P**

Penguin Pete

P is for penguin, Penguin Pete.
P /p/ /p/ /p/ /p/ /p/ /p/
Puppies, popcorn, porcupines.
P /p/ /p/ /p/ /p/ /p/ /p/
Pitter-patter, pumpkin pie.
P /p/ /p/ /p/ /p/ /p/ /p/
(Repeat the first two lines.)

POPCORN POP

Make popcorn with the children. Have them listen to the sound of the popcorn as it's popping, and imitate it with their lips. Introduce Penguin Pete as the alphabet animal friend whose name begins with the same sound as the popcorn makes as it pops. Then let the children munch.

PIZZA PARTY

Have a pizza party to celebrate the letter P. Ask the children to bring their favorite pizza toppings to share. On "Penguin Pete's Pizza Party Day," let the children create their own pizzas by putting toppings on flattened refrigerator biscuits that have been spread with small amounts of tomato sauce. Bake the pizzas for about 10 minutes in a 400° oven.

PENGUIN PETE'S Pp BOOK

Brainstorm with the class words that begin with the same sound as Penguin Pete. Distribute paper and let the children each choose a word to illustrate. Have them copy the following sentence frame onto the page and write their word in the blank space. Put the pages together to make a class book.

Penguin Pete put a _____ in his pocket.

Penguin Pete

Glue peanuts (or popcorn) on the Pp's.

Pp
Literature Connection

READ A BOOK
Pumpkin, Pumpkin by Jeanne Titherington (Greenwillow, 1986). A little boy named Jamie plants a pumpkin seed and watches it grow. The illustrations are charming and the text so simple that the children will soon be reading this book over and over for themselves.

Presentation
Gather a variety of seeds together and show them to the children. Ask what they are, then ask if any of the children has planted seeds. Have them tell what they did, and what happened to the seeds. Show the children the cover of the book. Ask them if they can tell what this book is about. Then read the book together.

Additional Books
Petunia by Roger Duvoisin (Knopf, 1950); *Pierre* by Maurice Sendak (Harper, 1962); *The Three Little Pigs* by Paul Galdone (Clarion, 1970); *Little Penguin's Tale* by Audrey Wood (Harcourt, 1989); *A Pocket for Corduroy* by Don Freeman (Viking, 1978).

RELATED ACTIVITIES

Write a Pumpkin Book
Discuss the sequence of events in the book. Ask the children questions such as, "What happened first in the story?" "What came next?"

Give all the children a piece of pumpkin-shaped paper, and have them choose one of the story events to illustrate. Encourage them to write or dictate a sentence about their drawing. Let the class organize the pictures in sequence. Then turn the pages into a book by binding them together and adding a cover.

Plant Some Pumpkin Seeds
The month of May is a good time to plant seeds in most parts of the country. Have the children plant three or four pumpkin seeds in plastic glasses. Show them how to make a hole in the potting soil by pressing their index finger into it to the first knuckle. Then have them drop a few seeds into the hole, sprinkling soil over each seed after it is added, and put the seed containers in a warm, sunny place. In a small blank book, have the children record their observations pictorially every two or three days.

The first two leaves that appear are called the "seedling leaves." The sprouted seeds can be transplanted outdoors when the more mature leaves appear. Transplanting and growing the pumpkins to maturity requires a lot of space, but if it's not available, the experience of watching even a small plant grow from a seed will be very rewarding.

Listen and Draw a Penguin

Give the children oral directions as you draw each step with them.

1. Draw an oval body. Put a round bump on top for the head.

2. Draw a wing on each side of the body.

3. Make a shape like a diamond on its side in the middle of the head. Put a line through the middle of the diamond.

4. Add two eyes on the head. Make two jagged feet under the body.

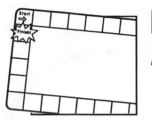

Pp
Phonics Connection

AT SCHOOL

Materials:

Two 8" circles of light brown construction paper, crayons, oaktag, scissors, circle-shaped beginning sound picture cards

To make the pizza: Have the children decorate the paper circles to look like pizza. Make two pizzas for each game.

To make the pepperoni: Copy the circle-shaped beginning sound picture cards onto oaktag for the children to color and cut out.

Show the children how to play the game. Include the "At Home" directions when the game goes home.

- -

AT HOME

Materials:

A set of circle-shaped beginning sound picture cards; a paper pizza for each player

Directions:

1. Shuffle the cards and put them in a pile face down between the players.
2. Take turns drawing cards. If a picture is drawn that begins with the sound of "p," put it on the pizza. If the picture begins with another letter sound, put it in a discard pile.
3. The winner is the person whose pizza has the most pepperoni after all the cards have been played.

 **Pp**
Math Connection

PUMPKIN MATH

During the fall, bring a pumpkin to class and have the children estimate its circumference by cutting string into lengths that they think will just fit around the pumpkin's fattest part. Make a graph by posting three signs on the wall. One sign should say "Too Short," another "Too Long," and the last "Just Right." Have the children check the accuracy of their estimates by wrapping their pieces of string around the pumpkin and taping their strings below the appropriate sign.

DID YOU COME TO SCHOOL WITH POCKETS TODAY?

(a graphing activity)

Make a living graph about pockets. After a brief discussion about pockets, ask the children who is wearing clothing with pockets today. Have the children who do have pockets get in one line, and those who do not in another, parallel, line. Have the children hold the hand of the child opposite them. Then tell them to drop hands and stand still. This makes the graph easier to "read." Explain that the two lines of children are like two columns of a graph. Ask them to tell you everything they can about what they see.

Write an experience story together after the discussion. Encourage someone to draw a picture of the graphing activity. Put a copy of the story with its illustration into an experience story book and place it in the classroom library.

Pp
Science Connection

PENGUINS

Class: Bird
Group: Colony
Habitat: Ocean, rocky and icy shorelines
Food: Fish, shellfish, shrimp, krill, squid
Baby: Chick
Color: Black and white

Penguins cannot fly like most other birds, but they swim so well they look like they're flying through the water. Some penguins make their nests with pebbles to keep their eggs from rolling away. Another type of female penguin actually places her egg on the male penguin's feet and leaves for two months while he holds and hatches it.

READ MORE ABOUT PENGUINS

Little Penguin by Patrick Benson (Philomel, 1990).

DO AND DISCOVER

Let the children discover why penguins have oily feathers. Hand out lidded baby food jars filled with water, a few drops of blue food coloring, and vegetable oil. Have the children shake the jars and try to mix the oil and water. After they discover that oil and water do not mix, show them two construction paper feathers, one of which has been brushed with vegetable oil. Have them predict what will happen when water is sprinkled on each feather. Then slowly drip about a tablespoon of water onto each paper feather and encourage the children to observe how the water soaks into the untreated feather and beads up or rolls off the oiled paper feather.

WRITE A BOOK ABOUT PENGUINS

Brainstorm all the things the children remember about penguins from their study. Make a list of the food penguins eat. Talk about their habitat. Discuss all the interesting things the children learned about penguins.

Put three pages together with a cover for a book for each child. Have the children draw a picture of a penguin on the cover and write a title for the book. (See "Listen and Draw A Penguin.") On the first page, have them draw the food that penguins eat. On the second, let them draw the penguin's habitat, and on the third draw something interesting they know about penguins. Have the children write or copy a sentence about the picture on each page.

Pp
Science Connection

PAPER

Take a poll of all the children who help their families recycle paper. Have them describe what they do to help. Talk about what recycling means (to use something over and over again).

Demonstrate how paper can be recycled by making usable paper from tissues.

1. Cut a piece of fine-gauge screen and fold the edges over twice to form a 4" by 6" rectangle.

2. Tear up three tissues and put the pieces into a mixing bowl. Fill the bowl about three quarters full of hot water.

3. Beat the tissue and water with an electric mixer. Add one tablespoon of liquid starch. This mixture is called "slurry."

4. Pour the slurry into a shallow pan.

5. Slide the screen frame into the bottom of the pan. Get an even layer of slurry on the frame, and carefully lift the frame up to drain.

6. Lay the screen with the pulp side up on a stack of newspapers. Cover with more newspapers, and run a rolling pin across the top to squeeze out the excess moisture.

7. Peel off the screen and allow the recycled paper to dry.

PLANTS

Start the study of plants by soaking some large lima beans in water overnight. Show the children how to carefully split one of these seeds open to see the baby plant inside. Discuss how the seed is like an egg: the seed's coating acts like an eggshell to protect the baby plant, and the material inside the seed provides food for it just as the egg yolk provides food for the unborn chick. Tell the children that many plants start from seeds.

Let the children each plant a seed in a clear plastic cup of potting soil. Choose seeds that germinate quickly, and choose a Wednesday or Thursday as planting day so that the children are in school the day the seedlings pop up from the soil. Prepare a plant growth chart for each child, ruling at least 14 vertical columns (each ½" wide) across the paper. Number the columns along the bottom from 1 to 14. The children will cross out #1 to indicate that no growth was seen on the first day, and perhaps the second and third. When a seedling is seen, have the child take a prepared ½" by 9" strip of green paper and cut it to match the seedling's height. Show the children how to glue the strip on their growth chart on the appropriate day. Encourage the children to measure their plants each day and to continue recording their growth.

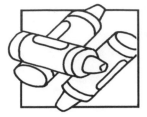

Pp
Arts and Crafts Connection

POTATO PRINTS

Materials:
Potatoes, plastic knives, sharp knife, metal spoons, liquid tempera paint, brushes, paint containers, paper

Procedure:
1. Give each child a precut potato half.
2. Show the children how to make a design on the sliced end by digging out small pieces or making notches with a plastic knife or metal spoon.
3. When the designs are satisfactory to the artists, have them brush liquid tempera onto the entire design end of the potato.
4. Show them how to press the potato's painted side down gently onto paper, lift straight up, and stamp again. The children will be able to get three or four prints each time they paint the potato surface. Have the children continue the process until they are satisfied with the effect.

Hints:
1. Have the children wash the surface of the potato before changing colors.
2. Encourage them to exchange potato stamps with others to get a variety of prints on their papers.
3. When a child has finished printing, you or another adult can slice the old design off the potato to create a fresh surface for a new design.

PUFFY PAINTS

Materials:
Flour, salt, water, bowl, spoon, liquid tempera paint, cardboard or heavy paper squares, plastic squeeze bottles (ketchup, mustard, honey containers)

Procedure:
1. Mix equal parts of flour, salt, and water in a bowl.
2. Add tempera paint
3. Pour the mixture into plastic squeeze bottles.
4. Show the children how to squeeze the puffy paint onto a piece of paper or cardboard in lines and dots. Encourage them to experiment with different designs and patterns. Puffy paint hardens when it dries.

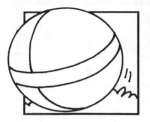

Pp
Movement Connection

POM, POM, PULL AWAY

Take the children out to a grassy area and establish two goal lines. Divide the children into two groups. Have one group line up shoulder to shoulder on one goal line, and have the other group do the same on the opposite goal.

Choose two children to be "It." Give them each a large rubber playground ball and have them crouch halfway between the two teams on opposite sidelines.

Play begins as the two teams chant "Pom, pom, pull away!", then run across the play area to exchange places with one another. The two "Its" roll their balls across the play area just as the groups run by. The children who are touched by either of the balls must join the two children on the sidelines. They help retrieve balls and try to touch others with the ball when they run by with each call of "Pom, pom, pull away!"

HOT POTATO PASS

Have the children sit down close together in a circle. A real potato is passed from child to child until the "Potato-Caller" (the teacher), who is standing outside the circle, facing away from it, shouts, "Hot potato!" The player with the potato in his or her hand at that moment gives it to the next person in the circle, and, facing away from the circle, sits down with the "Potato-Caller." He or she whispers a number to that person. The potato is then passed again around the circle as the "Potato-Caller" and the new helper quietly count to the number together before yelling "Hot potato!" in unison. The person holding the potato at that point gives it to the next person in the circle and joins the other callers. The game continues until other children have had a chance to join the callers and choose a "Hot potato" number to count to.

Pp

HOMEWORK

Name _____

Date Due _____

Put a √ by the activity you have chosen to do.

☐ Learn about the **p**resident of the United States. Ask a grownup to write what you find out. Draw a picture of the **p**resident. Bring the information and the picture to school.

☐ **P**repare something using **p**eanuts. Bring your **p**eanut creation to school.

☐ Make up a recipe for **p**ancakes. Ask a grownup to write it for you. Bring the **p**ancake recipe to school.

_____
Signature of grown up helper

PENGUIN PETE'S PRETZEL

Ingredients (serves 1)
yeast (dry)
warm water
salt
sugar
flour
Cheddar cheese
egg (beaten)
kosher salt

1. Dissolve 1/2 tsp. yeast in 3 T. warm water.

2. Add a pinch of salt and 1/2 tsp. sugar.

3. Add 1/2 cup flour.

4. Add 2 T. grated Cheddar cheese and mix well. (The dough will be stiff.)

5. Make into a ball, and knead 2-3 minutes.

6. Cut into 2-4 pieces. Roll each piece into a "worm" shape. Then twist together into any shape.

7. Brush with beaten egg, sprinkle with salt, and bake at 375° for 15 minutes. (You need a helping hand.)

Qq

RAP WITH QUINCY QUAIL

Sign Language **Q**

Q is for quail, Quincy Quail.
Q /q/ /q/ /q/ /q/ /q/ /q/
Quiet, queens, and quarterbacks.
Q /q/ /q/ /q/ /q/ /q/ /q/
Questions, quilts, and quarreling.
Q /q/ /q/ /q/ /q/ /q/ /q/
(Repeat the first two lines.)

Quincy Quail

QUILTING

Introduce Quincy Quail and his letter Q by displaying a real quilt or showing the children pictures of quilts. Tell the children the covering's name if they don't know it. Introduce Quincy Quail as the alphabet animal friend who will teach them the sound of the letter Q.

A QUILTING BEE

Celebrate the letter Q by making a class paper quilt during an old-fashioned quilting bee. Tell the children what a quilting bee is. Prepare colored construction paper triangle and diamond shapes for them to glue onto white 6" by 6" squares. When these quilt blocks are dry, let the children arrange them in a design on a large piece of colored butcher paper.

After the paper quilt has been made, tell the children how to play a game called "Who's Under The Quilt?" Have the children sit in a circle around a real quilt that is spread out on the floor and close their eyes. Choose one child by touching him or her on the shoulder, indicating that he or she should quietly hide under the quilt. When you ask, "Who's under the quilt?" the children open their eyes and guess who is hiding.

QUINCY QUAIL'S Qq BOOK

Brainstorm with the class words that begin with the same sound as Quincy Quail. Distribute paper and let the children each choose a word to illustrate. Have them copy the following sentence frame onto the page and write their word in the blank space. Put the pages together to make a class book.

Answer the question, Quincy Quail.

Do you like _____ ?

Quincy Quail

Glue uncooked Quaker oats on the Qq's.

220

Qq
Literature Connection

READ A BOOK
The Quilt Story by Tony Johnston (Putnam, 1985). This is the story of a quilt lovingly made by a pioneer mother to warm and comfort her little daughter. Many years later the same quilt is mended and restored by another mother for her little girl.

Presentation
Bring in a real patchwork quilt or a picture of one to show the children. Discuss how quilts are made. Encourage the children to tell about quilts they have seen or have owned. Talk about pioneer times, when people did not live near stores where they could buy warm coverings for their beds, but saved pieces of cloth from old clothing or scraps left over from making new garments to use to make quilts. Tell them that you are going to read a story about a quilt that was made a long time ago.

Additional Books
Quick as a Cricket by Audrey Wood (Child's Play, 1982); *The Very Quiet Cricket* by Eric Carle (Philomel, 1990); *The Keeping Quilt* by Patricia Polacco (Simon & Schuster, 1988); *The Patchwork Quilt* by Valerie Flourney (Dial, 1985).

RELATED ACTIVITY

Classroom Quilt
Gather as many pictures of different types of quilts as you can to show the children. Talk about the many ways in which shapes have been put together to make beautiful designs. Invite the children to bring in quilts to show and tell about.

Then encourage the children to make a quilt together. Have them bring in 5" by 5" scraps of material and have them sign their name on the corner of each of their squares with a laundry pen. Let the children arrange the squares in rows or designs on a piece of fabric; when the design is arranged, let the children glue down all the pieces with fabric glue (available at craft, needlework, and fabric stores). Remind the children to leave strips of the background fabric uncovered between designs for a patchwork quilt effect. Let the class enjoy the quilt in the playhouse, or displayed on the classroom wall.

Listen and Draw a Quail

Give the children oral directions as you draw each step with them.

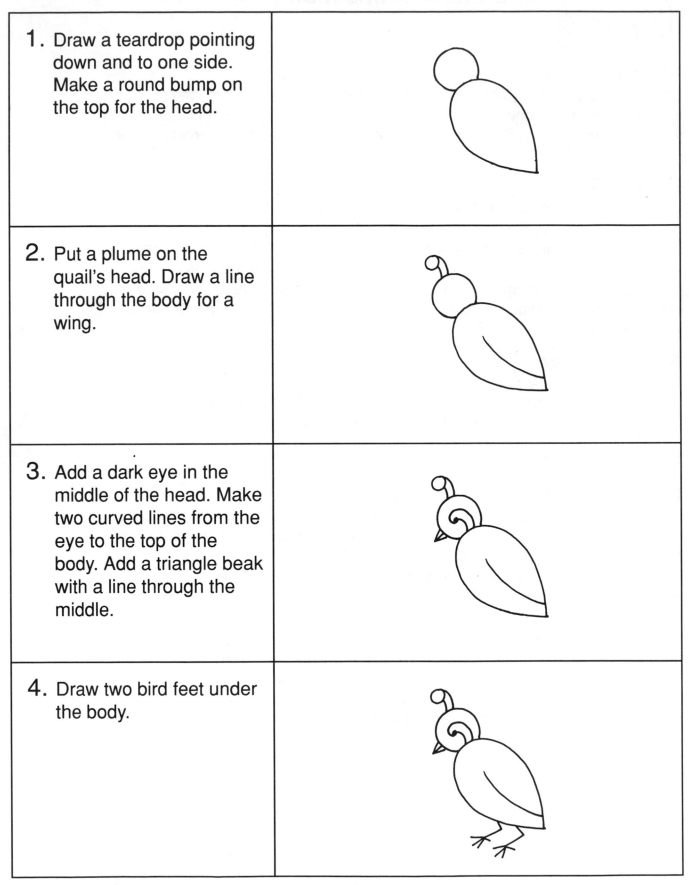

1. Draw a teardrop pointing down and to one side. Make a round bump on the top for the head.

2. Put a plume on the quail's head. Draw a line through the body for a wing.

3. Add a dark eye in the middle of the head. Make two curved lines from the eye to the top of the body. Add a triangle beak with a line through the middle.

4. Draw two bird feet under the body.

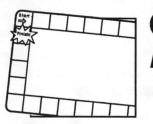

Qq
Phonics Connection

AT SCHOOL

Materials:
White construction paper, quilt block, crayons, oaktag, scissors, block-shaped beginning sound pictures cards

To make the quilts: Copy the quilt block onto white construction paper. Have the children color the squares different colors. Make two quilt blocks.

To make the quilt pieces: Make two copies of the quilt piece sound picture cards on oaktag for the children to color and cut out.

Show the children how to play the game. Include the "At Home" directions when the game goes home.

- -

AT HOME

Materials:
Two sets of the quilt piece beginning sound picture cards; a quilt game board for each player

Directions:
1. Shuffle the cards and put them in a pile face down between the players.
2. Take turns drawing cards. If a picture is drawn that begins with the sound of "q," put it on one of the quilt squares. If a picture begins with another letter sound, put it in a discard pile.
3. The winner is the player whose quilt block is filled in first.

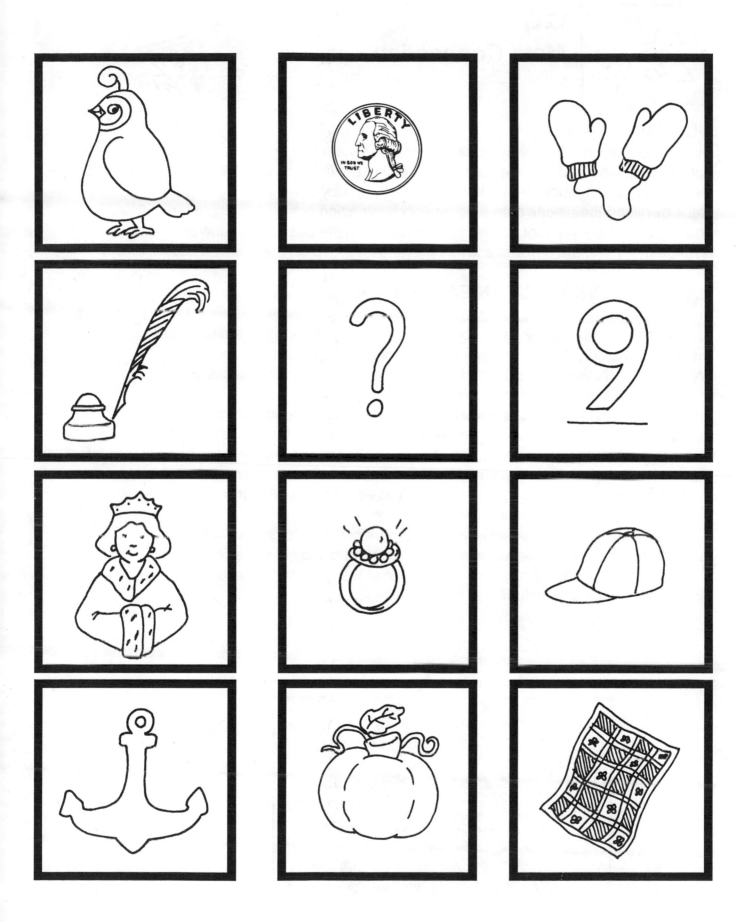

Qq
Math Connection

QUILT PATTERNS

Divide the class into four or five groups. Provide a variety of precut quilt pieces (fabric or wallpaper) and have each group design a quilt block with the pieces. Have one group member from each group make a copy of his or her group's block by gluing the pieces onto a square of construction paper. Assemble the finished blocks on the floor, taking suggestions from the class about how to arrange them. Pin the children's favorite arrangement up on the wall.

HAVE YOU EVER FELT AN EARTHQUAKE?

(a graphing activity)

Ask the children what they know about earthquakes. Encourage the discussion with questions like, "What happens in an earthquake?" "How does one feel?" "What do you think you should do if you feel one?" After a short discussion ask the children if any one of them has every felt an earthquake.

Make a living graph. Have the children who have felt an earthquake stand in one line, and the children who have not experienced one stand in another. Make the lines parallel to one another, and have each child in one line hold the hand of the child in the other line who is opposite him or her. Tell them to drop hands but not to move their feet. This makes the graph easier to "read." Ask the children to tell you everything they can about what they see.

After the graphing discussion, write an experience story together including as many of the children's observations as possible. Put a copy of the story into a book for the classroom library. Encourage one of the children to make a picture of the experience, and include it in the book.

Have You Ever Felt an Earthquake?

227

Qq
Science Connection

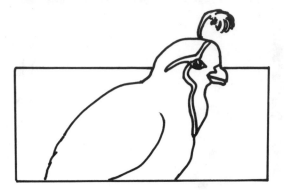

QUAILS
Class: Bird
Group: Covey (night) or bevy (day)
Habitat: Grassy areas, bushy fields
Food: Berries, grains, insects
Color: Brown, black, white, buff

A quail has very short wings so it can fly only short distances. But it can run quickly. Its coloring hides it from its enemies. Members of a covey (up to 100) arrange themselves in a closed circle at night with their heads turned outward. In this way they keep warm and can see danger approaching.

READ MORE ABOUT QUAILS
Bobwhite from Egg to Chick to Egg by E. and Charles Schwartz (Holiday, 1959).

DO AND DISCOVER
Quails remain motionless when they are in danger and don't want to be seen by their enemies. Let the children discover what it's like for quails to remain still. Play a version of Freeze Tag. "It" calls, "Move." The "quails" (players) may move around until "It" calls, "Freeze!" Then all the players must not move at all. "It" tags any "quail" that moves. After being tagged, that player becomes "It" and tags another player that moves after the call to freeze. The children will soon discover how hard it is to remain motionless for any length of time—something quails must often do for survival.

WRITE A BOOK ABOUT QUAILS
Brainstorm all the things the children remember about quails from their study. Make a list of the food quails eat. Talk about their habitat. Discuss all the interesting things the children learned about quails.

Put three pages together with a cover for a book for each child. Have the children draw a picture of a quail on the cover and write a title for the book. (See "Listen and Draw A Quail.") On the first page, have them draw the food that quails eat. On the second, let them draw the quail's habitat, and on the third draw something interesting they know about quails. Have the children write or copy a sentence about the picture on each page.

Qq
Science Connection

QUAKES

Ask the children if they know what a "crust" is. They will probably think of pie crust or bread crust, which are both good analogies to the earth's crust: they are both thin, somewhat hard layers that surround something softer. Tell the children that the earth's crust is divided into huge sections called plates. The plates slide very slowly over hot, soft rock under the earth's crust. Sometimes the plates bump into each other and cause the rocks of the plate to bend along the edges. There are also cracks in the crust called "faults." The rocks along the edges of the fault bend as well. When the rocks snap back, the earth shakes. This is called an earthquake.

Stretch a rubber band over a cardboard box. Pluck it and let the children feel the vibrations as the string settles back into place. Relate this action to the vibrations on the earth's surface as bent rock settles back into place.

QUEEN BEE

Ask the children to tell you all they know about queens. After the discussion, tell them that you know about a queen that is not human. Ask the children if they can guess what kind of a queen it might be. Then explain that honey bees have queens, called queen bees. Tell the children that a queen bee does not have a crown. She is not married to a king, nor does she do any of the things that human queens do.

Explain that every bee in a honey bee colony has a special job to do. The queen bee's job is to lay eggs. That is all that she does. Worker bees take care of the larva (baby bees), clean the hive, fan the hive with their wings to keep it cool, gather nectar and pollen, and take care of the queen. There is a special bee that guards the entrance of the colony, and special bees (drones) whose job is to mate with the queen.

There can be only one queen bee in the hive. Sometimes a hive has too many bees. Then the queen, some workers, and some drones fly away and form a new hive where a new queen is born. Demonstrate this to the children by standing in the middle of an area marked off with jump ropes. Choose children one at a time to join you. When the area is full, choose some of the children to follow you to a new designated area. Select one child as the new queen bee.

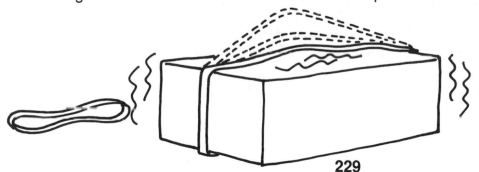

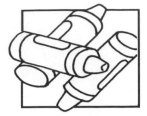

Qq
Arts and Crafts Connection

Q-TIP QUICKIES

Materials:
9" by 12" pieces of glossy freezer wrap or finger painting paper; red, yellow, and blue finger paints (see the recipes under the letter Ff); paint containers; damp sponges; Q-tip swabs

Procedure:
Tell the children that today they are going to learn a special art technique called pointillism. Tell them that a very famous artist named George Seurat invented it, and though he did not use Q-tips as they will, their paintings will be quite similar to his.

1. Fill each container with a different color paint.
2. Help the children wet their papers with a sponge.
3. Have the children think of a subject for their paintings, such as a flower, animal, house, boat, etc.
4. Dip a Q-tip in some paint and show the children how to press or dot it onto their paper without rubbing or stroking it as they would a brush.
5. Tell the children to create their entire paintings using only dots, just as George Seurat did. Show the children a print of one of Seurat's paintings, such as "La Grande Jatte."

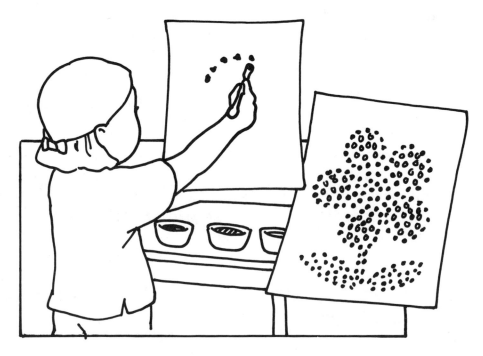

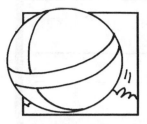

Qq
Movement Connection

QUICK AS A WINK

Have the children find partners, then scatter around the playground and stand back to back to wait for directions. Give the following touch commands one at a time, and tell the partners to respond as quickly as possible:

toes to toes	tummy to tummy	cheek to cheek
head to head	hand to hand	bottom to bottom
elbow to elbow	nose to nose	side to side
knee to knee	wrist to wrist	arm to arm
hip to hip	ankle to ankle	ear to ear

Occasionally call out, "Quick as a wink!" All the players must then change partners, stand back to back again, and get ready to continue as commanded.

QUESTIONS

Encourage the children to participate in movement activities by giving them plenty of opportunities to play without competing or conforming exactly to a set of rules. Here are some questions that children can make creative use of in movement activities that use balls, beanbags, jump ropes, walking boards, and just their own bodies:

Can you do. . .?
Can you think of another way to. . .?
What would happen if you added this?
Is there another way you can do it?
Can you do it with a friend?
Who can show me. . . ?
Let's see if you can. . . !
How high/low can you. . .?
How many times can you. . .?
How far can you make it go?
Who can make a. . .?
How do you think a_____looks when. . .?

Qq

HOMEWORK

Name _____

Date Due _____

Put a √ by the activity you have chosen to do.

☐ Draw a picture of a **q**ueen. Bring it to school and tell a story about your **q**ueen.

☐ Think up three **q**uestions to ask your school friends. Ask a grownup to write them down. Bring your **q**uestions to school to ask the class.

☐ Make crayon rubbings of **q**uarters. Bring your rubbings to school to share.

_____
Signature of grown up helper

QUINCY QUAIL'S QUILT BLOCK

Ingredients (serves 1)
  white bread slice (square)
  milk
  food coloring

1. Pour milk into 3 small cups.

2. Put 3 drops of food coloring into each.

3. Remove the crust from the bread.

4. Dip a Q-tip into the colored milk.

5. Draw a design on the bread. Color it in.

6. Toast.

RAP WITH RHINO RUTH

Sign Language **R**

R is for rhino, Rhino Ruth.
R /r/ /r/ /r/ /r/ /r/ /r/
Rattles, rocks, and radios.
R /r/ /r/ /r/ /r/ /r/ /r/
Running, races, rockets, roar.
R /r/ /r/ /r/ /r/ /r/ /r/
(Repeat the first two lines.)

Rhino Ruth

RINGS FROM RHINO RUTH

To introduce Rhino Ruth and her letter R, put an inexpensive ring (from a party supply store) at each child's place before school. Ask the class what alphabet animal friend they think might have brought them the rings.

A RHINO RUTH RUN

Plan "Rhino Ruth's Run" to celebrate the letter R. Start by designating a running course. Then make a runner's bib for each participant with two 8" by 11" pieces of paper glued or stapled together over the shoulders with narrow paper straps. Staple yarn ties to the bottoms of the papers. Have the children decorate their bibs with a picture of Rhino Ruth. Discuss the good health aspects of running and encourage the children to run for this reason, rather than simply to win. Award red ribbons to all runners.

RHINO RUTH'S Rr BOOK

Brainstorm with the class words that begin with the same sound as Rhino Ruth. Distribute paper and let the children each choose a word to illustrate. Have them copy the following sentence frame onto the page and write their word in the blank space. Put the pages together to make a class book.

Read, read, Rhino Ruth.

Read about _____.

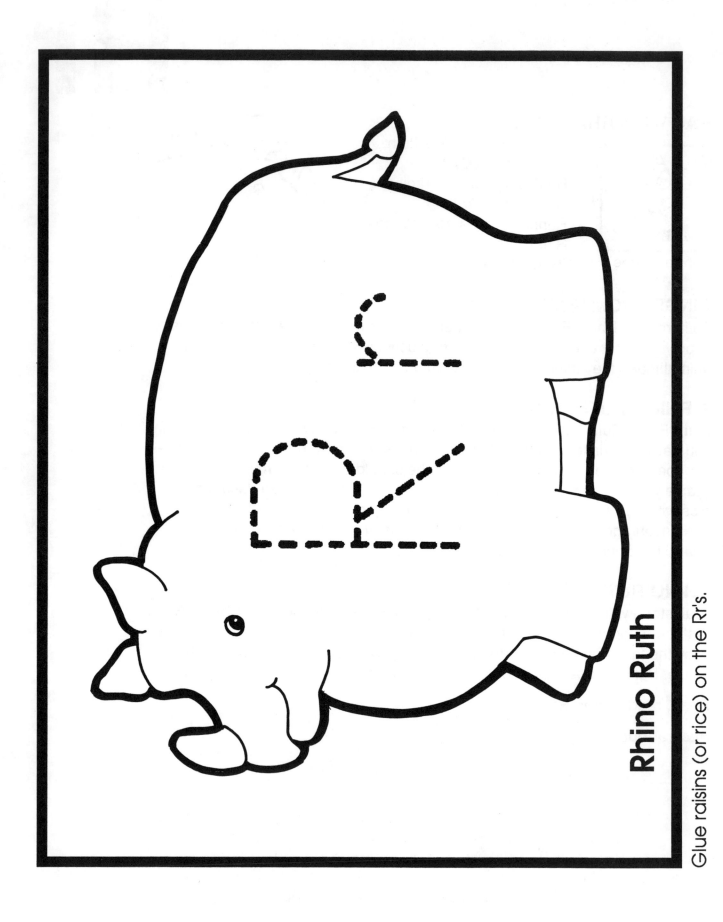

Rhino Ruth

Glue raisins (or rice) on the Rr's.

234

Rr
Literature Connection

READ A BOOK
Rosie's Walk by Pat Hutchins (Alladin, 1968). Rosie the hen goes for a walk around the barnyard. Over and over she escapes being captured by a fox that she doesn't realize is following her. The fox, however, does not have such good luck. The story humorously teaches positional concepts.

Presentation
Discuss farm animals with the children—the sounds they make and the way they walk. Ask some children to demonstrate how a chicken walks. Talk about the natural enemies of such farm animals as ducks, turkeys, and chickens. Tell the class that the story you are going to read, *Rosie's Walk*, is about a hen named Rosie who went for a walk around the barnyard.

Additional Books
Round Robin by Jack Kent (Prentice Hall, 1982); *Little Red Riding Hood,* retold by Mabel Watts (Golden, 1979); *Everybody Needs a Rock* by Byrd Baylor (Scribner's, 1974); *Rain* by Robert Kalan (Greenwillow, 1978).

RELATED ACTIVITIES

Dramatization
Have the children take turns pretending to be Rosie the hen. Give them directions to follow based upon the text, but adapted to your classroom or play yard. For example, "Rosie went *under* the table. She went *around* the desk."

Make a Book
Talk with the children about a farm; brainstorm all the things that they might see there. Discuss the places that Rosie went on her walk, and other places on the farm where she might have gone. Explain that the children are going to make their own books about Rosie, but in their books Rosie can go anywhere on the farm that they want her to go.

Make a blank book for each child. On the first page, have the children draw a farm scene and copy the sentence "Rosie the hen went for a walk." Give them construction paper scraps or a pattern from which to make a small cutout of a hen. Have them attach one end of a 12" length of yarn to their hen, and the other end of the yarn to the first page of their book.

On each of the following pages, have the children draw a place for Rosie to go on her walk. Then have them dictate a positional phrase sentence that matches each picture. For example, "Rosie climbed *over* the fence." When the books are complete, show the children how to move Rosie from page to page, putting her in the position indicated by the dictated sentence.

Listen and Draw a Rhino

Give the children oral directions as you draw each step with them.

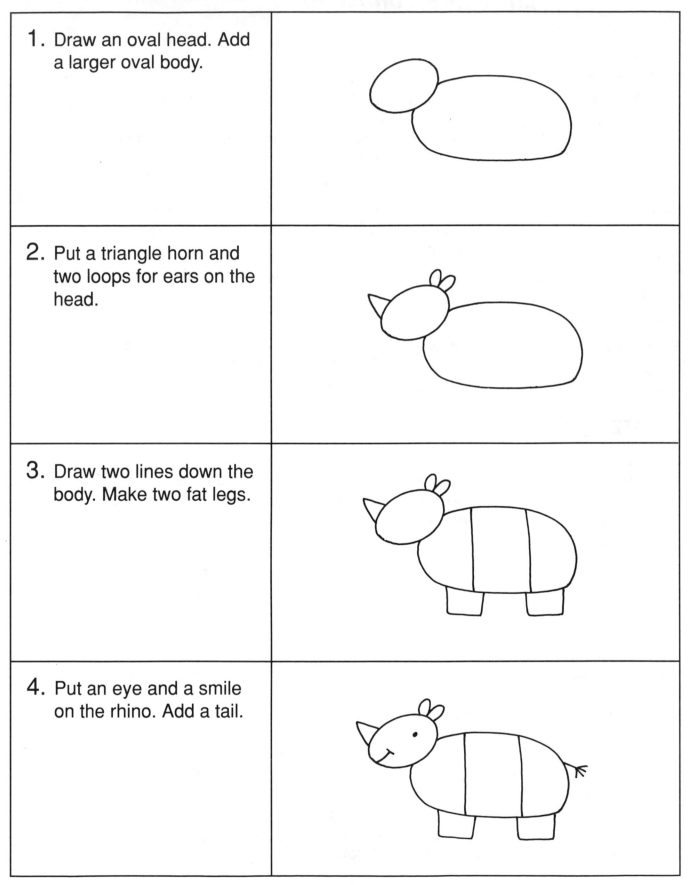

1. Draw an oval head. Add a larger oval body.

2. Put a triangle horn and two loops for ears on the head.

3. Draw two lines down the body. Make two fat legs.

4. Put an eye and a smile on the rhino. Add a tail.

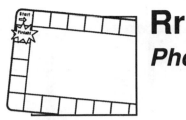

Rr
Phonics Connection

AT SCHOOL

Copy the game board and the set of sound picture cards for Rhino Ruth's "R" game onto oaktag for the children to color. Have them cut the cards out. Glue an envelope onto the back of the game board to store the cards and the directions for play.

Show the children how to play the game. Include the "At Home" directions when the game goes home.

AT HOME

Materials:
Rhino Ruth's game board and set of sound picture cards; a small marker for each player

Directions:
1. Place the cards face down in a pile between the players.
2. Take turns drawing from the pile. If the picture on the card begins with the sound of "r," move the marker forward one space. If the picture begins with another letter sound, no move is made. If a player is lucky enough to draw Rhino Ruth's card, move the marker forward two spaces.
3. Reshuffle the cards each time they have all been drawn, and continue playing until someone reaches the finish line. The player who finishes first is the winner.

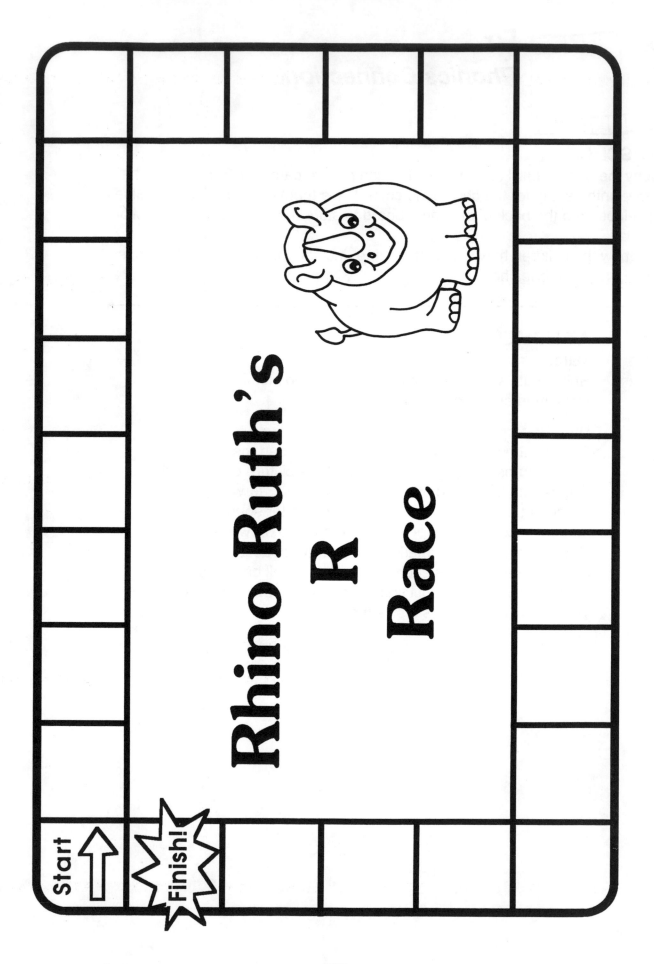

Rhino Ruth's R Race

Start

Finish!

238

Rr
Math Connection

RAMP ROLL

Let the children work in small groups or pairs to build ramps out of building blocks to use with small toy cars. Let a child from each group place a car at the top of the group's ramp and let it roll down until it comes to a natural stop. Show the children how to mark the stopping points with chalk or tape. Challenge the groups to rebuild their ramps to increase the distance their car will roll.

CAN YOU ROLLER SKATE?

(a graphing activity)

Talk about roller skating with the children. Ask if anyone in the class can roller skate. Then make a living graph. Have the children who can roller skate get into one line and those who cannot into another, parallel, line. Have the children in one line hold the hand of the child opposite them in the other line. Then tell them to drop hands but stand still. This makes the graph easier to "read." Explain that the two lines of children are like two columns of a graph. Ask the children to tell you everything they can about what they see.

Write an experience story together about the graph. Include as many of the children's observations as possible. Make a book of the class's graphing experience stories for the classroom library.

Can You Roller Skate?

Rr
Science Connection

RHINOCEROSES

Class: Mammal
Group: Crash or herd
Habitat: Grasslands, bushes, scrub
Food: Grass, leafy twigs, shrubs
Baby: Calf
Color: Black or gray

Rhinoceros means "nose horn." A rhino has either one or two horns. If the horn gets broken off, a new one will grow back quickly. Rhinos can't see very well, so they attack almost anything that moves. Little birds, called oxpeckers, follow rhinos around picking bugs off their backs.

READ MORE ABOUT RHINOCEROSES

Rhinoceros Mother by Toshi Yoshida (Philomel, 1991).

DO AND DISCOVER

Let the children discover why a rhinoceros might charge most anything that moves. Cover a child's eyes with a gauze cloth—one that allows a limited view. Hold up familiar objects and ask the child to identify them. Explain to the children that with limited vision it is often difficult to see what an object is. Since rhinos' sight is very limited, they are often unable to tell exactly what is moving, and think that it might be an enemy. They charge to protect themselves.

WRITE A BOOK ABOUT RHINOCEROSES

Brainstorm all the things the children remember about rhinos from their study. Make a list of the food rhinos eat. Talk about their habitat. Discuss all the interesting things the children learned about rhinos.

Put three pages together with a cover for a book for each child. Have the children draw a picture of a rhinoceros on the cover and write a title for the book. (See "Listen and Draw A Rhinoceros.") On the first page, have them draw the food that rhinos eat. On the second, let them draw the rhino's habitat, and on the third draw something interesting they know about rhinos. Have the children write or copy a sentence about the picture on each page.

Rr
Science Connection

ROCKS

Take the children on a rock hunt to see how many different kinds of rocks can be found around the school. (In some locations you may need to get a variety of rocks from a stream bed or park to secretly "seed" the school area before the children begin their hunt.) Tell the children that people who like to collect interesting rocks are called "rock hounds," and on this field trip that is what they are. Explain that "rock hounds" explore very carefully, and choose only the most interesting rocks they see. Give the children bags or empty egg cartons to hold the special rocks they choose.

When the rock hunt is finished, have the children bring their collections back to the classroom. Give each a small bowl of water and some toweling to wash and dry their rocks. As the children work with their rocks, ask them questions about what they observe: "Do your rocks change color when they're wet?" "Which rock is your favorite?" "What color is your favorite rock?" "Is your favorite rock rough or smooth? Hard or soft?" "What shape is your favorite rock most like—a circle, oval, square, rectangle, or triangle?" After they have observed their rocks, have the children sort them by size, shape, color, and texture.

If you have access to interesting rocks such as pumice (which floats), obsidian (volcanic glass), crystals, or petrified wood, bring them in. The children will be fascinated by them.

RAINBOWS

Children love rainbows. Even though it may not be raining, tell them that you are going to show them how to make rainbows. Explain that they must first learn to bend light, because that is where rainbows hide. Discuss the color of light. Say that though it seems to be white it really is a mixture of colors, and that the only way we can see these colors is to make the light bend. That is what raindrops do as sunlight shines through them. And that is why we often see a rainbow when there are rain showers and sunshine at the same time.

Give each small group of children a glass of water and a small mirror. Have them take turns putting the mirror into the water and turning it so that direct sunlight hits the mirror and reflects onto the ceiling or wall. Tell them that the mirror is bending the sunlight and making a rainbow on the wall. Ask them what colors they see.

Tell the children that in the sky a rainbow looks like an arch, but it is really a complete circle. If they were up in an airplane looking at a rainbow they would see this circle of colors.

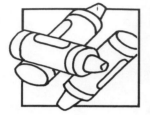

Rr
Arts and Crafts Connection

ROCK SCULPTURES

Materials:
Assortment of river rocks (have the children bring in their own, or purchase a bagful from a local rockery), 3" by 5" cardboard rectangles, squeeze bottles of glue, fine-tipped felt pens (in a variety of colors)

Procedure:
1. Let the children choose the rocks they want to use.
2. Tell them to decide where they would like to place their rocks on the cardboard to create a picture ("rock people" would be fun). Have them squeeze puddles of glue onto those spots.
3. Show the children how to put the rocks into the puddles.
4. When the rocks are secure, let the children add details such as eyes, nose, mouth, hair, and clothing with fine-tipped felt pens.
5. Free-form "sculptures," in which rocks are stacked, are also fun to make and can go three-dimensional if you add wheat paste to the glue till it's the consistency of oatmeal. Free-form sculptures take a bit more patience on the children's part, since they must hold each rock after applying glue to give the glue time to set.

RUBBINGS

Materials:
Newsprint or white tissue paper, peeled crayons
(fat ones are best)

Procedure:
1. Give each child a sheet of paper.
2. Provide lots of peeled crayons.
3. Show the children the technique of rubbing with the side of the crayon.
4. Take the children outside and let them explore the yard to find various textures with which to make rubbings. Tree bark, leaves, pine needles, stucco walls, and wire fencing all make wonderful rubbing surfaces.
5. Have the children place their chosen materials under the paper and rub gently to transfer the shapes to the paper.

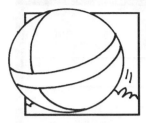

Rr
Movement Connection

RELAY RACES

Divide the children into two teams. Go to a grassy area and mark a start and finish line, and have half of the children on each team line up behind the start line and the other half directly opposite it, behind the finish line. Then choose one of the following activities to play as a relay game.

Sack Relay—Provide an old pillowcase for each team. On your signal, the first player on each team climbs into the pillowcase, jumps to the finish line, climbs out of the pillowcase, and gives it to the first person on his or her team. That child climbs into it and jumps back to the starting line, where the next player on the team repeats the process. Play continues until everyone has had a turn. The team whose players all have a turn first wins.

Spoon Relay—Provide a large spoon and a tennis ball or Ping-Pong ball for each group. Have the children take turns walking quickly from one line to the opposite line balancing the ball on the spoon. If the ball drops, the child must put it back on the spoon and resume walking. The team whose players have all had a turn first wins.

Back to Back Relay —The children run in pairs between the goals, back to back with their arms linked at the elbows. Each child carries a ball or beanbag to the receiving pair on the opposite line. The winning team is the one whose players all have a turn before the other team's players.

ROW, ROW, ROW YOUR BOAT

Take the children to a grassy or carpeted area. Establish a start line and a finish line about 15 feet apart. Have the children pair up. Have one partner (A) sit on the starting line with knees together and legs straight out. Have Partner B sit facing with the soles of his or her shoes pressed against the soles of Partner A's shoes. When the signal is given to begin "rowing," Partner B pulls Partner A into a bent-knee position. Partner B then pushes back to straighten his or her legs. Partner A then straightens his or her legs and pushes Partner B's legs into a bent position. This pushing and pulling motion resembles the movements of someone rowing a boat, and moves the players along. If the activity is done indoors, the children could sing "Row, Row, Row Your Boat."

Rr

HOMEWORK

Name _____

Date Due _____

Put a √ by the activity you have chosen to do.

☐ Make a picture or word list of all the things in your bedroom that have a **r**ectangular shape. Bring the list to school.

☐ **R**ead a book about something that begins with **R** (for example, Little **R**ed **R**iding Hood, **R**umplestiltskin, The Little **R**ed Hen, **R**osie's Walk). Tell about it at school.

☐ Have a **r**ace with a friend. Give the winner a **r**ed **r**ibbon. Tell about the **r**ace at school.

_____
Signature of grown up helper

RHINO RUTH'S RAISINS ON A RAFT

Ingredients (serves 1)
crackers
  (round and rectangular)
peanut butter
raisins

1. Sort some round and rectangular crackers.

2. Choose one to be your "raft."

3. Spread it with peanut butter.

4. Count out 10 raisins.

5. Put raisins on the raft.

RAP WITH SUZY SEAL

Sign Language **S**

S is for seal, Suzy Seal.
S /s/ /s/ /s/ /s/ /s/ /s/
Scissors, seesaw, sandwiches.
S /s/ /s/ /s/ /s/ /s/ /s/
Silly, soup, and Saturday.
S /s/ /s/ /s/ /s/ /s/ /s/
(Repeat the first two lines.)

Suzy Seal

SUPER SUITCASE

Introduce Suzy Seal and her letter S with a small suitcase filled with objects that begin with /s/. Choose some children to take things out of the suitcase one at a time and name them. Let everyone guess what alphabet animal friend brought the suitcase full of things that start with /s/.

SILLY SANDWICH SOCIAL

Hold a "Silly Sandwich Social" in honor of the letter S. Have the children bring sandwich fixings to share with everyone. Let each child make his or her own silly sandwich to eat. Then graph the children's answers to the question "What is your favorite sandwich?"

Read *The Giant Jam Sandwich* by John Vernon Lord.

SUZY SEAL'S Ss BOOK

Brainstorm with the class words that begin with the same sound as Suzy Seal. Distribute paper and let the children each choose a word to illustrate. Have them copy the following sentence frame onto the page and write their word in the blank space. Put the pages together to make a class book.

Suzy Seal saw _____ in her suitcase.

Suzy Seal

Glue sunflower seeds on the Ss's.

Ss
Literature Connection

READ A BOOK
Swimmy by Leo Lionni (Dragonfly, 1963). This beautifully illustrated book tells the story of an ingenious little fish who saves all his friends from being eaten by a bigger fish. It also teaches a valuable lesson about working together.

Presentation
Ask the children if any of them has ever been to an aquarium. Discuss what was seen there. Talk about the many different creatures that live under the sea. Tell the children that the book called *Swimmy* is about the beautiful undersea world.

Additional Books
The Snowy Day by Ezra Jack Keats (Puffin, 1962); *The Very Busy Spider* by Eric Carle (Philomel, 1984); *The Tiny Seed* by Eric Carle (Picture Book, 1987);*The Snowman* by Raymond Briggs (Random House, 1978); *Stone Soup* by Ann McGovern (Scholastic, 1968); *The Giant Jam Sandwich* by John Vernon Lord (Houghton, 1972).

RELATED ACTIVITIES

Underwater Pictures
Show the children the book's illustrations. Tell them that the artist used many different colors of paint called "watercolor" for the backgrounds. He also seems to have stamped different-shaped objects onto the background to create his under-water scenes.

Show the children how to make paintings like Leo Lionni did for this book. Apply a thin layer of water to white drawing paper with a sponge. Demonstrate how to paint watercolors on the wet paper to create an undersea look. Use blue, purple, and green.

When the paper has dried completely, cut flat household sponges into fish shapes and collect different-colored stamp pads. Then stamp swimming fish onto the watercolor sea. After watching the demonstration, let the children create undersea watercolors of their own.

Swimming Book
Discuss with the children what can swim and what cannot. Distribute four-page books with the following sentence frames to complete and illustrate:
(Page 1) _____ **can swim.**
(Page 2) _____ **can swim.**
(Page 3) _____ **can swim.**
(Page 4) **But a** _____ **cannot.**

249

Listen and Draw a Seal

Give the children oral directions as you draw each step with them.

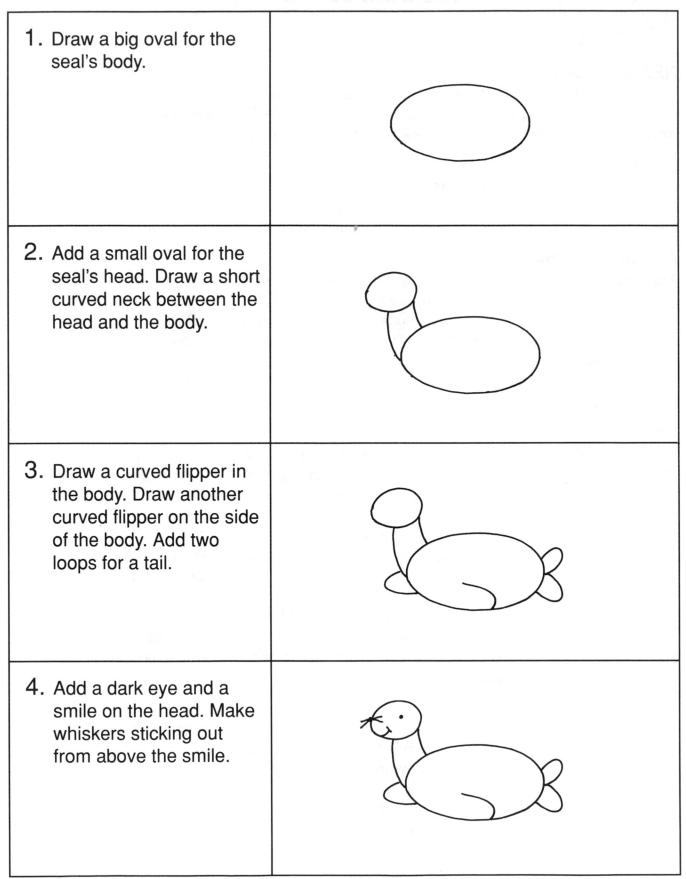

1. Draw a big oval for the seal's body.

2. Add a small oval for the seal's head. Draw a short curved neck between the head and the body.

3. Draw a curved flipper in the body. Draw another curved flipper on the side of the body. Add two loops for a tail.

4. Add a dark eye and a smile on the head. Make whiskers sticking out from above the smile.

Ss
Phonics Connection

AT SCHOOL
Materials:
4" by 7" envelopes, pieces of brown construction paper, scissors, glue, oaktag, crayons, sock-shaped beginning sound picture cards

To make the suitcases: Have the children cut off and discard the flap from an envelope. Give the children each a piece of 8" by 7" brown construction paper and show them how to fold it in half the short way. Have the children glue the paper around the envelope so that the top will still open. Then have them cut a 3" by 1" block shape from brown construction paper. Have them glue this handle to the back edge of the envelope's top opening. Let the children add Suzy Seal's initials to their suitcases.

To make the socks: Copy the sock-shaped beginning sound cards onto oaktag for the children to color and cut out.

Show the children how to play the game. Include the "At Home" directions when the game goes home.

- -

AT HOME
Materials:
A set of sock-shaped beginning sound picture cards; one envelope suitcase for each player

Directions:
1. Shuffle the cards and put them in a pile face down between the players.
2. Take turns drawing cards. If a picture is drawn that begins with the sound of "s," put it in the suitcase. If the picture begins with another letter sound, put it in a discard pile.
3. The winner is the person whose suitcase contains the most socks after all the cards have been played.

Ss
Math Connection

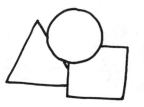

SORTING SHAPES

Seat the children on the floor in a large circle and place several classroom objects of the same shape in the center of the circle. (Some examples might be an eraser, a book, and a sheet of paper.) Ask the children how all of the objects are alike. When the shape attribute has been identified, challenge the children to find another object in the room to add to the sorting pile. Repeat the activity using objects of a different shape.

WHAT IS YOUR FAVORITE SANDWICH?

(a graphing activity)

Brainstorm with the children all the different kinds of sandwiches they can think of. Make a list on the chalkboard or a chart. Make a four-column graph according to the directions in the Introduction, and label three of the columns according to the three most popular kinds of sandwiches (perhaps "Tuna," "Egg Salad," and "Peanut Butter and Jelly"). Label the last column "Others," and explain that this is the place to put sandwich choices that are not named in the first three columns.

Have each child draw a picture of his or her favorite sandwich on a 3" by 3" paper and tape it onto the appropriate column on the graph. When everyone has recorded a choice, ask the children to tell you everything that they can about what they see. Record their observations on big paper "bubbles" (like dialogue bubbles in a comic strip). Post the bubbles around the graph for an informative bulletin board display.

253

Ss
Science Connection

SEALS

Class: Mammal
Group: Herd or pod
Habitat: Ocean
Food: Fish, squid, seabirds, krill
Baby: Pup
Color: Gray, white, brown

Most seals live in cold water, and their bodies are built to deal with the problems this creates. Their fur is coarse and waterproof, and they are fat, which keeps them warm. Their large eyes help them see well under water. Seals are born knowing how to do most everything they need to do, because their mothers don't stay with them very long. They don't make friends with each other either.

READ MORE ABOUT SEALS

The Seals by Iona Serbert Hiser (Steck-Vaughn, 1975).

DO AND DISCOVER

Let the children discover how difficult it is for seals to move on land. Using a short rope or piece of rug yarn, tie a child's feet together at the ankles. Also tie the child's elbows to his or her sides or have the child hold them in so that they touch his or her body. Then have the child try to crawl from one point to another.

WRITE A BOOK ABOUT SEALS

Brainstorm all the things the children remember about seals from their study. Make a list of the food seals eat. Talk about their habitat. Discuss all the interesting things the children learned about seals.

Put three pages together with a cover for a book for each child. Have the children draw a picture of a seal on the cover and write a title for the book. (See "Listen and Draw A Seal.") On the first page, have them draw the food that seals eat. On the second, let them draw the seal's habitat, and on the third draw something interesting that they know about seals. Have the children write or copy a sentence about the picture on each page.

Ss
Science Connection

SUN AND SOLAR ENERGY

Take the children outside on a warm sunny day. Stand in the sun and have them feel its heat. Stand in the shade and talk about the difference. Use the term "solar energy" in the discussion.

Bring a piece of black or dark blue construction paper out and place it where the sun will hit it for a while. Keep another piece indoors to compare results after several hours. Also give the children small squares of dark colored construction paper and have them place interesting shapes on them, such as leaves, flat flowers, and keys. Lay the papers out in the sun. After several hours, remove the objects from the papers and encourage the children to observe what happened.

SPIDERS

Children are intrigued by spiders, but are often fearful of them. Begin the study of spiders by acknowledging the fear. Make a graph of who is afraid of spiders and who is not. Inform the children about any spiders in your area that are dangerous. Make them aware that some precautions are needed when observing spiders, but that most spiders are not poisonous and all spiders are helpful to us.

Take the children on a spider web walk. Tell them that they will only be observing webs, not touching them, because spider webs can be easily destroyed. Take a spray bottle of water on the walk. When a web is located, spray it with a fine mist. The web will glisten as if covered with morning dew, and the children will be able to see its delicate beauty and design.

Try catching a spider to watch for a short time in the classroom. Put it in a commercial "bug box" or a jar with air holes poked in the lid. Leave out magnifying glasses for the children to make closer observations.

255

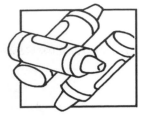

Ss
Arts and Crafts Connection

SANDPAPER PRINTS

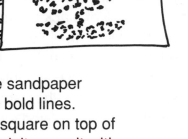

Materials:
Sandpaper squares (fine grained), crayons, white drawing paper squares (same size as sandpaper), electric iron

Procedure:
1. Have the children draw bright crayon pictures directly onto the sandpaper squares. Encourage them to use a variety of colors and to make bold lines.
2. When the drawing is completed, place a white drawing paper square on top of each sandpaper picture (crayoned side up) and you or another adult press it with an electric iron set on medium heat. The crayon will show through the back of the paper when the print is ready. Due to the roughness of the sandpaper, the picture on the white drawing paper will resemble the work of the famous painter George Seurat, who created his masterpieces by painting them all in dots.

STRING PAINTING

Materials:
2' lengths of thin string, liquid tempera paint (mixed thin), paint containers, construction paper, heavy books

Procedure:
1. Show the children how to dip a piece of string into one color of tempera paint, pull it between their first finger and thumb to squeeze out excess paint, and lay it on a piece of paper in a wavy pattern or some other interesting way. Have them leave a "tail" of string hanging over the edge of the paper.
2. Encourage the children to add additional strings dipped into a variety of colors, making sure that the end of each one is left hanging over the side of the paper.
3. Have them cover their string creations with another piece of construction paper and lay a heavy book on top of it.
4. Show them how to carefully pull each string out from under the book. Hold the book for them so it will not move as they remove the strings.
5. When all the strings have been pulled out, remove the book, lift off the top paper, and enjoy the sensational string designs that have been created.

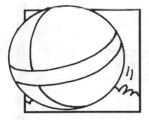

Ss
Movement Connection

SIMON SAYS

Have the children spread out over the play area so that they can swing both arms without bumping another child. Make sure that they can see and hear you or whoever is the leader.

Start giving commands, some of which you preface with the words "Simon says" and some of which you do not. The players must do everything that is preceded by "Simon says" but they must not obey commands that do not start that way. If a child makes a mistake, everyone simply enjoys a good laugh together and proceeds with the game.

Some suggested commands:
Flap your arms in the air.
Clap your hands behind you.
Pat your tummy.
Wobble your knees.
Shrug your shoulders.
Stamp your feet.

STICKS

Rhythm sticks can give children good manipulative and sensory experiences; they're also fun to use. Make a pair of sticks with ¾" doweling cut to 12" lengths, or use the brightly colored commercial variety.

To use the sticks, have the children scatter around the area, finding places where they will not bump into anyone or anything but where they can see and hear you. Give each child one stick to begin with, then have them go to two.

One-stick activities: Ask—
How many ways can you balance your stick?
Can you balance your stick between your knees?
Can you repeat my pattern? (Tap out a simple pattern.)
Can you hold your stick up high in front of you, then drop it and catch it with your other hand?
Can you balance your stick on one hand in front of you, and gradually raise it above your head without dropping it? Can you start it out up high and lower it?

Two-stick activities (the children should be seated on the floor for these): Ask—
Can you close your eyes and bring the ends of the sticks together in front of you?
Can you hammer one stick with the other stick?
Can you tap your sticks together up high? Down low?
Can you tap your sticks together behind your back?

When the children have had practice, add music and marching, and put on a "Sensational Stick Show!"

Ss

HOMEWORK

Name _____

Date Due _____

Put a √ by the activity you have chosen to do.

☐ Tell how to make your favorite **s**andwich. Ask someone to write down your directions. Make a picture of your **s**andwich. Bring the picture and the directions to school to tell about.

☐ Count your **s**ocks. Think of many ways to **s**ort them. At **s**chool, tell how you **s**orted them.

☐ Think of things with **s**eeds inside. Bring a picture or word list to **s**chool.

_____

Signature of grown up helper

SUZY SEAL'S SILLY SANDWICH

Ingredients (serves 1)
bread
fillings:

		spreads:
cheese slice	peanut butter	mayonnaise
bologna	sprouts	mustard
jam or jelly	banana slices	catsup
sliced pickles	raisins	butter

1. Cut a slice of bread in half.

2. Choose a spread to put on your bread.

3. Choose fillings for your sandwich.

4. Put the sandwich halves together.

5. Enjoy!

RAP WITH TIGER TIM

Sign Language **T**

T is for tiger, Tiger Tim.
T /t/ /t/ /t/ /t/ /t/ /t/
Tummies, toys, and tambourines.
T /t/ /t/ /t/ /t/ /t/ /t/
Talking, tables, tattletales.
T /t/ /t/ /t/ /t/ /t/ /t/
(Repeat the first two lines.)

Tiger Tim

TOY TRUCKLOAD

Introduce Tiger Tim and his letter T with a toy truckload of things that begin with /t/ (for example, a tea bag, a top, tissue, tape, a golf tee, a triangle, and a tack). Choose children to take the objects out of the truck one at a time and name them. Ask everyone to guess what alphabet animal friend's name begins the same way as all the things in the truck.

TALENT-SHOW TIME

Put on a "Talent Show" in the classroom to celebrate the letter T. Plan ahead, asking parents to help their child learn a dance, song, magic trick, or poem to present to the class on that special day. Invite the parents to come and watch.

TIGER TIM'S Tt BOOK

Brainstorm with the class words that begin with the same sound as Tiger Tim. Distribute paper and let the children each choose a word to illustrate. Have them copy the following sentence frame onto the page and write their word in the blank space. Put the pages together to make a class book.

Tiger Tim talks about _____.

Tiger Tim

Glue toothpicks on the Tt's.

Tt
Literature Connection

READ A BOOK

Tikki Tikki Tembo by Arlene Mosel (Holt, 1968). This Chinese folk tale is about a little boy with a very long name. The story goes that because of his name the boy very nearly loses his life, and from that day to this, the Chinese have always thought it wise to give their children short names.

Presentation

Before reading this story, talk about China and point it out on the globe. Explain that it is a very old country. Be sure the children understand what a well is before reading the story.

Additional Books

A Tree is Nice by Janice M. Udry (Harper, 1956); *Teeny Tiny* by Jill Bennett (Putnam, 1986); *The Enormous Turnip* by Leo Tolstoy (Heinemann, 1978); *The Train* by David McPhail (Atlantic, 1977); *Trains* by Gail Gibbons (Scholastic, 1987).

RELATED ACTIVITY

Book of Names

Tikki Tikki Tembo had a very long name. Write his whole name on a sentence strip so that the children have a picture of how long it was. Count the number of words in his name, then the number of letters. Give each child a sentence strip with his or her whole name on it. Have the children count the number of words and the number of letters in their names. Record the information, and find out who has the longest and who has the shortest name in the class. Bind the sentence strips together into a book of names for the classroom library.

Listen and Draw a Tiger

Give the children oral directions as you draw each step with them.

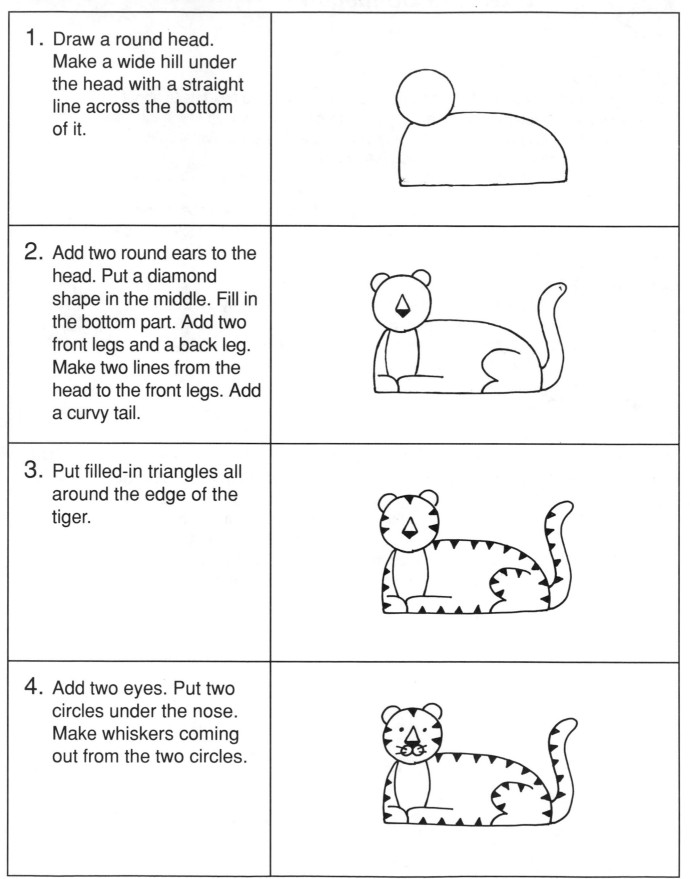

1. Draw a round head. Make a wide hill under the head with a straight line across the bottom of it.

2. Add two round ears to the head. Put a diamond shape in the middle. Fill in the bottom part. Add two front legs and a back leg. Make two lines from the head to the front legs. Add a curvy tail.

3. Put filled-in triangles all around the edge of the tiger.

4. Add two eyes. Put two circles under the nose. Make whiskers coming out from the two circles.

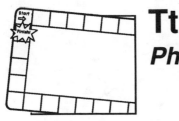

Tt
Phonics Connection

AT SCHOOL

Copy the game board and the set of sound picture cards for Tiger Tim's "T" Game onto oaktag for the children to color. Have them cut the cards out. Glue an envelope onto the back of the game board to store the cards and the directions for play.

Show the children how to play the game. Include the "At Home" directions when the game goes home.

- -

AT HOME
Materials:
Tiger Tim's game board and set of sound picture cards; a small marker for each player

Directions:
1. Place the cards face down in a pile between the players.
2. Take turns drawing from the pile. If the picture on the card begins with the sound of "t," move the marker forward one space. If the picture begins with another letter sound, no move is made. If a player is lucky enough to draw Tiger Tim's card, the marker is moved forward two spaces.
3. Reshuffle the cards each time they have all been drawn, and continue playing until someone reaches the finish line. The player who finishes first is the winner.

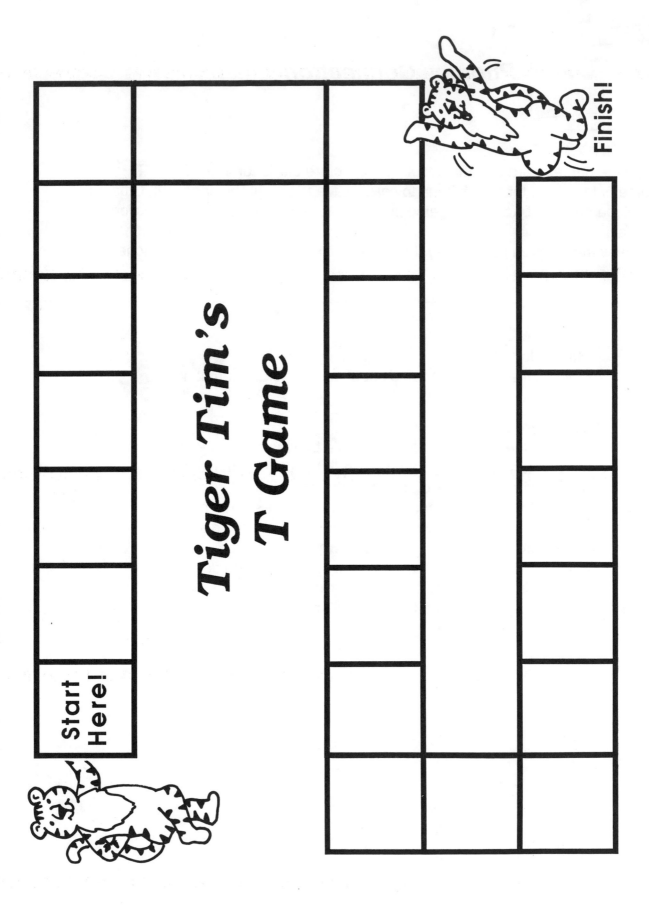

Tiger Tim's
T Game

Start Here!

Finish!

Tt
Math Connection

TOOTHPICK NUMBER DESIGNS

Have the class choose a "Number of the Day." Give each child some toothpicks and several four-inch squares of construction paper, and have them make designs using just that special number of toothpicks for each. Each toothpick in each design must also touch at least one other toothpick. When the children have decided on a design, show them how to hold a toothpick in the center and dip the ends one at a time into a puddle of glue to press into position on the paper square. When the designs have dried, display all the variations of the "Number of the Day."

WHAT KIND OF TOOTHPASTE DOES YOUR FAMILY USE?

(a graphing activity)

Discuss dental health with the children, emphasizing the need to take good care of their teeth. Tell them that one of the most important ways to take care of their teeth is to brush them often.

Bring in three of the more popular brands of toothpaste for the children to see, and ask them if their families use one of them. Make a four-column graphing grid according to the directions in the Introduction. Label three of the columns with the actual toothpaste boxes, and one with the word "Others." Then ask the graphing question: "What kind of toothpaste does your family use?"

Reproduce the toothpaste tube graphing symbols on the following page, one for each child. Have the children draw the logo of their family's toothpaste choice on their toothpaste tube, and tape it onto the appropriate column on the graph. When everyone has recorded a choice, ask the children to tell you everything that they can about what they see.

After discussing the graph, write an experience story together, including as many of the children's observations as possible. Put a copy of the story into an experience story book and place it in the classroom library.

What Kind of Toothpaste Does Your Family Use?

Tt
Science Connection

TIGERS

Class: Mammal
Group: Solitary
Habitat: Rain forests, swamps, mountains
Food: Fish, turtles, crocodiles, deer, monkeys, antelopes
Baby: Cub
Color: Orange, red, or yellowish with black stripes

Water is very important to tigers. They often take "dips" to cool off on hot days. They also drink large amounts of water when they eat. Tiger mothers teach their cubs what they will need to live on their own. The white tufts of fur on their ears let them signal to their cubs to follow them.

READ MORE ABOUT TIGERS

Tiger by Jill Bailey (Gallery, 1990).

DO AND DISCOVER

Let the children discover how tigers are able to see well at night. Have a child shine a flashlight on a wall or into a large box. Then show the child how to remove the silver reflector behind the flashlight bulb, and shine the light again. The change in light will be dramatic. Explain that tigers, as well as all other cats, have a special layer behind their eyes that reflects light much the same way as the silver part does for the flashlight. This layer helps them make good use of light, so they can see even when it's dim.

WRITE A BOOK ABOUT TIGERS

Brainstorm all the things the children remember about tigers from their study. Make a list of the food tigers eat. Talk about their habitat. Discuss all the interesting things the children learned about tigers.

Put three pages together with a cover for a book for each child. Have the children draw a picture of a tiger on the cover and write a title for the book. (See "Listen and Draw A Tiger.") On the first page, have them draw the food that tigers eat. On the second, let them draw the tiger's habitat, and on the third draw something interesting that they know about tigers. Have the children write or copy a sentence about the picture on each page.

Tt
Science Connection

TREES

Give the children paper and crayons and ask them to draw trees. When they have finished their pictures, talk about the different parts of the trees, helping them to identify those on their own pictures. Use the terms trunk, branches, and leaves. Explain that there is a very important part of the tree that we don't usually see—the roots. These are mostly underground, holding the tree in place and helping it get water from the soil. Give one of the children a glass of water and a straw to demonstrate how we sip liquids through straws into our mouths. Relate the straw to roots bringing water up to the other parts of a tree.

Go for a science walk with the children to observe trees. Take along some paper and crayons to do bark rubbings of various trees. (Hold a piece of paper against the trunk of a tree and rub it with the side of a peeled crayon.) Explain to the children how bark protects the tree's soft inner parts, much like our skin protects us. Take bags along on the walk for the children to collect interesting leaves, seed pods, and cones.

TEETH

Give each of the children a mirror and tell each to look at his or her own teeth. Ask, "Are all your teeth alike?" "Are all teeth the same size, or are some bigger than others?" "Are all of your teeth the same shape, or are some pointed, some flat, and some bumpy?" "Why do you think that your teeth are different shapes?"

Then ask the children what they think their teeth are for. They'll probably answer that they help them eat their food. Explain that each of the different-shaped teeth is needed for eating, and that each has a different job to do. The front teeth (incisors) are straight across. They help us cut into food and take bites. Behind these teeth are the sharp, pointed teeth (cuspids) that we use for ripping food. At the back are the bumpy, big, flat teeth (molars) that we use for grinding food into tiny pieces that can be swallowed.

Let the children discover how their teeth do different jobs. Give them each an apple slice to eat. Ask them what they did first to eat the apple. (They took a bite by cutting into the apple with their front teeth, or incisors.) Next give them a piece of fruit leather to eat. Ask them what they had to do first to get some of the fruit leather in their mouths. (They tore it using their pointed teeth, or cuspids.) Finally, give them some raisins to eat and have them describe how they ate them. (They used the big, bumpy teeth in the back of their mouths—molars—to grind the raisins.)

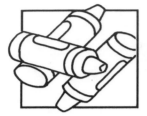

Tt
Arts and Crafts Connection

TOOTHPICK TOWERS

Materials:
Cardboard squares, toothpicks, plasticine clay

Procedure:
1. Show the children how to take a small pinch of clay and roll it into a ball.
Tell them to make a big pile of clay balls before they begin their towers.
2. Give each of the children a cardboard base and show them how to press some clay balls onto it to begin their towers.
3. Show them how they can build tall, tall towers by connecting toothpicks and clay balls "Tinker Toy" style.

TWIST AND TURN PAINTING

Materials:
Squeeze bottles (plastic ketchup and mustard bottles) filled with liquid tempera paint, freezer wrap or finger painting paper, table top

Procedure:
1. For each painting, let the children squeeze three or four dots of paint fairly close together, though not touching, directly onto a table top. Encourage them to use more than one color.
2. Have the children place a 6" or 7" piece of paper on top of the paint dots, press their hand on the paper, and give it a half turn.
3. When they lift the paper they will see a terrific twist and turn design.

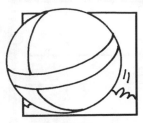

Tt
Movement Connection

TORNADO TWISTERS

Take the class outside to an open grassy field and set up a start and finish line about 20 feet apart. Have the children line up at the starting line, leaving plenty of room between themselves. For children who may not have heard of tornadoes, explain that they are storms that are sometimes called "twisters," because the wind twists around and around as it blows. Use a tambourine to signal the start of the game, and have the children spin around and around like tornadoes as they move from the start to the finish line.

TIPTOE TAG

Have the children sit in a circle. Choose one child to be "It." Blindfold the child and have him or her sit on a chair in the center of the circle. Place a small toy under "It's" chair. Point to someone seated in the circle. That player tiptoes quietly toward the chair and attempts to grab the toy and take it back to his or her place in the circle. "It," in the meantime, listens for sounds of footsteps and, without moving off the chair, tries to tag the "Tiptoer." If the tag is successful, the "Tiptoer" becomes the new "It." If not, the old "It" remains in the chair and the successful "Tiptoer" points to someone else in the circle to try to take the toy.

Tt

HOMEWORK

Name _____

Date Due _____

Put a √ by the activity you have chosen to do.

☐ Glue **t**oothpicks onto some cardboard in **t**errific **t**riangle designs. Add color and bring the designs to school.

☐ Play **T**ic-**T**ac-**T**oe **t**en **t**imes with someone in your family. Bring the game papers to school to share.

☐ Learn your **t**elephone number. **T**ell it to your **t**eacher.

_____
Signature of grown up helper

TIGER TIM'S TASTY TORTILLA

Ingredients (serves 1)
masa flour
water
cooking spray
butter (optional)

1. Put 3 T. flour into a bowl.

2. Add 1 T. water.

3. Stir.

4. Pat it flat.

5. Spray the skillet with cooking spray. Heat the tortilla in the skillet. (You need a helping hand.)

6. Eat it plain or with butter.

RAP WITH UMBRELLA BIRD

Sign Language **U**

U is for Umbrella Bird, Umbrella Bird.
U /u/ /u/ /u/ /u/ /u/ /u/
Upset, uncles, underwear.
U /u/ /u/ /u/ /u/ /u/ /u/
Up and under, ugliness.
U /u/ /u/ /u/ /u/ /u/ /u/
(Repeat the first two lines.)

Umbrella Bird

UPSIDE-DOWN DAY

Before class, turn some things in the room (chairs, name tags, toys) upside down. Put other things under the tables or desks. When the children come in, discuss what has happened. Use the terms "upside down" and "under" frequently in the discussion. Ask the children to listen to the beginning sound of the terms. Then ask if they can think of other words that begin with that sound. Tell them that sometimes we say /u/ when we read the letter u. Introduce the Umbrella Bird. Them tell the children that sometimes we read the letter u by saying its name. Ask if anyone can think of an alphabet fantasy animal that begins with this sound (unicorn).

UGLY DAY

Have an "Ugly Day Celebration" for the letter U. Invite the children to join you in coming to school dressed in ugly clothes and wearing an ugly hair style. Have an "Ugly Day Parade" with you leading the way.

Ask the principal to judge class participants in an "Ugly Face-Making Contest." Have him or her give an award to every child who makes an ugly face in front of the class.

Decorate cookies in an ugly way for refreshments. Take pictures and make an "Ugly Book" for the library corner.

UMBRELLA BIRD'S Uu BOOK

Brainstorm with the class words that begin with the same sound as Umbrella Bird. Distribute paper and let the children each choose a word to illustrate. Have them copy the following sentence frame onto the page and write their word in the blank space. Put the pages together to make a class book.

Umbrellas go up. Can _____ go up?

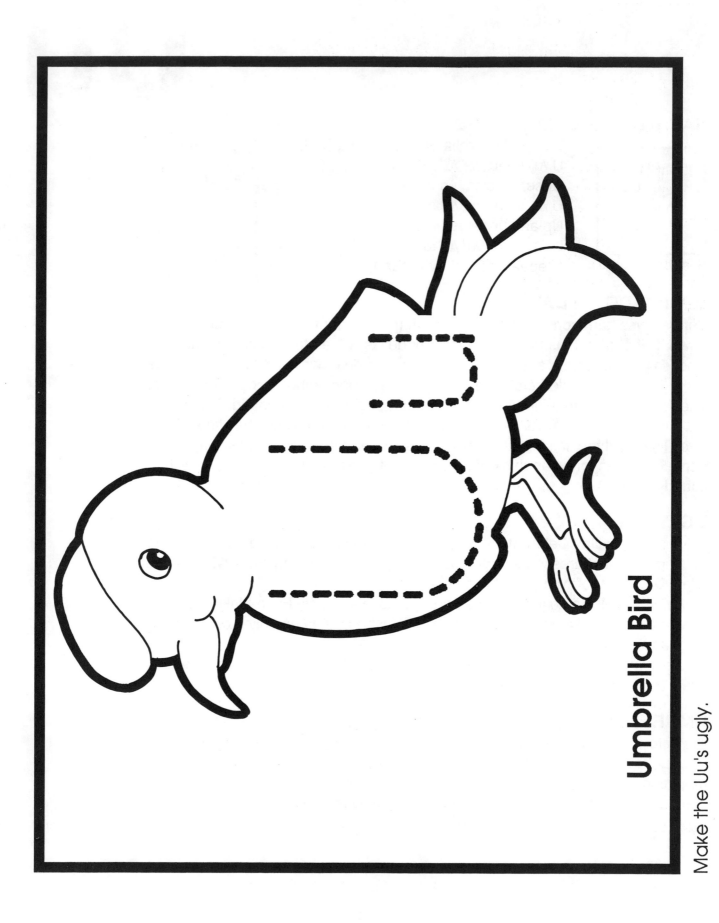

Umbrella Bird

Make the Uu's ugly.

Uu
Literature Connection

READ A STORY
Umbrella by Taro Yashima (Puffin, 1958). This story is about a little Japanese girl who anxiously waits for the first rain, and is overjoyed when it finally comes.

Presentation
Show the children the picture of Momo on the cover of the book. Tell them that she lives in Japan in a very large city. Show them the picture of the city, and talk about how it's like the place where they live and how it's different. Then read the book together.

Additional Books
Great Day for Up by Theo Seig (Random House, 1974); *Ugly Duckling* by Hans Christian Anderson (Harcourt, 1979).

RELATED ACTIVITIES

Umbrella Collages
Have the children create umbrella collages. Have them start by cutting out a number of umbrella shapes from a variety of papers (wallpaper, gift wrap, construction paper, etc.). Then have them glue the shapes onto a piece of drawing paper. Encourage the children to draw legs showing beneath some of the umbrellas, as in a street scene. Let them spray glue onto the picture and then shower the glue with silver glitter raindrops.

Umbrella Shape Books
Give each of the children an umbrella-shaped piece of paper with the following sentence frame on it:

Under my umbrella _____.

Have the children draw a picture on the paper of a place they might go or something they might do when it's raining and they're walking with their umbrella. Encourage them to complete the sentence frame either by themselves or by dictating to you or another adult. They might say, for example, "Under my umbrella I like to splash in puddles."

Bind the pages together with a cover, and put the umbrella book in the classroom book corner.

Listen and Draw an Umbrella Bird

Give the children oral directions as you draw each step with them.

1. Draw a circle for the head with a small oval on top. Make a long bib under the umbrella bird's chin.

2. Draw a half-circle for the body. Add a curved line for a wing.

3. Make three long tail feathers at the bottom of the body. Draw a triangle beak on the side of the head with a line through the middle.

4. Add one dark eye. Add two bird feet.

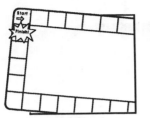

Uu
Phonics Connection

AT SCHOOL

Copy the game board and the set of sound picture cards for The "U" Game onto oaktag for the children to color. Have them cut the cards out. Glue an envelope onto the back of the game board to store the cards and the directions for play.

Show the children how to play the game. Include the "At Home" directions when the game goes home.

- -

AT HOME

Materials:

The "U" Game game board and set of sound picture cards; a small marker for each player

Directions:

1. Place the cards face down in a pile between the players.
2. Take turns drawing from the pile. If the picture on the card begins with the long or short sound of "u," move the marker forward one space. If the picture begins with another letter sound, no move is made. If a player is lucky enough to draw Umbrella Bird's card, the marker is moved forward two spaces.
3. Reshuffle the cards each time they have all been drawn, and continue playing until someone reaches the finish line. The player who finishes first is the winner.

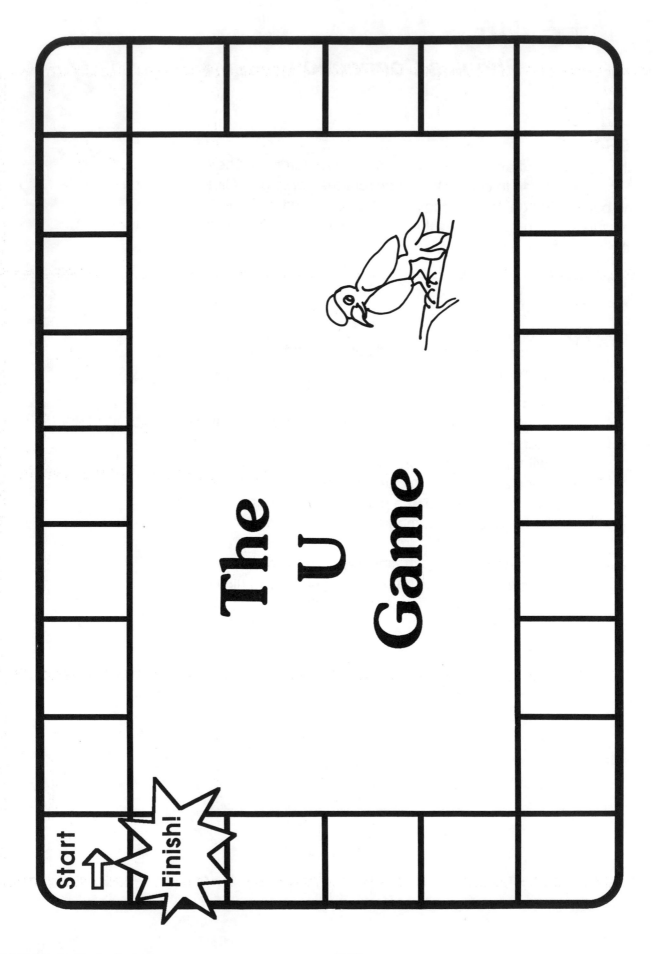

The U Game

Start

Finish!

Umbrella Bird

Uni Unicorn

Uu
Math Connection

UMBRELLAS UNLIMITED

Ask the children to bring an umbrella to school on a certain day (have some extras on hand). On that day, have them sit in a circle with their umbrella on their lap. Walk around the circle gathering all the umbrellas that are alike in some way. Start out collecting umbrellas with an obvious attribute, such as color. Put all the umbrellas you gather in the center of the circle, and ask the children to tell you how they are all alike.

Repeat the sorting activity using a less obvious attribute. This time select the umbrellas one at a time and have their owners bring them to the center of the circle. Allow the children to guess what the common attribute is each time an umbrella is brought to the center. Continue sorting by additional attributes. The more skilled the children are at sorting by attribute, the more creative you can be in those you collect; for example, you could sort umbrellas by the shape of their handle, those with pictures, those that are solid colors, and those that have folding handles.

DO YOU HAVE AN UMBRELLA?

(a graphing activity)

Talk about what people need when they go out in the rain. Ask the children if any of them has an umbrella of his or her own. Make a living graph. Have the children who do have their own umbrella get into one line, and those who do not get into another, parallel, line. Have the children in one line hold the hand of the child opposite them in the other line. Then tell them to drop their hands and stand still. This makes the graph easier to "read." Have the children tell you everything that they can about what they see.

Write an experience story together about the graph. Include as many of the children's observations as possible. Put a copy of the story into an experience story book and place it in the classroom library.

Do You Have an Umbrella?

Uu
Science Connection

UMBRELLA BIRDS

Class: Bird
Group: Solitary
Habitat: Rain forests
Food: Fruit
Baby: Chick
Color: Male, bluish black; female, brown

The umbrella bird gets its name from a curving crest of feathers that stands up to look like an umbrella over the bird's head. It also has another unusual arrangement of feathers—a long feathered wattle that hangs under the bird's chin. Very little is known about the umbrella bird because it lives in the very tops of rain forest trees.

READ MORE ABOUT UMBRELLA BIRDS

"Umbrella Bird" by Rodolphe Meyer de Schauensee, *World Book Encyclopedia*, vol. 20, (World Book, 1987).

DO AND DISCOVER

Let the children discover why male umbrella birds have crests on their heads. Match each child with a partner, but don't tell the children who their partners are. Explain that you will tell one child of each pair a visual clue to use to find his or her partner (for example, "He has on a red cap"). When one child in each pair has been told a clue, give a signal and let the children find their partners. Later, tell the children that the umbrella bird's crest is a visual clue that helps his partner to find him.

WRITE A BOOK ABOUT UMBRELLA BIRDS

Brainstorm all the things the children remember about umbrella birds from their study. Make a list of the food umbrella birds eat. Talk about their habitat. Discuss all the interesting things the children learned about umbrella birds.

Put three pages together with a cover for a book for each child. Have the children draw a picture of an umbrella bird on the cover and write a title for the book. (See "Listen and Draw An Umbrella Bird.") On the first page, have them draw the food that umbrella birds eat. On the second, let them draw the umbrella bird's habitat, and on the third draw something interesting that they know about umbrella birds. Have the children write or copy a sentence about the picture on each page.

Uu
Science Connection

UNDERGROUND

Go on a science walk with the class to look for signs of animals that live underground. Ask what the children think some of the signs might be (a hole, a mound of dirt, a bump in the grass). Caution the children not to stick their hands or fingers into any hole in the ground.

When you return to the classroom, discuss what the children saw. Ask if they know some animals that live underground. Make a chart list. If pictures of underground animals, such as moles, gophers, prairie dogs, ants, insects, worms, ground squirrels, etc., are available, show them to the children. Ask if they saw any signs of those animals on their walk. Also ask the children what they think the animals do underground (sleep, hide, store food, etc.).

Cover the bottom of a large jar with a thin layer of gravel, then fill the jar with rich soil. Collect some earthworms and put them in the jar. Let the children bring in "worm food" (lettuce, oatmeal or other cereals). Have them observe the worms as they burrow and tunnel underground. Be sure to moisten the soil very lightly now and then.

UNDERWATER

Pose the question, "If you could go underwater and travel across the ocean floor, what do you think you would see?" The children will undoubtedly talk about the various sea animals they know. But they may be surprised to find out that they would also see mountains, valleys, volcanoes, plains, and even rivers under the water. Tell them that they would see the same forms that they see on land.

Have the children work in groups to make models of the ocean floor. Give each group a clear plastic shoe box and some plasticine clay. Have them mold mountains, canyons, volcanoes, etc., and place their creations on the bottom of the plastic box. Help the children add water until their models are underwater.

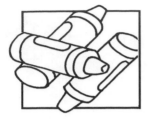

Uu
Arts and Crafts Connection

UPSIDE-DOWN PUPPETS

Materials:
2" by 8" strips of lightweight cardboard, 4" by 4" fabric squares, felt pens, stapler

Procedure:
1. Lightly mark the halfway point on each cardboard strip. Gather a fabric square and staple it across each strip at the line. This will be the puppet characters' skirts.
2. Give each child a skirted cardboard strip and felt pens and let the children draw the head and torso of a puppet on the cardboard strip just above the skirt.
3. Have the children flip the puppet upside down, so that the skirt covers the puppet face and torso just drawn, and have them draw the head and torso of another puppet character on the other end of the strip.

Suggested story characters for the upside-down puppets:

1. Red Riding Hood and her grandmother. (Have the children draw the wolf full length on the back side of the cardboard strip.)
2. The little girl with a curl in the middle of her forehead. (Put the good little girl on one end and the horrid girl on the other.)
3. Cinderella as a ragged maid and as a beautiful princess. (The prince could be on the back.)

UNIDENTIFIED FLYING OBJECTS

Materials:
Glue, paper plates, felt pens, assortment of scrap paper, sequins, glitter, stapler

Procedure:
1. For each UFO, staple two paper plates together so that the top sides of the plates are facing each other.
2. Discuss the children's ideas about what UFO's look like. Then give them the stapled paper plates and the rest of the materials and have them create their own unidentified flying objects. Remind them that their UFO's must be able to fly.
3. Take the children outside to fly their constructions Frisbee style.

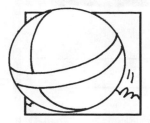

Uu
Movement Connection

UNDER AND OVER

Divide the children into groups of equal number. Arrange the groups in straight lines with the children standing one behind the other. Each group will need a small rubber playground ball.

Hand a ball to the first person in each line. When a signal is given, those players pass their ball under (between) their legs to the person behind them, until the balls reach the last person in the line. Each last player who receives a ball runs to the front of the line and begins to pass the ball back in the same manner. This continues until the original leader stands once again at the beginning of each line.

The activity can be repeated with the ball passed overhead from player to player. Then the activity can be repeated with the ball passed under the legs of the first player, over the head of the next player, and so on, under and over, under and over until it reaches the last player in line.

UP ON TOP

Give the children each a beanbag to put on top of their head. Play some music and have them move around a designated area balancing their beanbags. Encourage them to move without touching anyone. If a beanbag falls off a child's head, she or he must freeze until the music stops. Stop the music periodically for those who dropped their beanbags to "defrost" and rebalance. Continue the game by starting the music again.

Uu

HOMEWORK

Name _____

Date Due _____

Put a √ by the activity you have chosen to do.

☐ Tell a story about one of your **u**ncles, and ask someone to write it for you. Make a picture to bring to school with your story.

☐ Make a picture and word list of things that go **u**p. Bring it to school.

☐ Make a picture of something **u**gly to bring to school. Tell a story about the **u**gly thing.

_____
Signature of grown up helper

UMBRELLA BIRD'S NEST

Ingredients (serves 1)
 peanut butter
 powdered milk
 Chinese noodles
  (commercially
  prepared)
 powdered sugar
 honey
 shelled peanuts

1. Put 1 T. peanut butter into a bowl.

2. Add 1 T. powdered milk.

3. Add 1 T. sugar.

4. Mix in 1 T. honey. Stir well.

5. Mold the dough into a nest shape.

6. Press Chinese noodles into the dough.

7. Put 3 peanut "eggs" into the nest.

RAP WITH VULTURE VIC

Sign Language **V**

V is for vulture, Vulture Vic.
V /v/ /v/ /v/ /v/ /v/ /v/
Velvet, voices, valentines.
V /v/ /v/ /v/ /v/ /v/ /v/
Vim and vigor, vitamins.
V /v/ /v/ /v/ /v/ /v/ /v/
(Repeat the first two lines.)

Vulture Vic

VIOLIN MUSIC

Introduce Vulture Vic and his letter V by playing some violin music for the children. Ask them if they know the name of the musical instrument they are listening to. Have them guess what alphabet animal friend begins with the same sound as "violin."

VEGETABLE VARIETY SHOW

Celebrate the letter V with a "Vegetable Variety Show." Have the children bring fresh, unprepared vegetables to class. Then use the food in a classification activity. Sort the vegetables in as many different ways as the children can think of (by color, shape, texture of the skin, size, whether you eat the skin or not, and so on). Have a raw-vegetable tasting party before making vegetable soup. After the children have sampled the different foods, make a graph that displays the answers to the question "What is your favorite vegetable?"

VULTURE VIC'S Vv BOOK

Brainstorm with the class words that begin with the same sound as Vulture Vic. Distribute paper and let the children each choose a word to illustrate. Have them copy the following sentence frame onto the page and write their word in the blank space. Put the pages together to make a class book.

Vulture Vic thinks _____ are valuable.

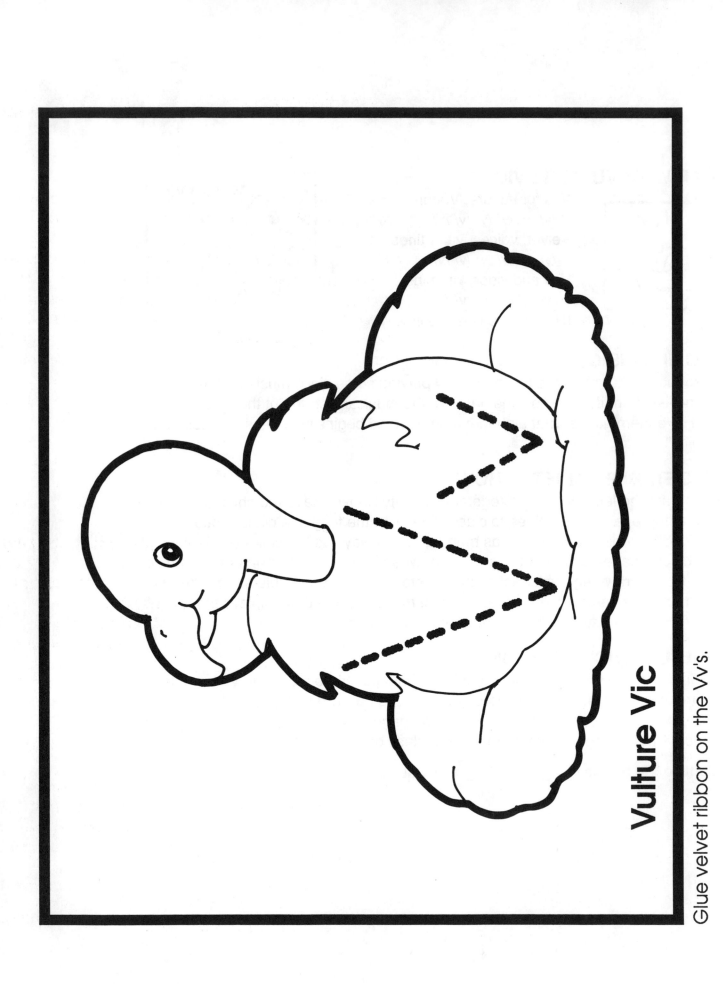

Vulture Vic

Glue velvet ribbon on the Vv's.

Vv
Literature Connection

READ A BOOK

Growing Vegetable Soup by Lois Ehlert (Harcourt, 1987). This brightly illustrated book with simple text is a wonderful way to introduce children to how vegetables grow in a garden.

Presentation

Read the book slowly, lingering over each page after reading the text to talk about the illustrations. Name the tools, the seeds, the things that need to be done for seeds to grow. Discuss the cooking tools used to make the vegetable soup.

Read the book again, pausing to recall the kinds of vegetables that were planted and the procedures used to grow them.

Additional Books

Velveteen Rabbit by Marjorie Williams (Running Press, 1984); *Valentine Bears* by Eve Bunting (Clarion, 1983).

RELATED ACTIVITY

Make a Big Book About Where Vegetables Grow

Bring a variety of vegetables to school for the children to identify and taste. Talk about which of the vegetables grow under the ground and which grow above the ground, and then make a list of each kind.

Ask each child to choose a vegetable. Provide each with the appropriate color of construction paper and have them all cut out their vegetable shape. Give each child a piece of brown paper on which to glue his or her cutout. The children who have made a vegetable that grows above the ground should copy the following sentence frame onto the brown page and then complete or dictate the answer:

_____ **grow above the ground.**

For the children who made a vegetable that grows under the ground, make a slit in the middle of their brown page, glue an envelope to the back with the opening flush with the slit, and have the children fill in or dictate their answer to the following sentence frame:

But _____ **grow below the ground.**

Let the children slip their vegetable that grows under the ground into the pocket with only the leafy part showing.

Bind all the pages together so that every fourth page or so is about a vegetable that grows under the ground. The children will enjoy pulling that vegetable "out of the soil" each time they read the book.

Listen and Draw a Vulture

Give the children oral directions as you draw each step with them.

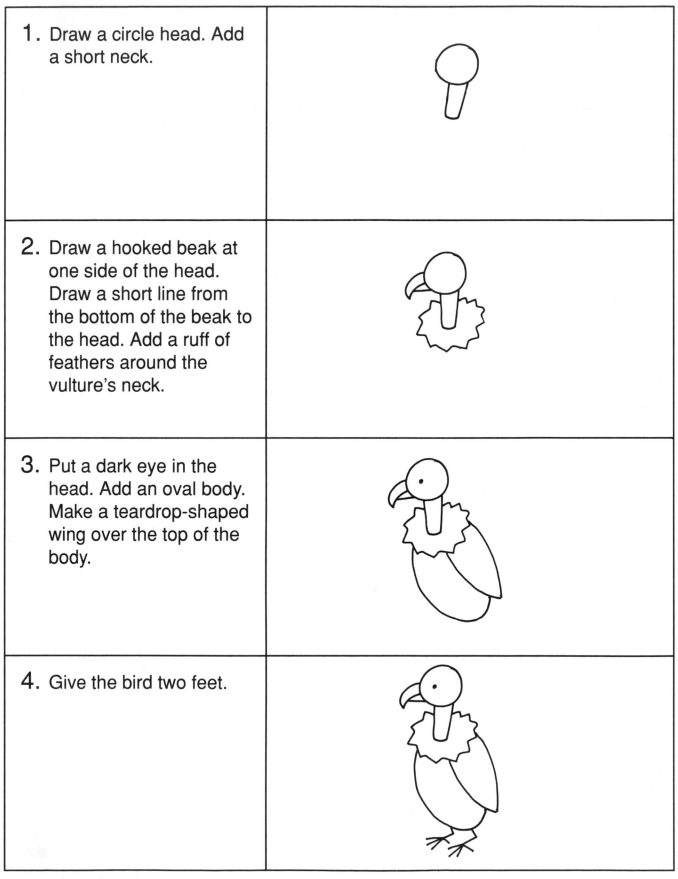

1. Draw a circle head. Add a short neck.

2. Draw a hooked beak at one side of the head. Draw a short line from the bottom of the beak to the head. Add a ruff of feathers around the vulture's neck.

3. Put a dark eye in the head. Add an oval body. Make a teardrop-shaped wing over the top of the body.

4. Give the bird two feet.

Vv
Phonics Connection

AT SCHOOL
Materials:
White lunch bags, pink and red construction paper scraps, commercial valentine stickers, small white paper doilies, scissors, crayons, glue, heart-shaped beginning sound picture cards

To make the valentine bags: Let the children decorate their bags with stickers, construction paper hearts, and white paper doilies. Have them put Vulture Vic's Vv's on their bags. Make two bags for each game.

To make the hearts: Copy the heart-shaped sound picture cards for the children to color and cut out.

Show the children how to play the game. Include the "At Home" directions when the game goes home.

AT HOME
Materials:
A set of heart-shaped sound picture cards; a valentine bag for each player

Directions:
1. Shuffle the cards and put them in a pile face down between the players.
2. Take turns drawing cards. If a picture is drawn that begins with the sound of "v," put it in the valentine bag. If the picture begins with another letter sound, put it in a discard pile.
3. The winner is the person whose valentine bag contains the most hearts after all the cards have been played.

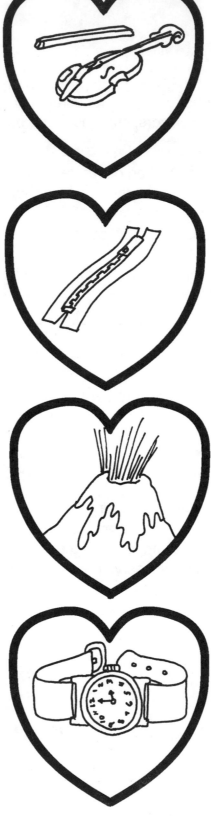

Vv
Math Connection

VEGETABLE SORTING

Bring to class an assortment of vegetables, such as a carrot, an ear of corn, a head of cabbage, a head of cauliflower, a tomato, a zucchini, etc. Pull them out of a shopping bag one at a time for the children to name and discuss. Then have the children take turns grouping vegetables that are alike in some way, while the others try to guess the way in which they're alike.

WHAT'S YOUR FAVORITE VEGETABLE?

(a graphing activity)

Brainstorm with the children a list of all the vegetables they can think of. Then ask the graphing question: "What is your favorite vegetable?" Give each child crayons and a piece of drawing paper about three inches square on which to draw a picture of his or her choice

Make a four-column graphing grid according to the directions in the Introduction. Label three of the columns with the names of the three most popular vegetable choices. Label the last column "Others," explaining that this is where to put pictures of vegetables that are not named on the other graph columns. Have the children tape their pictures onto the appropriate columns.

When everyone has recorded a choice, ask the children to tell you as many things as they can about what they see on the favorite vegetable graph. Then write an experience story together, including as many of the children's observations as possible. Put a copy of the story in an experience story book and place it in the library.

293

Vv
Science Connection

VULTURES

Class: Bird
Group: Solitary or in flocks (for feeding)
Habitat: Forests, rocky cliffs
Food: Carrion (dead, often rotten, animals)
Baby: Chick
Color: Black with red, gray, yellow, or orange head

Vultures are very graceful in the air as they glide in circles over the dead animals they see from high in the sky; when they land, however, they seem awkward. Vultures are like garbage collectors, cleaning up waste that other animals won't touch. They have few feathers on their heads so that when they stick their heads into the carcasses (dead bodies) the blood and other gore slip right off.

READ MORE ABOUT VULTURES

Vultures by Lynn M. Stone (Rourke, 1989).

DO AND DISCOVER

Let the children discover how the vulture's extra-wide wingspan helps it glide for long periods of time on air currents. Have the children fold two different kinds of paper airplanes, one with a narrow wingspan and one with a wide wingspan. Have them compare the lengths of time the two types stay in the air. Make sure the wingspan is the only difference between the two paper planes.

WRITE A BOOK ABOUT VULTURES

Brainstorm all the things the children remember about vultures from their study. Make a list of the food vultures eat. Talk about their habitat. Discuss all the interesting things the children learned about vultures.

Put three pages together with a cover for a book for each child. Have the children draw a picture of a vulture on the cover and write a title for the book. (See "Listen and Draw A Vulture.") On the first page, have them draw the food that vultures eat. On the second, let them draw the vulture's habitat, and on the third draw something interesting that they know about vultures. Have the children write or copy a sentence about the picture on each page.

Vv
Science Connection

VOLCANOES

Hold a bottle of soda pop or carbonated water over a sink or dishpan. Shake the bottle vigorously. Ask the children to predict what will happen when you open the bottle. They will delight in the fact that the liquid comes spewing out of the top when you do open it. Tell the children that as you shook the bottle, more and more gas bubbles formed in the liquid, making it press harder and harder on the bottle. The bubbles wanted to escape because there was less and less room for them inside. As soon as the top was taken off, the gases rushed to get out, taking the liquid with them. Tell the children that this is much the same way a volcano erupts. Gases inside the earth push hot, melted rock up through holes in the earth.

Let the children work together in small groups to make their own volcano models. Each group will need a box lid, newspapers, an empty can with the top removed, sand, ½ cup water, ¾ cup vinegar, 2-3 drops of red food coloring, and ¼ cup baking soda. Have the children place the newspaper in the box lid, set the can in the center, and make a mound of sand around the can. Have them add the baking soda, water, and food coloring to the can. When the group is ready for the eruption, add the vinegar. What happens?

VACUUM

Bring a vacuum cleaner with a hose to school. Turn it on and let the children feel air being sucked in. Explain that before people understood how to create a vacuum, they had to sweep things up with brooms. Tell the children that "vacuum" means empty space, which the machine creates. Air then rushes in to fill the space, carrying dirt with it.

Tell the class that you can create a vacuum without a machine. Put a playing card over the opening of an empty paper cup. When you turn the cup over, the card falls off. Next, fill the cup with water and again place the card over the cup's opening, this time holding the card in place with your finger. Turn the cup completely upside down and then remove your finger. The card will stick to the cup. Tell the children that this is not a magic trick, but is an example of a vacuum. The air in the cup was absorbed into the water, and a vacuum (empty space) was formed where the air had been.

Furnish the children with cups, cards, and water, and let them try the experiment. Have the children work at a water table, sink, or over a dishpan.

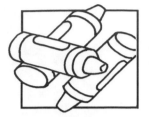

Vv
Arts and Crafts Connection

VEGETABLE PRINTS

Materials:

Variety of vegetables (such as carrots, green peppers, small cabbages, potatoes, broccoli, artichokes), knife, white drawing paper, brushes, liquid tempera paint

Procedure:

1. Cut the vegetables in half to provide a flat surface and lines that will show up in the prints.

2. Show the children how to paint the cut surface of the vegetable they choose and press it to a piece of paper to create a print. Remind them that they can print three or four times before painting the vegetable surface again.

3. Encourage the children to repeat the process with other vegetables and colors until they are pleased with their design.

VASES

Materials:

Small clean bottles of various shapes, masking tape, brown or black liquid shoe polish, brushes, paper towels or facial tissue, newspaper, clear fixative (optional)

Procedure:

1. Show the children how to tear masking tape into small pieces (not more than a half inch in diameter) and stick them onto a bottle, covering the surface so that no glass shows. Check to see that all the edges of the tape pieces are securely stuck to the bottle.

2. Cover the work surface with newspaper and have the children paint their bottle with liquid shoe polish.

3. Before the polish dries, give the children pads of soft paper towels or facial tissue to wipe over the surface of the bottles, drying the polish and creating a beautiful antiqued look.

4. When the vases are dry, you may spray them with a clear art fixative. Caution: Do this step outside or in a well-ventilated area after the children have gone home.

Vv
Movement Connection

VOLCANO

Take the children out to a playground area with a large circle painted on it. Have the children stand with their toes touching the circle. Choose one child to be the "Volcano" and have him or her squat down in the center of the circle. No one is allowed to move until the "Volcano" shouts "Hot lava!" and pops up from the squatting position. The children then scatter as the "Volcano" chases them, trying to tag someone. The player who is tagged becomes the new "Volcano," and the game begins again with the other children enclosing the "Volcano" in a circle.

VEHICLES

Explain to the children that a vehicle is something used to carry or move people or things. Brainstorm a list of vehicles with them, such as plane or jet, car, truck, van, jeep, train, bicycle or Big Wheel, wheelbarrow, rowboat, tractor, and bus.

To play the game, have the children sit in a circle. Invite someone to come into the circle and pretend to be one of the vehicles on the list (it's a good idea to have the child whisper the name of his or her vehicle in your ear first). Then have the others guess what the vehicle is. Once the vehicle is guessed, the child may choose four or five other children to join in and act out the vehicle together. Have all those children return to the outside circle and choose someone else to act out a different vehicle.

Vv

HOMEWORK

Name _____

Date Due _____

Put a √ by the activity you have chosen to do.

☐ Draw a picture of where you would like to go on **v**acation. Ask a grownup to write about it. Bring the picture and the story to school.

☐ Make a picture list of all the **v**egetables you can think of. Ask a grownup to label each vegetable pictured. Bring the list to school.

☐ Find out about **v**olcanoes. Bring the facts to school. Make a picture of a **v**olcano to bring too.

_____

Signature of grown up helper

VULTURE VIC'S VARIETY VEGETABLE SOUP

Ingredients (serves a group)
    vegetables (each child brings one)
    soup stock (prepare ahead by a grown-up)

1. Peel and cut the vegetables.

2. Add them to a big pot of simmering soup stock.

3. Cover and simmer for 1 hour.

4. Serve with a variety of crackers.

Ww

RAP WITH WALRUS WALT

Sign Language **W**

W is for walrus, Walrus Walt.
W /w/ /w/ /w/ /w/ /w/ /w/
Watermelon, wonderful.
W /w/ /w/ /w/ /w/ /w/ /w/
Windy weather, wiggling worms.
W /w/ /w/ /w/ /w/ /w/ /w/
(Repeat the first two lines.)

Walrus Walt

A WAGON FULL OF W'S

Introduce Walrus Walt and his letter W with a wagon filled with things that begin with /w/. Have the children name each object as it's taken from the wagon. Ask them how all the names are alike, and let them guess what alphabet animal begins with that sound.

WACKY WEDNESDAY

Celebrate W by turning the middle of the week into "Wacky Wednesday." Encourage the children to do wacky things, such as wearing a sweater or shirt backward to school, and do some yourself, such as starting the day with end-of-the-day activities and ending with school-day starters. Sing songs like "Willaby, Wallaby, Woo" and read together the book *Wacky Wednesday* by Theo Steig. Have the children make and serve "Wacky Waffles" by adding food coloring to the batter.

WALRUS WALT'S Ww BOOK

Brainstorm with the class words that begin with the same sound as Walrus Walt. Distribute paper and let the children each choose a word to illustrate. Have them copy the following sentence frame onto the page and write their word in the blank space. Put the pages together to make a class book.

Where, oh, where can Walrus Walt be?

He's looking through the window at a _____ and me.

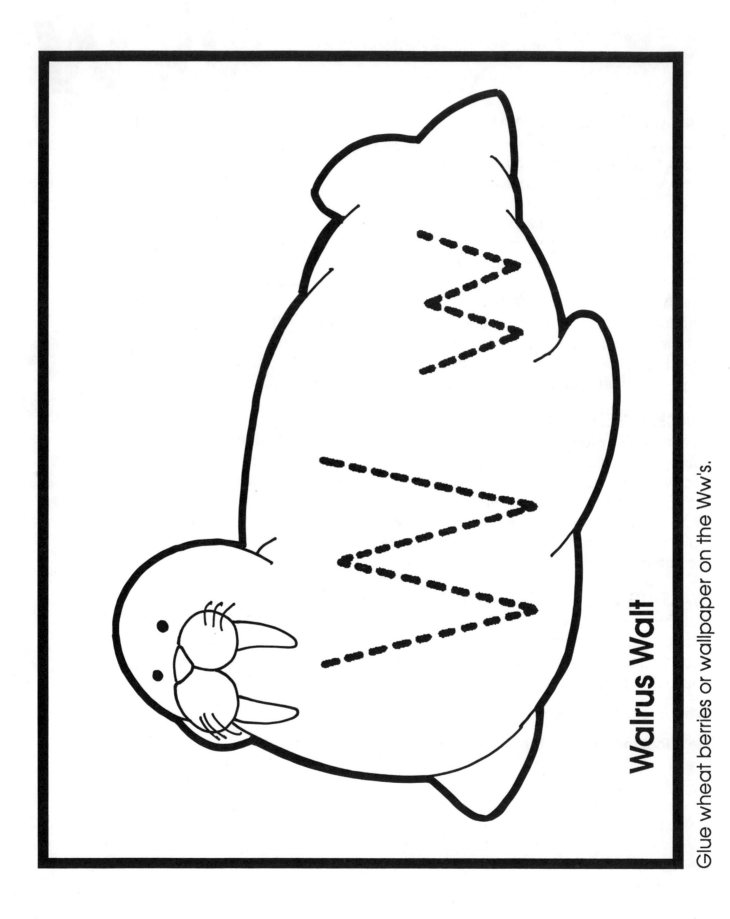

Walrus Walt

Glue wheat berries or wallpaper on the Ww's.

Ww
Literature Connection

READ A BOOK

Where the Wild Things Are by Maurice Sendak (Harper, 1963). This is a book that is both exciting and reassuring to children. It tells of Max, who was sent to bed without any supper for making a smart remark to his mother. He dreams of a faraway land where he becomes king of the terrible wild things who live there. Maurice Sendak's wonderful illustrations won him the Caldecott Medal.

Presentation

Ask the children if they have ever had a bad dream. Give each an opportunity to tell about a dream. Many may tell of frightening monsters. Show the class *Where the Wild Things Are* and tell them that this is a book about a little boy named Max who had a bad dream.

Additional Books

Whistle for Willie by Ezra Jack Keats (Viking, 1964); *The Wheels on the Bus* by Maryann Kovalski (Little, Brown, 1987); *The Wind Blew* by Pat Hutchins (Puffin, 1974); *Gilberto and the Wind* by Marie Hall Ets (Viking, 1963); *Wheels Away* by Dayle Ann Dodds (Harper, 1989).

RELATED ACTIVITIES

A Book of Wild Things

Discuss the vivid artwork in the book. Talk about the "wild things" and ask the children to imagine one of their own. Tell them that they are going to illustrate a class book of wild things using an art technique called crayon resist.

Give each child a piece of drawing paper and crayons. Explain that they need to press very hard with their crayons as they make their drawing, and fill in most of the space. Encourage the children to be imaginative in their creations.

When the drawings are finished, have the children paint over them with a light wash of black watercolor paint. Be sure the paint is well watered down. When the drawings are dry, bind the finished art together into a "Wild Things" class book.

A Wild Thing Mural

Tape up a long piece of butcher paper and let the children paint their version of the place where the wild things live. To guide them, show them the book illustrations of the trees, grass, and the night sky.

When the mural is completed, give each child a large piece of drawing paper, felt pens, crayons, and scraps of various kinds of art papers. Ask each to create a "wild thing" to glue to the painted background.

Listen and Draw a Walrus

Give the children oral directions as you draw each step with them.

1. Draw a tall hill leaning to one side. Draw a straight line across the bottom.

2. Make a round flipper in the front of the body. Make another round flipper on the side of the body. Make a short up and down line between the two flippers.

3. Draw two circles for the nose. Make a triangle pointing down from the bottom of each circle. Add two loops to the end of the body for a tail.

4. Add two eyes above the nose. Make whiskers coming out the sides of the circles.

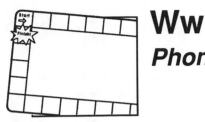

Ww
Phonics Connection

AT SCHOOL

Materials:

9" by 6" pieces of brown construction paper, stapler, crayons, light green construction paper, scissors, w-dollar beginning sound picture cards

To make the wallets: Have the children fold the pieces of brown construction paper the long way to look like wallets. Help them staple the short ends to form the pocket for the w-dollars. Let the children decorate their wallets with Walrus Walt's initials. Make two wallets for each game.

To make the w-dollars: Copy tho w-dollar beginning sound picture cards onto light green paper for the children to cut out.

Show the children how to play the game. Include the "At Home" directions when the game goes home.

- -

AT HOME

Materials:

A set of w-dollar beginning sound picture cards; a paper wallet for each player

Directions:

1. Shuffle the cards and put them in a pile face down between the players.

2. Take turns drawing cards. If a picture is drawn that begins with the sound of "w," put it in the wallet. If the picture begins with another letter sound, put it in a discard pile.

3. The winner is the person whose wallet contains the most w-dollars after all the cards have been played.

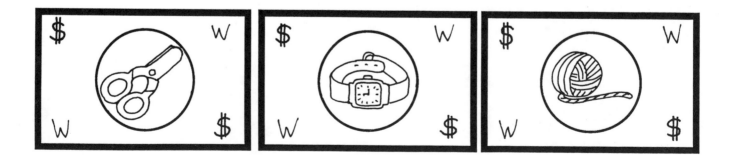

Ww
Math Connection

WATERMELON IS WONDERFUL

During the early fall or late spring, bring a watermelon to class. Have the children estimate how much it weighs, and write their estimates on the chalkboard. Then weigh the watermelon to find out how close the estimates are. Count the number of estimates that are too heavy, too light, and just right.

Slice the watermelon and divide the pieces among the children. Have them estimate the number of seeds they think are in their portion and record the numbers on the chalkboard. When the children eat their watermelon, remind them to save their seeds. Encourage them to divide their seeds into groups of 10 and count them. Finally, challenge the children to figure out how many seeds were in the whole watermelon.

WHAT KIND OF WEATHER DO YOU LIKE BEST?

(a graphing activity)

Talk about different kinds of weather with the children. Then ask them, "What kind of weather do you like best?" Make copies of the weather graphing symbols on the following page, and have each child select and color his or her favorite.

Make a four-column graphing grid according to the directions in the Introduction. Print the graphing question across the top, and label each column with one of the symbols. Have the children tape their graphing symbols onto the appropriate columns on the graph.

When everyone has recorded a choice, ask the children to tell you everything they can about what they see. Write an experience story together, including as many of the children's observations as possible. Put a copy of the story into an experience story book and place it in the classroom library.

What Kind of Weather Do You Like Best?

Snowy

Rainy

Cloudy

Sunny

Ww
Science Connection

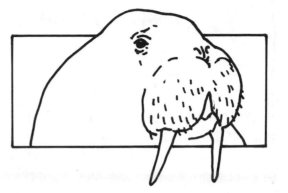

WALRUSES

Class: Mammal
Group: Herd
Habitat: Ocean and ice near North Pole
Food: Shellfish, clams
Color: Reddish brown

Walruses use their two long tusks to drag themselves up from the water and over the ice and land. There are about 700 sensitive hairs in a walrus's mustache that are used as "forks" to hold shellfish in place while he eats them. The moustache is also used to help the walrus feel its way around in dark, murky waters.

READ MORE ABOUT WALRUSES
Walruses by Sarah Palmer (Rourke, 1989).

DO AND DISCOVER
Let the children discover how a walrus's thick layer of blubber helps to keep it warm. Fill a large jar or pan with ice water. Have the children take turns sticking their fingers into the water. Then have them put on a rubber glove and try it again. The glove insulates their fingers much the same as blubber insulates the walrus.

WRITE A BOOK ABOUT WALRUSES
Brainstorm all the things the children remember about walruses from their study. Make a list of the food walruses eat. Talk about their habitat. Discuss all the interesting things the children learned about walruses.

Put three pages together with a cover for a book for each child. Have the children draw a picture of a walrus on the cover and write a title for the book. (See "Listen and Draw A Walrus.") On the first page, have them draw the food that walruses eat. On the second, let them draw the walrus's habitat, and on the third draw something interesting that they know about walruses. Have the children write or copy a sentence about the picture on each page.

Ww
Science Connection

WATER

Water holds a wonderful fascination for children. Have a tub of water available, and let the children explore its effects on a variety of things. Give them several different sizes of plastic bottles and jars to fill and pour from. Provide some different substances such as salt, sugar, oil, beans, cotton, tissue, rocks, and dirt for them to add to the water to see what happens.

After a period of free exploration, help the children set up a controlled experiment much like scientists do. Explain that they will be observing their experiments daily to see what happens. Give the children open baby food jars three quarters full of water. Show them how to mark the water level with a permanent marker, and have them place their jars in a safe place. Tell them that they will mark the water level each day. After several days, ask the children what they have observed. (The water level will go down.) Also ask how they think this happened and where they think the water has gone.

WIND

Ask the children to show you lots of different ways that they can make wind. They may flap their arms, bow, or wave a piece of paper or a folded-paper fan. Ask them if they can see the wind they are making. Then ask, "How do you know when the wind is blowing if you can't see it?" "What is wind?" Also ask, "How do you think the air moves outside? Is there a big fan in the sky?" Tell the children that there is not a big fan making the air move, but that in some places air gets packed in like air in a balloon and must move out and away. Weather persons call these places "high pressure systems." Inflate a balloon and let the "wind" blow in the children's faces.

Have the children work in small groups to make windsocks. For each one, have the children:

1. Cut off the sleeve of an old shirt.
2. Bend a thin, flexible wire into a circle to fit the shoulder end of the cut-off sleeve.
3. Staple the sleeve over the wire.

Make and pin up a class wind calendar. Tie the windsocks to tree branches and have the class observe them each day over a several-day period. Let the children decide whether to mark "windy" or "still" on the calendar each day.

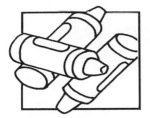

Ww
Arts and Crafts Connection

WATERCOLORS

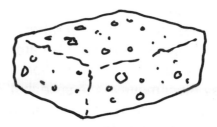

Materials:
Sets of watercolor paints, cups of water, white drawing paper, brushes, paper towels, sponges (optional)

Procedure:
1. If the children have not worked with watercolors before, there are a few techniques you will need to demonstrate for them. The first thing they will need to know is how to prepare the paints for use. Show them how to dip their brushes into clear water to fill them and then gently touch a paint pan (cake of watercolor) to release the water onto the color. Also show them how to dip their brushes into the cups of water after using a color to keep the colors from getting "muddy." They will need to be reminded to get fresh water occasionally, so that their colors stay clear and bright.

2. Let the children experiment with the effects of painting on wet paper (dampened with brushes or a sponge and clear water) versus painting on dry paper.

3. Have them try painting with a brush full of paint and then painting with a brush when most of the paint is gone (dry brush).

4. Show them how to mix colors in the lid of the paint box so that the paint pans will not become muddied.

5. Cleanup is very important when finished with watercolor painting. Show the children how to wash their brushes and shape them back to a point with their fingers. Demonstrate how to soak up unused mixed paints with a paper towel, leaving the paint box lid open so that the paint pans can dry thoroughly.

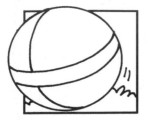

Ww
Movement Connection

WHISTLE STOP

Go outside to a grassy area where there are established boundaries. Have the children scatter about within the play area. Tell them that when you give the signal they are to move in any direction within the boundaries without touching anyone. They must move in the style that is stated. When they hear the whistle they must stop. Designate a "sit-out" area for players who touch, but have them sit out for only one turn before joining the play again.

Movement styles:

run on tiptoes	gallop
skip	walk like a. . . (name an animal)
hop (or jump)	slide sideways
run backward	walk with giant steps

WALK THE BOARD

Place a board on the floor. This is the "walking board." (Wooden balance beams are also available commercially.) Establish some guidelines with the children before giving them specific challenges as they take turns walking the board.

Tell the children to keep their chin up and look at something at the end of the board, so that they will not watch their feet. Show them how to take steps on the board, placing their toes down, then their heel, keeping their feet pointing straight ahead on the board without overhanging. Encourage the children to walk slowly.

Challenges for walking the board: Say—

Walk forward on the board with your arms held out to the sides (over your head, flapping, clapping, etc.).

Walk forward to the middle of the board. Stop, turn around, and walk the rest of the way backward.

Walk sideways on the balls of your feet all the way down the board.

Walk forward with your hands on your. . . (hips, head, shoulders, knees, etc.).

Balance a beanbag on your. . . (head, shoulder, etc.) as you walk.

Ww

HOMEWORK

Name _____

Date Due _____

Put a √ by the activity you have chosen to do.

☐ Be a **w**eather **w**atcher. Record the **w**eather with pictures each day for a **w**eek. Bring the pictures to school.

☐ Make three **w**ishes. Draw pictures that show your **w**ishes. Bring your pictures to school to tell about.

☐ Count and make a picture record of all the **w**indows in your house. Bring your pictures to school.

_____
Signature of grown up helper

WALRUS WALT'S WAFFLE

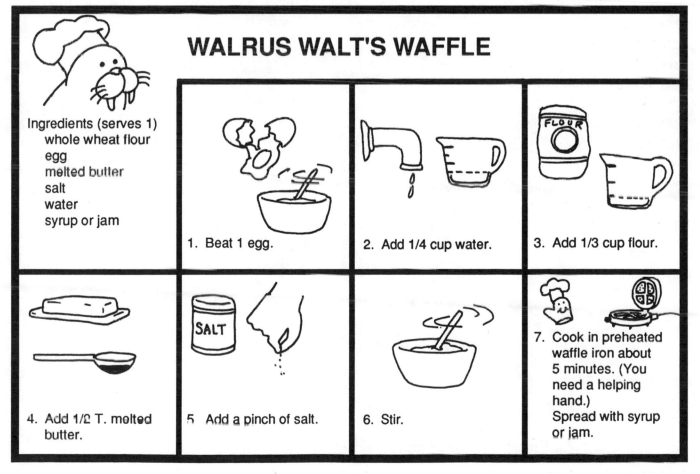

Ingredients (serves 1)
whole wheat flour
egg
melted butter
salt
water
syrup or jam

1. Beat 1 egg.

2. Add 1/4 cup water.

3. Add 1/3 cup flour.

4. Add 1/2 T. melted butter.

5. Add a pinch of salt.

6. Stir.

7. Cook in preheated waffle iron about 5 minutes. (You need a helping hand.) Spread with syrup or jam.

Sign Language **X**

INTRODUCING X

Show the children a xylophone. Play it and ask the class if they know what the instrument is called. Discuss how the name "xylophone" begins with the sound /z/, but does not begin with the letter z. Tell them that the alphabet letter x is read /z/ at the beginning of most words, and /cks/ at the end of words such as "fox." Then tell them that there are no alphabet animals that begin with x in English, so they are going to make one up.

Brainstorm some imaginary animal names that begin with x, for example, xeradon and xox. Make a list. Have the mask patterns (pages 343) and a variety of colored construction paper and crayons available to the children, and let them go to work making their own x animal masks. Write each child's chosen alphabet animal name on his or her creation.

Yy

RAP WITH YOLANDA YAK

Sign Language **Y**

Y is for yak, Yolanda Yak.
Y /y/ /y/ /y/ /y/ /y/ /y/
Yippy, yo-yo, yummy, yam.
Y /y/ /y/ /y/ /y/ /y/ /y/
Yucky, yellow, yarn, and you.
Y /y/ /y/ /y/ /y/ /y/ /y/
(Repeat the first two lines.)

Yolanda Yak

YARD HUNT

To introduce Yolanda Yak and her letter Y, hide some yellow yarn, a yam, a yo-yo, and a yogurt container in the school yard. Choose some children to go to the yard and find four things that begin with the same sound as "yard." When they return, have everyone name the objects, then guess what alphabet animal begins with the same sound. Tell them that /y/ is the sound you say when you read the letter y.

YUMMY YOGURT PARTY

To celebrate the letter Y, have a "Yummy Yogurt Party." Ask the children to bring a carton of their favorite yogurt to share. Let everyone take a taste of each kind. Ask the question, "Which yogurt did you like best?" Graph the children's answers.

YOLANDA YAK'S Yy BOOK

Brainstorm with the class words that begin with the same sound as Yolanda Yak. Distribute paper and let the children each choose a word to illustrate. Have them copy the following sentence frame onto the page and write their word in the blank space. Put the pages together to make a class book.

Yes, Yolanda Yak likes you and your _____.

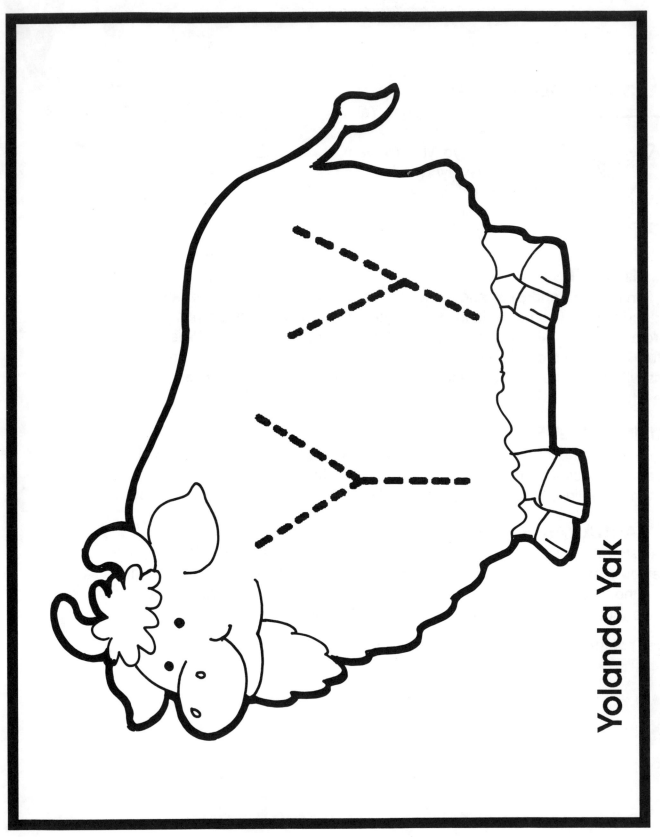

Yolanda Yak

Glue yellow yarn on the Yy's.

Yy
Literature Connection

READ A BOOK
Yummers by James Marshall (Houghton, 1973). This is the light-hearted story of a little pig named Emily who loves to eat.

Presentation
Ask the children about their favorite foods. Make a list. Show them the book, and tell them that the pig in the story named Emily has so many favorite foods that she cannot stop eating.

Additional Books
Yummers Too by James Marshall (Houghton, 1986), *Little Blue and Little Yellow* by Leo Lionni (Greenwillow, 1978); *Yertle, the Turtle* by Dr. Seuss (Random House, 1950); *Chicken Soup With Rice* by Maurice Sendak (Harper, 1962).

RELATED ACTIVITY

Yummy Big Book
Put together a class big book of the children's favorite foods. Give each child a page with the following sentence frame to complete and illustrate:

Yummy (name of favorite food). **Yummy** (another favorite food). **Yummy, yummy in my tummy!**

Bind the pages together for the classroom book corner.

Listen and Draw a Yak

Give the children oral directions as you draw each step with them.

1. Draw a tall hill for the body. Make the bottom of the hill shaggy. Draw a circle in the top of the hill for the head. Draw an oval at the bottom of the circle.

2. Make two horns on the top of the head. Make an oval ear below each horn. Add a shaggy beard at the bottom of the head. Make a rectangle at the bottom of the body.

3. Make a line down the middle of the rectangle. Draw another line across the middle of the rectangle. Add two circles to the head for nostrils. Add curvy hair to the top of the yak's head.

4. Give the yak two eyes. Draw two short lines for toes.

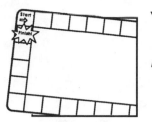

Yy
Phonics Connection

AT SCHOOL

Copy the game board and the set of sound picture cards for Yolanda Yak's "Y" Game onto oaktag for the children to color. Have them cut the cards out. Glue an envelope onto the back of the game board to store the cards and the directions for play.

Show the children how to play the game. Include the "At Home" directions when the game goes home.

AT HOME
Materials:

Yolanda Yak's game board and set of sound picture cards; a small marker for each player

Directions:

1. Place the cards face down in a pile between the players.
2. Take turns drawing from the pile. If the picture on the card begins with the sound of "y," move the marker forward one space. If the picture begins with another letter sound, no move is made. If a player is lucky enough to draw Yolanda Yak's card, the marker may be moved forward two spaces.
3. Reshuffle the cards each time they have all been drawn, and continue playing until someone reaches the finish line. The player who finishes first is the winner.

Start
Here!

Yolanda Yak's Y Game

Finish!

Yy
Math Connection

YELLOW YARN MEASURING

Hang four or five small poster-sized pieces of heavy paper or tag board at easy reaching height around the classroom. Draw a horizontal line across the center of each poster, making each line a different length. Cut pieces of yellow yarn the same lengths as the various lines, making five or six pieces to match each line. Hold all the pieces of yarn in your fist, resting the ends in your lap so that the children can't see how long they are. Then, one at a time, have the children pull a piece of yarn from your hand and match it with the correct poster line. Have them tape their yellow yarn directly under the line.

WHAT KIND OF YOGURT DO YOU LIKE BEST?

(a graphing activity)

Hold a "Yogurt Tasting." Ask the children to each bring a small carton of yogurt to class to share. Give the children paper plates and spoons and let them serve themselves a "taste" of each yogurt that they would like to try. When everyone has tasted, ask, "Which kind of yogurt do you like best?"

Make a four-column graphing grid according to the directions in the Introduction. Print the graphing question across the top, and label each column with one of the yogurt cup graphing symbols from the following page. Make copies of the symbols for the children to select and color, then tape onto the appropriate columns of the grid.

When everyone has recorded a choice, ask the children to tell you everything they can about what they see on the graph. Write an experience story and include as many of the children's observations as possible. Include the story in a book of other graphing experience stories.

What Kind of Yogurt Do You Like Best?

Yy
Science Connection

YAKS
Class: Mammal
Group: Herd
Habitat: Mountains
Food: Grass
Baby: Calf
Color: Black

Yaks, the mammals that live at the highest elevations in the world, are found in the mountains of Tibet, where it gets extremely cold. To keep warm, yaks have very heavy coats of fur, and few sweat glands. Yaks in Tibet are like cows here. They are raised for milk, cheese, butter, curd, meat, and hide. They are very strong, and are often used to carry heavy loads.

READ MORE ABOUT YAKS
"Yaks" by C. Richard Taylor, *World Book Encyclopedia*, vol. 21 (World Book, 1988).

DO AND DISCOVER
Let the children discover some of the interesting uses of butter, which, in Tibet, is the main product made from yak milk. First, have the children make butter by shaking a small amount of heavy whipping cream in a jar. Help them remove the lump of butter that forms, and let the children taste it. Then have them sculpt their butter lump into a shape. Tell them that Tibetans make butter sculptures for religious purposes. Explain that yak butter is also burned for fuel in lamps and used to pay for things as we pay with money.

WRITE A BOOK ABOUT YAKS
Brainstorm all the things the children remember about yaks from their study. Make a list of the food yaks eat. Talk about their habitat. Discuss all the interesting things the children learned about yaks.

Put three pages together with a cover for a book for each child. Have the children draw a picture of a yak on the cover and write a title for the book. (See "Listen and Draw A Yak.") On the first page, have them draw the food that yaks eat. On the second, let them draw the yak's habitat, and on the third draw something interesting that they know about yaks. Have the children write or copy a sentence about the picture on each page.

Yy
Science Connection

YOUNG AND OLD

Have the children bring in pictures of themselves as babies. Tell them to bring their picture in an envelope so that no one else will get to see it. Put each child's name on the back of his or her picture.

Play a "Mystery Baby" game. Each day, have the children try to guess the identity of the baby in one of the pictures. Also take pictures of the children as they are in the classroom, and pin this set up on a bulletin board. Ask the children to try to match the baby pictures with the current pictures. Talk about how each child has changed from when he or she was a baby to the present.

Explain that all living creatures begin as babies, and that we say an animal's babies are its "young." Show as many different examples of animal babies and adults as you can. Compare the young of humans to the young of other living things. Ask, "Do caterpillars look as much like butterflies as human young look like human grownups?"

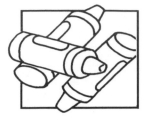

Yy
Arts and Crafts Connection

YARN PICTURES

The Huichol Indians, a tribe in central Mexico, have used this art form for many centuries.

Materials:

Yarn (assorted colors, lengths, and thicknesses),
coarse sandpaper, lightweight cardboard, pencils,
white glue, brushes, paper towel squares

Procedure:

Method #1 (for younger children)

1. Give the children each a piece of sandpaper and a variety of yarn pieces from which to create their masterpieces.

2. Show them how to lay the yarn onto the sandpaper in the design or picture they would like, and press on it gently to make it stick.

Method #2 (for older children)

1. Have the children draw a simple design or picture with lots of open space on a piece of cardboard.

2. Show them how to brush glue evenly over their pictures.

3. Be sure they wash or wipe their hands often, particularly after brushing the glue onto the cardboard. This will keep the yarn from sticking to their fingers and pulling back up from their pictures.

4. Show the children how to lay pieces of yarn onto the glued surface following the lines of their drawings, pushing the yarn as close together as possible, thus filling the open spaces with color and texture. Have them cover their entire picture with yarn.

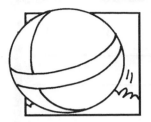

Yy
Movement Connection

YOO-HOO

This game is similar to the old game of Hide and Seek, but good listening skills help the children find the hiding child. The game can be played inside or out.

Choose one child to be "It." The other players hide their eyes while "It" finds a hiding place. The players who are hiding their eyes count to 50 (or to 10 five times), and then call out in unison, "Yoo-hoo!" The hiding child answers, "Yoo-hoo!" from his or her hiding place. The "Seekers" continue to call out in unison, and "It" continues to answer until found. Praise the children for being good listeners, and thank "It" for using a loud, clear voice.

YOGA EXERCISES

Demonstrate each exercise for the children. Caution them never to force their bodies to do something that hurts.

Yoga Bend

Have the children take a slow breath in, stand up tall, reach toward the ceiling, and breathe out as they bend forward at the waist, keeping their back straight. Tell them to bend until their hands are near their feet. Have them hold their hands behind their knees and stay in that position while you count to 30. (Increase the count as the children become comfortable with this stretch.)

Yoga Stand

Have the children stand with their legs straight. Show them how to bend their right knee and put the bottom of their right foot on the inside of their left thigh. Have them raise their arms over their head and clasp their hands. Have them hold the position briefly, and then repeat it standing on the other leg.

Yy

HOMEWORK

Name _____

Date Due _____

Put a √ by the activity you have chosen to do.

☐ Have a grownup help you cook **y**ams for your family. Make a list of the people who thought the **y**ams were **y**ummy. Bring the list to school.

☐ Learn about what a **y**ear is. Find out how many months are in a **y**ear, how many weeks, and how many days. Bring the facts to school.

☐ Collect **y**ellow things. Bring them to school to share.

_____
Signature of grown up helper

YOLANDA YAK'S YOGURT

Ingredients (serves 1)
vanilla yogurt
granola
sunflower seeds
jam
raisins

1. Put 4 T. vanilla yogurt into a bowl.

2. Add 2 tsp. granola.

3. Add 1/2 tsp. sunflower seeds.

4. Add 2 tsp. jam.

5. Add 10 raisins.

6. Fold ingredients in gently to mix.

RAP WITH ZEBRA ZACH

Sign Language **Z**

Z is for zebra, Zebra Zach.
Z /z/ /z/ /z/ /z/ /z/ /z/
Zooming, zombies, zinnias.
Z /z/ /z/ /z/ /z/ /z/ /z/
Zigzag, zippers, zero, zoo.
Z /z/ /z/ /z/ /z/ /z/ /z/
(Repeat the first two lines.)

Zebra Zach

3 Z'S

Introduce Zebra Zach and his letter Z by showing the children a zucchini, a zipper, and the numeral 0. Name the objects and ask how they are all alike. Let the children guess the name of the alphabet animal that begins with the same sound as each of those words.

A ZOO TRIP

To celebrate the letter z, go on a field trip to the local zoo. Be sure to visit the zebras. Make a class book of the trip for the library corner.

ZEBRA ZACH'S Zz BOOK

Brainstorm with the class words that begin with the same sound as Zebra Zach. Distribute paper and let the children each choose a word to illustrate. Have them copy the following sentence frame onto the page and write their word in the blank space. Put the pages together to make a class book.

Zebra Zach begins with z, and so does _____.

Zebra Zach

Draw zeroes on the Zz's.

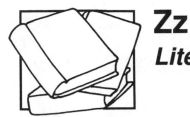

Zz
Literature Connection

READ A BOOK
If I Ran the Zoo by Dr. Seuss (Random House, 1977). Dr. Seuss captivates children with his outrageous rhymes and pictures in this book about a new kind of zoo. The animals in this zoo inspire the imagination of all who read the book.

Presentation
Ask the children if they have ever been to a zoo. Discuss what they saw, and what zoos are like. Make a list of all the animals that the children can think of that might live in a zoo.

Additional Books
Put Me in the Zoo by Robert Lopshire (Random House, 1960); *The Greedy Zebra* by Mwenye Hadithi (Little, Brown, 1984).

RELATED ACTIVITY

Zoo Big Book
Ask the children to pretend that they are young Gerald McGrew, who let all the real animals out of the zoo and replaced them by creating his own zoo with animals from his imagination. Discuss the parts of animals that make them unique, such as elephants' trunks, giraffes' long necks, lions' manes, and monkeys' tails. Then give the children some drawing paper and crayons or markers to create special animals for their own zoo.

Have each child complete the following sentence frame on the page with their make-believe animal:

If I ran the zoo, I'd put a _____ in it.

Bind the pages into a book for the classroom book corner.

Listen and Draw a Zebra

Give the children oral directions as you draw each step with them.

1. Draw a small oval for the zebra's head. Draw a large oval for the body.

2. Draw two pointed ears. Add a straight neck between the head and the body. Make a zigzaggy mane along the top of the neck. Put a short tail at the end of the body.

3. Add some hairs to the end of the tail. Draw two legs under the body. Make triangle stripes all over the zebra's head, neck, tail, and body.

4. Give the zebra an eye, a nose, and a smile.

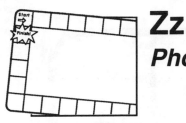

Zz
Phonics Connection

AT SCHOOL

Copy the game board and the set of sound picture cards for Zebra Zach's "Z" Game onto oaktag for the children to color. Have them cut the cards out. Glue an envelope onto the back of the game board to store the cards and the directions for play.

Show the children how to play the game. Include the "At Home" directions when the game goes home.

- -

AT HOME
Materials:
Zebra Zach's game board and set of sound picture cards; a small marker for each player

Directions:
1. Place the cards face down in a pile between the players.
2. Take turns drawing from the pile. If the picture on the card begins with the sound of "z," move the marker forward one space. If the picture begins with another letter sound, no move is made. If a player is lucky enough to draw Zebra Zach's picture, the marker is moved forward two spaces.
3. Reshuffle the cards each time they have all been drawn, and continue playing until someone reaches the finish line. The player who finishes first is the winner.

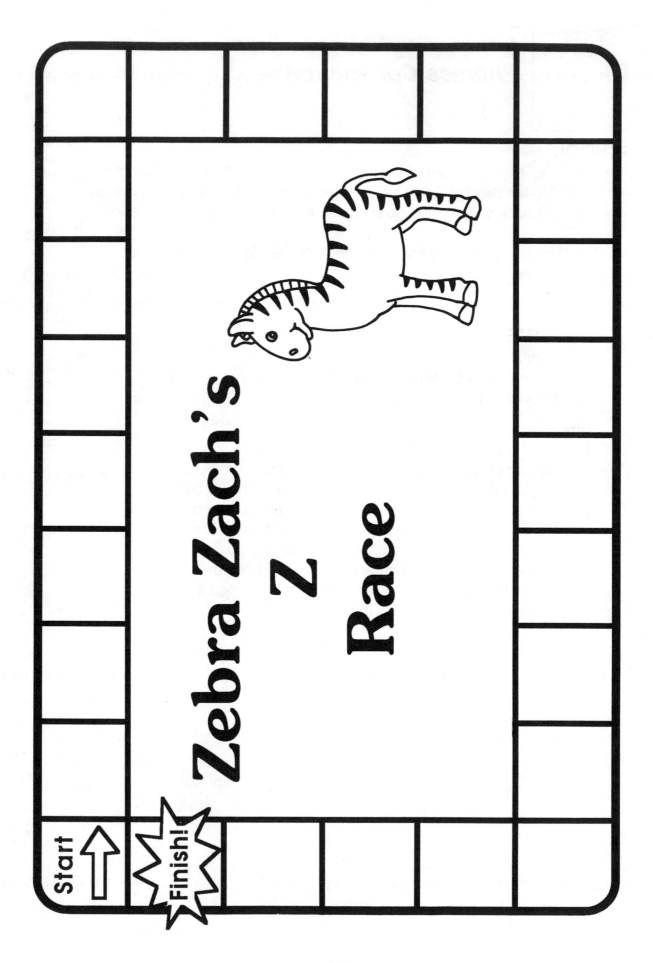

Zebra Zach's
Z
Race

Start

Finish!

Zz
Math Connection

ZERO

To help the children begin to understand the importance that the numeral zero has as a place holder, give them sections of the daily newspaper that include large retail store advertisements. Set a timer for 60 seconds, and ask the children to circle as many zeros as they can find in that time. Discuss how much each item costs with the zeros in place, and how much each would cost if the zeros were missing.

ARE YOU WEARING A ZIPPER TODAY?

(a graphing activity)

Ask the children if any of them is wearing clothing that has a zipper in it. Then have the children who do have zippers get in one line, and those who don't get in another, parallel, line. Have the children in one line hold the hand of the child opposite them in the other line. Then have them drop hands but stand still. This makes it easier to "read" the graph. Ask the children to tell you everything that they can about what they see in their living graph.

   Write an experience story together about the graph. Include as many of the children's observations as possible. Put a copy of the story in a book of experience stories and place it in the classroom library.

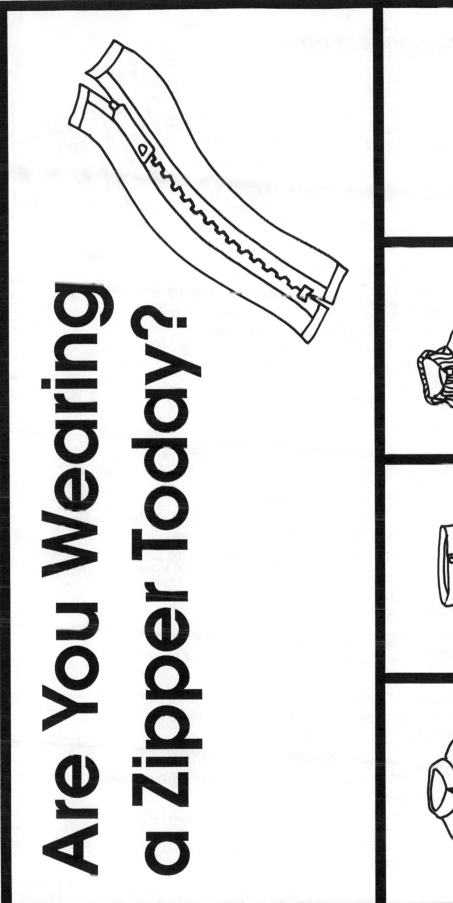

Are You Wearing a Zipper Today?

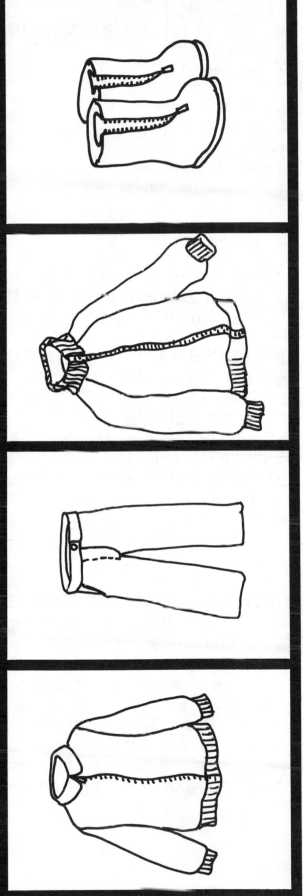

335

Zz
Science Connection

ZEBRAS
Class: Mammal
Group: Herd
Habitat: Grassy plains
Food: Grass, hay, grains
Baby: Foal
Color: Black and white

The stripes on a zebra are like people's fingerprints: no two zebras have the same pattern. Zebras are shy but fast. They like to stay together, but if they must run the males lag behind so the females and babies can get away. If one of the group is missing, the others become concerned and go looking for it.

READ MORE ABOUT ZEBRAS
Zebra by Caroline Arnold (William Morrow, 1987).

DO AND DISCOVER
Let the children discover why zebras have stripes that run up and down instead of across the animals' bodies. Draw vertical black stripes on a 4" by 5" white card, and draw horizontal black stripes on another white card the same size. Make sure the stripes are spaced evenly on both cards. Set the cards out side by side in an area of tall grass. Have the children stand back to observe which card is more easily seen. The vertical stripes provide camouflage for the card just as the stripes on a zebra do.

WRITE A BOOK ABOUT ZEBRAS
Brainstorm all the things the children remember about zebras from their study. Make a list of the food zebras eat. Talk about their habitat. Discuss all the interesting things the children learned about zebras.

Put three pages together with a cover for a book for each child. Have the children draw a picture of a zebra on the cover and write a title for the book. (See "Listen and Draw A Zebra.") On the first page, have them draw the food that zebras eat. On the second, let them draw the zebra's habitat, and on the third draw something interesting that they know about zebras. Have the children write or copy a sentence about the picture on each page.

Zz
Science Connection

ZOOS

Ask the children how many of them have been to a zoo. Put the resulting information on a chart graph. Tell the children that scientists helped set up the first zoos almost 200 years ago to study animals. Then people who were not scientists saw how interested everyone was to see animals from all over the world, and began to put wild animals into tiny cages along pathways and charge admission to see them. Today, people are more concerned about learning how to take care of the world and protect its wildlife. And now zookeepers try to put wild animals into areas that are like their real habitats, not cages.

Plan a field trip to the zoo. Before going, make a list with the children of the animals that they will see. Have each child "adopt" an animal for the day. This animal will be the one that the child will pay special attention to, and learn as much as possible about its needs and habits. When the class returns to school, take time for "adopted animal" reports.

©1993 Monday Morning Books, Inc.

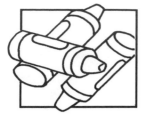

Zz
Arts and Crafts Connection

ZIGZAG SCULPTURES

Materials:
Construction paper, lightweight cardboard squares,
scissors, glue, brushes

Procedure:
1. Show the children how to cut strips of paper, or provide them with precut 1"-wide strips of a variety of colors of construction paper.
2. Demonstrate how to accordion-pleat the strips. Hint: Tell the children to fold, flip, fold, flip, over and over until the paper is used up. With this technique the strips will be the proper zigzag shape.
3. Have the children make several zigzag strips to begin their sculptures. Then show them how to twist, loop, and curl their strips around and through each other, gluing the ends wherever they choose.
4. Show the children how to apply a small amount of glue where they want it, and hold the pieces together while they count to five slowly.
5. They may wish to use one of the cardboard squares as a base, gluing the ends of some of the beginning strips to it.

ZANY ZOO ANIMALS

Materials:
9" by 12" pieces of construction paper in various
colors, yarn scraps, scissors, glue

Procedure:
Read together the book *If I Ran the Zoo* by Dr. Seuss. Tell the children that they are going to make their own zoo animals as zany as Dr. Seuss's.
1. Show the children how to make a fold about 1" deep along the two opposite ends of a piece of construction paper. The folds can be along the short ends or along the long ends, depending upon whether the animal is to be long or short.
2. Have the children keep the end folds in place and fold the paper again, this time in half so that the newly formed middle fold crosses the ones on the ends.
3. Show the children how to cut a half circle out of the open edge of the folded construction paper. (If the paper is folded lengthwise, the cutout will be shaped more like a half oval.) Tell them to keep the scraps to use for other parts.
4. Have the children carefully unfold their paper and cut a 1" slit from each end along the middle fold line. When the paper is refolded it will stand up.
5. Give the children the paper scraps and yarn scraps and let them create their zany zoo animal's head, ears, horns, trunk, beard, tail, etc.

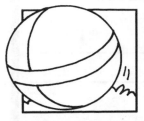

Zz
Movement Connection

ZIPPY ZIGZAGS

Lay out a zigzag pattern on the playground with jump ropes or chalk. Choose someone to be the leader, and have the other children line up behind him or her. Have the children follow the leader along the zigzag path, imitating the way he or she moves.

Movement suggestions:

hopping on one foot
jumping on two feet
walking backward
straddling the line
"balancing" on the line
jumping side to side

galloping
jogging
skipping
flapping arms

ZERO THE HERO

Have the children stand in a large circle a distance apart, ready to move around it in the same direction. Choose someone to be "Zero the Hero" and stand in the center of the circle. To begin the game, the child calls out "Zero!" and the children begin running around the circle in a clockwise direction. Each player tries to pass the player ahead of him or her, tagging the child as he or she goes by. Tagged players go into the middle of the circle and sit down. "Zero the Hero" can shout "Zero!" periodically, at which time the players must reverse direction. This turns the tables on the runner who is just about to overtake someone.

ZOO

Make a list of all the zoo animals the children can think of. Select six students to stand in a line in front of the class, and have each choose a different zoo animal to imitate. Have the six children say the name of their animal. Then, on your signal, have each child in line imitate his or her animal for about 20 seconds, staying in the assigned place in line. The other five children wave their arms and jump around. When the time is up, the rest of the class sits down and covers their eyes with their hands while you change the order of the six children in line. When they uncover their eyes, the seated children try to put the "Zoo Animals" in their original order and name each one. If interest continues, play the game with six new animal imitators.

Zz HOMEWORK

Put a √ by the activity you have chosen to do.

☐ Count the **zi**ppers you find on all your clothes.
Record the number and bring it to school. Tell what
kind of clothes have **zi**ppers in them.

☐ Draw as many **zo**o animals as you can. Bring your
pictures to school.

☐ Make a colorful design with **zig**zags and **zero**s.
Show it at school.

_____
Signature of grown up helper

ZEBRA ZACH'S ZUCCHINI ZEROS

Ingredients (serves 1)
  zucchini half
  egg
  milk
  bread or cracker crumbs
  Parmesan cheese
  cooking spray

1. Cut the zucchini half into 1/4" thick "zeros".

2. Mix together 1 T. crumbs and 1 T. Parmesan cheese.

3. Dip the zucchini slices into a mixture of the egg and 2 T. milk.

4. Dip the zucchini slices into the crumb and cheese mixture.

5. Put the slices on a cookie sheet sprayed with cooking spray.

6. Bake at 375° for 10 minutes. Turn over the zeros and bake for 10 more minutes. (You need a helping hand.)

Resources

Letters to Parents

PHONICS CONNECTION

Dear Mom and Dad,

I made a game at school today. It is fun to play, and will help me learn to read. Will you play it with me?

Thank you,

HOMEWORK

Dear Parents,

We have begun our study of the letters of the alphabet. The children are learning the sounds that we say when we read the letters, as well as what the letters are called. Using as the base of our study an animal mascot for each letter and alliterative chants we call "raps," the children are participating in a variety of activities at school that will help them develop this knowledge.

The children will also be given activities to do at home. They are designed for you and your child to do together. Three activities are listed on the homework contract for each letter of the alphabet. Please read them all to your child, and together choose the one you both would like to do. When the project is finished, sign the contract and have your child return it to school with the completed assignment by the due date given. Be sure your child signs the contract too.

We think you will find these activities to be a lot of fun.

Sincerely,

Make a Hat or Mask

In this section you'll find the patterns necessary to make hats or masks of all the alphabet letter animals. In addition there is a diagram of each animal's face, as well as a list of all the pattern pieces required and suggested construction paper colors to use.

Begin by duplicating the pattern pieces onto lightweight cardboard stock and cutting them out. Then let the children use them as tracing patterns, or duplicate them onto the appropriate colors of construction paper for the children to cut out and assemble.

To make the animal face

Give the children the appropriate patterns and colored construction paper. Have them trace the patterns and cut them out. Show them how to assemble the pieces according to the diagram, attaching the muzzle between the eyes with a small piece of transparent tape. (This acts as a hinge when making a hat, allowing that part of the face to lift slightly when the face is attached to the visor headband.) If making a mask, make a hole through each eye with a hole punch as close as possible to the eye place indicated on the pattern.

To make the mask

Attach a tongue depressor or craft stick to one side of the completed animal face to serve as a holder. Or fasten a piece of string or yarn to each side to tie around the child's head.

To make the hat

Attach the completed animal face to the completed visor headband by centering it over the visor as shown. Glue the bottom of the head part along the headband. Do not glue the muzzle part.

To make the visor

Duplicate the visor pattern and two headband strips onto construction paper the same color as the animal's head. Have the children cut out the patterns. Show them how to cut slits along the inner edge of the visor on the solid lines, and fold the resulting tabs up on the dotted fold lines. Staple the headband strips together to make a length that fits each child's head, and show the children how to glue the tabs to the inside of the headband.

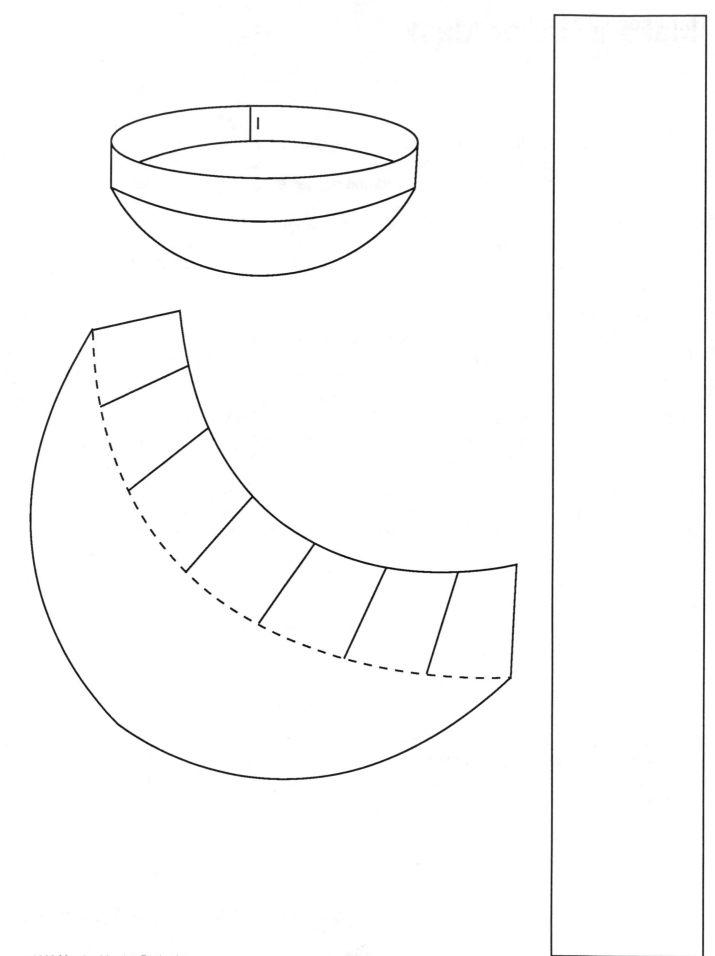

Hat Face Pattern #1

Mask Face Pattern #1

345

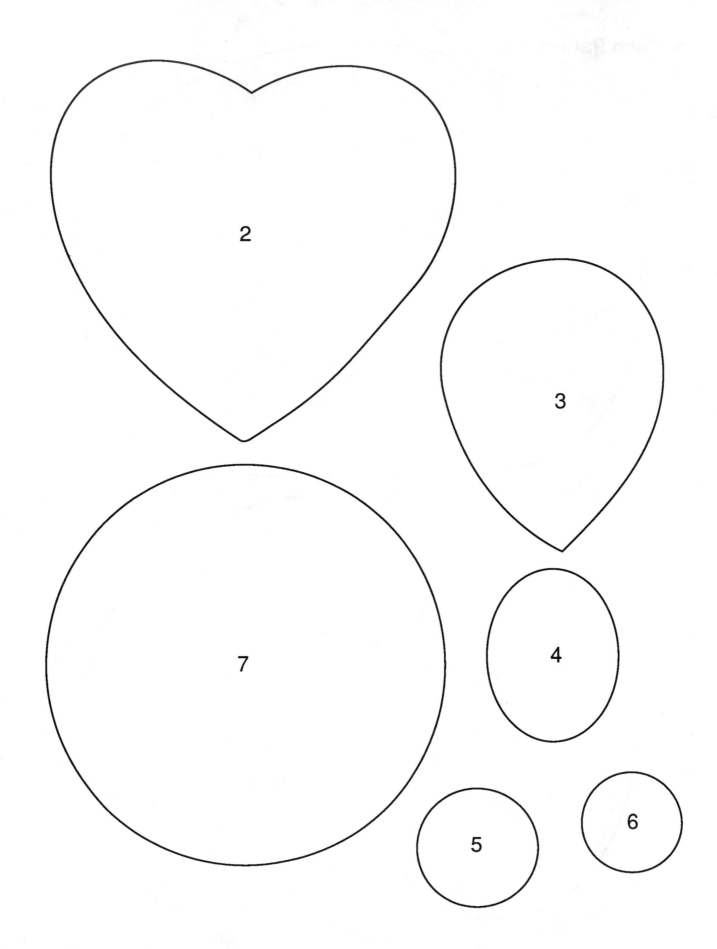

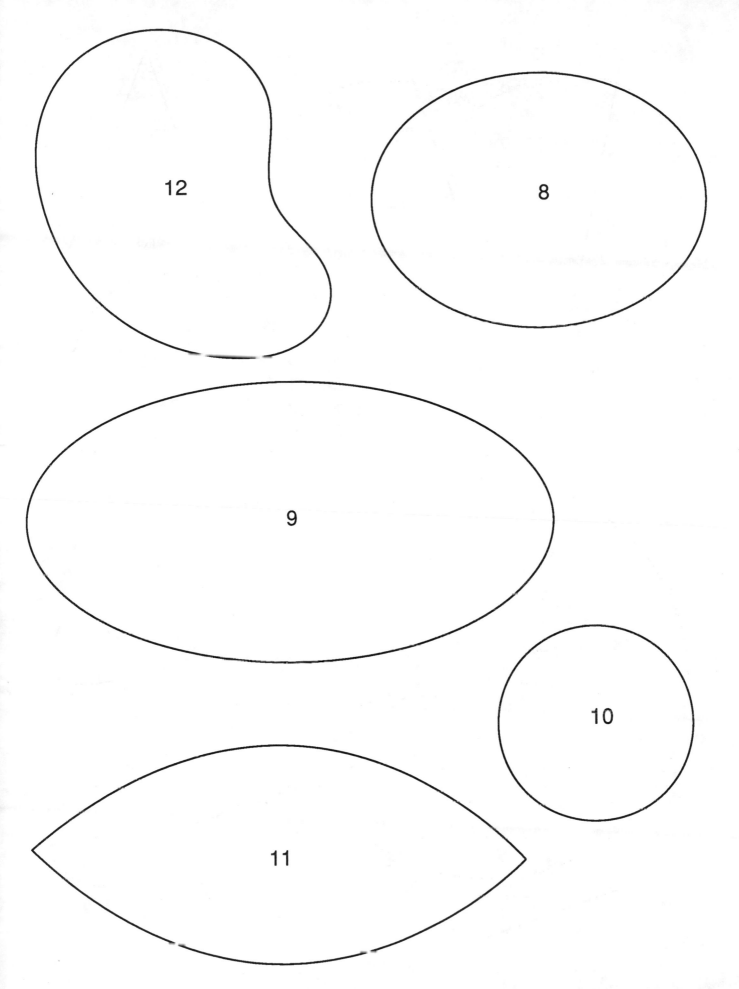

347

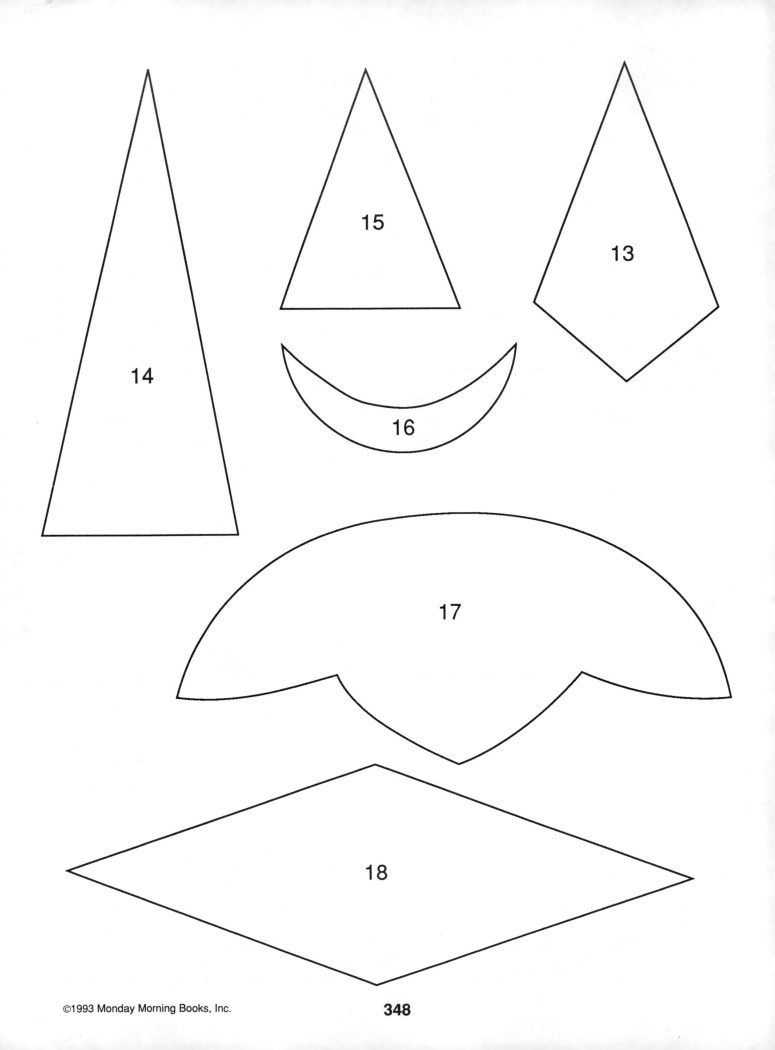

ALLIGATOR ANN

head	1	green
snout	9	green
eyes	4	yellow
pupils	5	black
eyelids	4	black (1 cut in half)
nostrils	6	black (1 cut in half)
spots		orange (free cut)
teeth		white (free-cut triangles)

BOBBY BEAR

head	1	brown
ears	3	brown (round side up)
muzzle	13	brown (long point up)
nose	4	black
inside ear	10	pink
eyes	6	black

CAMEL CAL

head	1	brown
bangs	17	yellow
muzzle	2	yellow (point up)
ears	3	brown (point up)
eyes	4	white
pupils	5	black
eyelids	4	black (1 cut in half)
nose/mouth		black (free-cut strips)

DINOSAUR DAWN

head	1	green
eyes	4	white
pupils	5	black
plates	15	orange
nostrils	6	orange

ELEPHANT ED

head	1	pink
ears	7	turquoise
eyes	4	white
trunk	12	orange
pupils	5	black

FENTON FOX

head	1	orange
face marking	2	white (point down)
ears	3	orange (point up)
snout	13	orange (long point down)
eyes	6	green
nose	5	black
whiskers		black (free cut)

GERTIE GOOSE

head	1	yellow
bill	9	orange
bill top	16	dark blue
eyes	4	white
pupils	5	black
nostrils	6	black (1 cut in half)

HIPPO HAL

head	1	royal blue
muzzle	1	turquoise (flat side up)
ears	3	turquoise (round side up)
eyes	4	white
pupils	5	black
nostrils	6	black
teeth		white (free-cut rectangles)

ICHABOD INDRI

head	1	black
ears	3	black (round side up)
muzzle	3	pink (point up)
nose	15	black
eyes	5	white
pupils	6	black

JAGUAR JAN

head	1	brown
ears	3	brown (round side up)
muzzle	2	yellow (point up)
nose	13	black (long point up)
whiskers		black (free cut)
eyes	4	yellow
pupils		black (free-cut triangles)
spots		(free cut)

KATY KANGAROO

head	1	green
ears	11	green
muzzle	8	purple
nose	4	black
eyes	4	white
pupils	5	black
mouth	16	white

LION LOU

head	1	brown
ears	3	brown (round side up)
muzzle	2	yellow (point up)
nose	13	black (long point up)
eyes	6	black
whiskers		black (free cut)
mane		orange (free-cut strips)

MOE MONKEY

head	1	brown
face	2	white (point down)
muzzle	7	yellow
ears	8	brown
nose	4	black
eyes	6	black
mouth	16	black

NARWHAL NED

head	1	dark blue
eyes	4	white
pupils	5	black
tusk	14	yellow (point down)

OLIVER OSTRICH

head	1	purple
cheeks	10	yellow
beak	18	orange
eyes	4	white
pupils	5	black
eyelids	4	black (1 cut in half)
nostrils	6	black (1 cut in half)

PENGUIN PETE

head	1	black
beak	13	yellow (long point down)
eyes	4	white
pupils	5	black

QUINCY QUAIL

head	1	turquoise
face	2	orange (point down)
beak	13	yellow (long point down)
plume	11	orange
eyes	4	white
pupils	5	black

RHINO RUTH

head	1	dark blue
muzzle	9	yellow
horn	13	orange (long point up)
ears	3	dark blue (round side up)
eyes	4	white
pupils	5	black
nostrils	6	black

SUZY SEAL

head	1	black
cheeks	10	white
nose	5	turquoise
eyes	4	white
pupils	5	black
whiskers		black (free cut)

TIGER TIM

head	1	orange
muzzle	2	orange (point up)
nose	13	black (long point up)
ears	3	orange (round side up)
eyes	6	black
stripes		black (free-cut triangles)
whiskers		black (free cut)

UMBRELLA BIRD

head	1	green
wattle	3	purple
crest	17	purple
beak	13	yellow
		(long point down)
eyes	6	black

VULTURE VIC

head	1	black
beak	2	orange
		(point down)
eyes	4	white
pupils	5	black
nostrils	5	black
		(1 cut in half)

WALRUS WALT

head	1	black
jowls	2	white
		(fringe curves)
nose	5	turquoise
eyes	4	white
pupils	5	black
tusks	15	white

YOLANDA YAK

head	1	turquoise
nostrils	6	black
muzzle	9	purple
bangs	17	purple
ears	11	turquoise
horns	16	white
eyes	5	black

ZEBRA ZACH

head	1	white
muzzle	9	pink
ears	11	black
mane	14	pink (point down)
nose	14	black (point up)
nostrils	6	black
stripes		black (free-cut triangles)
eyes	6	black